CALEB T. FRIEDEMAN

GOSPEL BIRTH NARRATIVES AND HISTORIOGRAPHY

Reopening a Closed Case

BAYLOR UNIVERSITY PRESS

© 2025 by Baylor University Press
Waco, Texas 76798

All Rights Reserved. No part of this publication may be reproduced, stored in a retrieval system, or transmitted, in any form or by any means, electronic, mechanical, photocopying, recording, or otherwise, without the prior permission in writing of Baylor University Press.

Unless otherwise stated, Scripture quotations are from the New Revised Standard Version Bible, copyright 1989, Division of Christian Education of the National Council of the Churches of Christ in the United States of America. Used by permission. All rights reserved.

Cover design by Elyxandra Encarnación
Cover image: Alsatian Master, "Nativity," 16th century. Sculpture-Wood. Rogers Fund, 1906. Object # 06.161, The Met. https://www.metmuseum.org/art/collection/.

Paperback ISBN 978-1-4813-2060-3
Printed case ISBN: 978-1-4813-2421-2

Library of Congress Control Number: 2024056194

"Unlike most books today, this one actually breaks new ground. Caleb Friedeman makes a compelling argument that authors of full biographies near the first century based the primary features of their birth narratives on prior information. He also provides evidence that Matthew and Luke likewise depend on prior sources. If Friedeman is correct, scholars will need to begin to reevaluate historical memory in our first-century stories about Jesus's infancy."
—**CRAIG S. KEENER**, *F.M. and Ada Thompson Professor of Biblical Studies, Asbury Theological Seminary*

"Thoroughly engaging with scholarship in such a way that allows readers to see the substance of the arguments, Friedeman demonstrates why history matters to theology. An insightful trip through several pertinent ancient biographies situates the Gospels in their historical context and also demonstrates the power of what they achieved. As someone with a keen interest in the reliability of Jesus' conception and birth—an interest all Christians should share—I cannot wait to share this vital contribution with others. *Gospel Birth Narratives and Historiography* leaves me more confident and more in awe of how God chose to enter the world."
—**AMY PEELER**, *Kenneth T. Wessner Professor of New Testament, Wheaton College*

"Caleb Friedeman's *Gospel Birth Narratives and Historiography* is a groundbreaking work that reclaims the Gospel birth narratives as serious contributions to ancient historiography. With scholarly precision and literary insight, Friedeman challenges long-standing assumptions about the birth narratives and invites a fresh reading of Jesus' origins. Matthew and Luke composed their accounts with genuine historical intent, creatively combining Jewish scriptural tropes with Greco-Roman biographical conventions. They intended their birth narratives to be understood as historically true. This book is essential for anyone seeking to understand the Gospels as both theology and history."
—**MICHAEL LICONA**, *Professor of New Testament Studies, Houston Christian University*

To my son Paul.
May you increase in wisdom
and in stature and in favor
with God and man (Luke 2:52).

CONTENTS

Acknowledgments ix
Abbreviations xi

Introduction 1

I Ancient Birth Narratives and Historiography

1 Cornelius Nepos 27

2 Philo 47

3 Plutarch 67

4 Suetonius 93

5 Ancient Birth Narratives and
   Historiography: Conclusions 125

II Gospel Birth Narratives and Historiography

6 Matthew 135

7 Luke 169

Conclusion 199

Appendix A: Historiographic Features in Ancient Historians 205
Appendix B: Historiographic Data for Cornelius Nepos,
   De viris illustribus 209

Appendix C: Historiographic Data for Philo, *On the Life of Moses*	213
Appendix D: Historiographic Data for Plutarch, *Lives*	215
Appendix E: Historiographic Data for Suetonius, *Lives of the Caesars* and *Lives of Illustrious Men*	225
Appendix F: Historiographic Data for Other Ancient Biographers	229
Bibliography	233
Index of Modern Authors	249
Index of Ancient Sources	253

ACKNOWLEDGMENTS

The present book began as a chapter in my original dissertation project at Wheaton College. As I studied the relationship between the Gospel birth narratives and historiography, however, I realized that the issue deserved a book of its own. This is that book. I want to thank my doctoral mentor, Nicholas Perrin, and my second reader, Daniel Treier, for their help both in developing that original project and in narrowing it to what became my actual dissertation—now published as *The Revelation of the Messiah* (Cambridge UP, 2023).

I would also like to express my gratitude to the many who have helped to bring this book to fruition in the decade since my initial research at Wheaton. As my intern, Olivia Bennett located reference numbers for historiographic features I had marked in Plutarch's *Lives*. My (now former) students Noah Bennett and Steven Best assisted with the research on Cornelius Nepos and Philo, respectively, during a summer study group. Tina Craft and her staff at Ohio Christian University's Melvin and Laura Maxwell Library went above and beyond in helping me obtain sources. The Ohio Christian University administration graciously granted me a research professor position in 2023 that has allowed me to complete this book much sooner than I would have otherwise. Joel Archer sharpened my thoughts through numerous conversations about the project and provided helpful feedback on the entire manuscript. My mother Mary also read the whole manuscript and helped improve my writing at numerous points. Susan Rieske read and offered valuable comments on the chapter on Matthew. All errors that remain are, of course, my own.

I am grateful for the opportunity to publish this book with Baylor University Press. Dave Nelson expressed interest in the project from the first and has been a wise and encouraging guide throughout the process. The two anonymous peer reviewers provided constructive feedback that helped to improve the project. The production team at Baylor has been a pleasure to work with, and I am grateful to each member for their work in crafting the manuscript into the book you now hold.

Finally, I want to thank my wife Isabella for her constant support and for graciously listening to me go on about historiographic features, ancient genealogies, and such over meals. I dedicate this book to our son Paul, who will be arriving not long after I write these words.

ABBREVIATIONS

MODERN SOURCES

AB	Anchor Bible
ABRL	Anchor Bible Reference Library
ANRW	*Aufstieg und Niedergang der römischen Welt: Geschichte und Kultur Roms im Spiegel der neueren Forschung.* Part 2, *Principat.* Edited by Hildegard Temporini and Wolfgang Haase. de Gruyter, 1972–
BBR	*Bulletin for Biblical Research*
BECNT	Baker Exegetical Commentary on the New Testament
Bib	*Biblica*
BNP	*Brill's New Pauly: Encyclopaedia of the Ancient World.* Edited by Hubert Cancik. 22 vols. Brill, 2002–2011
BZNW	Beihefte zur Zeitschrift für die neutestamentliche Wissenschaft
CBQ	*Catholic Biblical Quarterly*
CSB	Christian Standard Bible
ESV	English Standard Version

ETL	*Ephemerides Theologicae Lovanienses*
ExpTim	*Expository Times*
HThKNT	Herders theologischer Kommentar zum Neuen Testament
ICC	International Critical Commentary
JBL	*Journal of Biblical Literature*
JETS	*Journal of the Evangelical Theological Society*
JGRChJ	*Journal of Greco-Roman Christianity and Judaism*
JSHJ	*Journal for the Study of the Historical Jesus*
JSNTSup	Journal for the Study of the New Testament Supplement Series
JTS	*Journal of Theological Studies*
LCL	Loeb Classical Library
LNTS	Library of New Testament Studies
NA[28]	*Novum Testamentum Graece*, Nestle-Aland, 28th ed.
Neot	*Neotestamentica*
NETS	*A New English Translation of the Septuagint.* Edited by Albert Pietersma and Benjamin G. Wright. Oxford University Press, 2007
NICNT	New International Commentary on the New Testament
NICOT	New International Commentary on the Old Testament
NIGTC	New International Greek Testament Commentary
NIV	New International Version
NovT	*Novum Testamentum*
NRSV	New Revised Standard Version
NTD	Das Neue Testament Deutsch
NTS	*New Testament Studies*
OCD	*The Oxford Classical Dictionary.* Edited by Simon Hornblower, Antony Spawforth, and Esther Eidinow. 4th ed. Oxford University Press, 2012

OTP	*Old Testament Pseudepigrapha*. Edited by James H. Charlesworth. 2 vols. Doubleday, 1983, 1985
SNTSMS	Society for New Testament Studies Monograph Series
THKNT	Theologischer Handkommentar zum Neuen Testament
UBS⁵	*The Greek New Testament*, United Bible Societies, 5th ed.
WBC	Word Biblical Commentary
WUNT	Wissenschaftliche Untersuchungen zum Neuen Testament
ZECNT	Zondervan Exegetical Commentary on the New Testament
ZNW	*Zeitschrift für die neutestamentliche Wissenschaft und die Kunde der älteren Kirche*

ANCIENT SOURCES (NONBIBLICAL)

Aem.	Plutarch, *Aemilius Paulus*
Ag.	Nepos, *Agesilaus*; Xenophon, *Agesilaus*
Ag. Ap.	Josephus, *Against Apion*
Agr.	Tacitus, *Agricola*
Alc.	Nepos, *Alcibiades*
Alex.	Plutarch, *Alexander*
Ann.	Tacitus, *Annales*
Ant.	Josephus, *Jewish Antiquities*
Att.	Nepos, *Atticus*
Avot R. Nat.	Avot of Rabbi Nathan
Aug.	Suetonius, *Augustus*
b.	Babylonian Talmud
B. Bat.	Bava Batra
Ber.	Berakhot
Cal.	Suetonius, *Gaius Caligula*
Cat.	Nepos, *Cato*

Cic.	Plutarch, *Cicero*
Deut. Rab.	Deuteronomy Rabbah
Eccl. Rab.	Ecclesiastes Rabbah
Epam.	Nepos, *Epaminondas*
Exod. Rab.	Exodus Rabbah
Ezek. Trag.	Ezekiel the Tragedian
Gen. Rab.	Genesis Rabbah
Han.	Nepos, *Hannibal*
Hell.	Xenophon, *Hellenica*
Hist.	Herodotus, *Histories*; Livy, *History of Rome*; Polybius, *Histories*
Hist. eccl.	Eusebius, *Historia ecclesiastica*
Joseph	Philo, *On the Life of Joseph*
Jub.	Jubilees
Jul.	Suetonius, *Julius*
LAB	Liber antiquitatum biblicarum
Lev. Rab.	Leviticus Rabbah
Life	Josephus, *The Life*
Luc.	Plutarch, *Lucullus*
LXX	Septuagint
Lyc.	Plutarch, *Lycurgus*
Meg.	Megillah
Mekh. R. Ish.	Mekhilta of Rabbi Ishmael
Mekh. R. Sim.	Mekhilta of Rabbi Simeon
Midr. Pss.	Midrash Psalms
Midr. Tanh. B	Midrash Tanhuma Buber
Midr. Tanh. PV	Midrash Tanhuma Printed Version
Migration	Philo, *On the Migration of Abraham*
Milt.	Nepos, *Miltiades*
Moses	Philo, *On the Life of Moses*
Num. Rab.	Numbers Rabbah
Paus.	Nepos, *Pausanias*
Pel.	Plutarch, *Pelopidas*

Pel. War	Thucydides, *Peloponnesian War*
Pesiq. Rav Kah.	Pesiqta of Rav Kahana
Pirqe R. El.	Pirqe Rabbi Eliezer
Posterity	Philo, *On the Posterity of Cain*
Praep. ev.	Eusebius, *Praeparatio evangelica*
Qidd.	Qiddushin
Quint. Fratr.	Cicero, *Epistulae ad Quintum fratrem*
Rom.	Plutarch, *Romulus*
Rom. Hist.	Cassius Dio, *Roman History*
Shir.	Shirata
Sol.	Plutarch, *Solon*
Song Rab.	Song of Songs Rabbah
t.	Tosefta
Tg. Ps.-J.	Targum Pseudo-Jonathan
Them.	Nepos, *Themistocles*; Plutarch, *Themistocles*
Thes.	Plutarch, *Theseus*
Tib.	Suetonius, *Tiberius*
Unchangeable	Philo, *That God Is Unchangeable*
Vesp.	Suetonius, *Vespasian*
Vir.	Suetonius, *Virgil*
Vit.	Suetonius, *Vitellius*
Yevam.	Yevamot

INTRODUCTION

Most readers of the Bible do not realize that when they turn to the birth narratives of Jesus (Matt 1–2; Luke 1–2), they are looking at what modern scholarship regards as some of the most historically unreliable material in the Gospels.[1] Scholars, of course, have questioned the historicity of all sorts of events and details throughout the Gospels, but modern scholarship generally views the birth narratives as substantially less reliable than the rest of the Gospels. Indeed, many recent accounts of the historical Jesus pass over his birth altogether or provide only scant details about it.

---

[1] Here I use Matt 1–2 and Luke 1–2 as a shorthand for Matt 1:2–2:23 and Luke 1:5–2:52. The phrase "birth narrative" is admittedly an imperfect way of describing this material, since it deals not only with Jesus's birth but also his genealogy (Matt 1:2–17), early childhood, and early adolescence (Luke 2:41–52). It is even less ideal for describing similar material in ancient biographies, since such material often is not a narrative. However, the English alternatives are also flawed: "infancy narrative" and "childhood narrative" are somewhat broader but still do not easily encompass early adolescence, and neither of these terms is as commonly used as "birth narrative." Here I use "birth narrative" to refer to narrative (or mostly narrative) material about a subject's origins through their childhood and "birth material" to refer to such material that is not necessarily in story form, while recognizing that both terms have their flaws.

In this book, I challenge the unique skepticism that scholars have directed toward the Gospel birth narratives and argue that these stories should be regarded as on par with the rest of the Gospels from a historiographic perspective. To grasp the contribution of this book, however, we first need to understand why modern interpreters have been so skeptical of the Gospel birth narratives.

SKEPTICISM TOWARD THE GOSPEL BIRTH NARRATIVES

We must distinguish at the outset between two kinds of historiographic skepticism.[2] The first is what we might call skepticism of *intent*, which in essence says, "Author X narrates event Y but does not intend Y to be historically true." For example, suppose someone is using *Don Quixote* as a source for reconstructing the historical Don Quixote. I might protest that *Don Quixote* is a fictional novel and that its author Miguel de Cervantes did not intend to communicate that the man of La Mancha actually existed.[3] The second kind of skepticism might be called skepticism of *truth*, which declares, "Author X narrates event Y and intends Y to be historically true, but Y is not historically true."[4] For instance,

---

[2] The distinction below between skepticism of intent and skepticism of truth is my own. It simply attempts to describe the different sorts of historiographic skepticism that one finds in scholarly literature on the Gospel birth narratives. For a similar distinction between intended historicity and actual historicity, see Gregory W. Dawes, "Why Historicity Still Matters: Raymond Brown and the Infancy Narratives," *Pacifica* 19.2 (2006): 156–76. Dawes notes that Raymond Brown fails to distinguish sufficiently between these two concepts in *Birth of the Messiah* and that Brown's exegesis implies more intended historicity than he acknowledges. See Raymond E. Brown, *The Birth of the Messiah: A Commentary on the Infancy Narratives in the Gospels of Matthew and Luke*, rev. ed., ABRL (Doubleday, 1993).

[3] Of course, one might use a fictional work as a source for investigating the views or life of its author, and a fictional work might inadvertently contain details that are true to reality. Skepticism of intent, as I am using it, simply questions the usefulness of a source for reconstructing the events it recounts.

[4] I am here using "skepticism of truth" to refer specifically to skepticism of historical truth, or truth about historical information, as opposed to the kind of truth one might find in a novel or in poetry.

someone might argue that while Thucydides intends to report historical events in his *Peloponnesian War*, he gets certain events or details wrong.

Both sorts of skepticism are valuable to historical inquiry. However, it is crucial to recognize that while the two types of skepticism arrive at similar conclusions (the event in question did not happen), they function quite differently. Skepticism of truth is most effective when it can provide evidence that discredits the source altogether. However, such evidence is hard to come by, so this sort of skepticism can often provide grounds only for doubting the historicity of individual events or details, not entire sources.[5] By contrast, skepticism of intent must provide initial reasons for regarding a source as ahistorical, but once it has done so it can disregard the source (or relevant portion of the source) entirely: once one has convinced the would-be scholar of the historical Don Quixote that her primary (and, in this case, only) source is a fictional novel, it is no longer necessary to discuss the historicity of individual events. Thus, skepticism of intent, if successful, is often more efficient than skepticism of truth in discrediting a source.

Much of the skepticism that scholars have leveled at the Gospel birth narratives is skepticism of intent. For example, John Meier asserts in *A Marginal Jew*, his magisterial work on the historical Jesus,

> Little or nothing can be said with certitude or high probability about the birth, infancy, and early years of the vast majority of historical figures in the ancient Mediterranean world. In the exceptional cases of towering figures like Alexander the Great or the Emperor Octavian Augustus, some facts were preserved, though even these were often interwoven with mythical and legendary motifs. This same pattern can be found in the OT. . . . Some great figures, like Isaac, Jacob, the twelve patriarchs, Samson, Samuel, David, and most notably Moses are favored with stories about their birth or youth. These narratives often display

---

[5] Consider, for example, how difficult it would be to demonstrate that a given historical source is so unreliable that one should disbelieve everything it says.

common themes.... The drive to expand these "midrashic" elements continues beyond the canonical Scriptures into various "retellings" of the OT narratives, e.g., in Josephus' *The Jewish Antiquities* and Philo's *Life of Moses*, as well as in the later midrashim of the rabbis.

Granted this phenomenon of stories of wondrous birth or childhood, composed to celebrate ancient heroes, pagan and Jewish alike, one must approach with caution the Infancy Narratives found in Chapters 1–2 of both Matthew and Luke. Such caution need not betoken an anti-supernatural bias that rejects a priori any extraordinary action of God in human history. One can maintain the theoretical possibility of miracles while being wary of individual claims, especially when such claims occur in a type of literature (i.e., infancy narratives of the ancient Mediterranean world) where angelic annunciations and miraculous births were stock motifs. One can take such motifs seriously—inquiring after their religious message—without necessarily taking them literally. All this simply reminds us that the truth-claims of any literature must be judged according to the specific genre or form of the literature in question.[6]

Meier's argument seems to be something like this:

1. Ancient birth/childhood stories were meant to be legendary but in rare cases preserved some facts.
2. Stories that are legendary must be approached with caution by the historian.
3. The Gospel birth narratives are ancient birth/childhood stories.
4. Therefore, the Gospel birth narratives must be approached with caution by the historian.[7]

Note that the argument hinges on the first premise. However, Meier provides little substantiation for this claim about ancient birth narratives. He notes a few examples, but he does not discuss

---

[6] John P. Meier, *A Marginal Jew: Rethinking the Historical Jesus*, 5 vols., ABRL (Doubleday, 1991–2016), 1:208–9.

[7] Meier does conclude that one can obtain some minimal facts from the birth narratives—see below.

these in detail or cite other scholars who do so.⁸ On the basis of this minimal evidence, Meier is able to dismiss much of Matthew 1–2 and Luke 1–2. His actual conclusions about Jesus's birth and childhood are as follows:

1. Jesus was born around 7–4 BC.
2. Jesus was born perhaps in Bethlehem but more likely in Nazareth.
3. Jesus's mother was named Mary, and his (putative) father Joseph.
4. Jesus was probably a descendant of David.⁹

Meier's view that the birth narratives are largely legendary thus leads him to find only the barest of historical details in them. Interestingly, his suggestion that Jesus was born in Nazareth directly contradicts Matthew and Luke's witness that Jesus was born in Bethlehem.¹⁰

Robert Miller presents a similar view of the Gospel birth narratives in *Born Divine: The Births of Jesus and Other Sons of God*, which contains three chapters on ancient birth narratives and their implications for interpreting the Gospels.¹¹ In his chapter on Hellenistic birth narratives, Miller asserts,

> People in the ancient world believed that heroes were the sons of gods because of the extraordinary qualities of their adult lives, not because there was public information about the intimate details of how their mothers became pregnant. In fact, in some biographies the god takes on the physical form of the woman's husband in order to have sex with her. This plot device is a transparent admission that there was no information, not even any rumors, about

---

⁸ Meier briefly discusses Plutarch, *Alex.* 1–2, 6–7, and Suetonius, *Aug.* 94, in a note (*Marginal Jew*, 1:234n14). However, his discussion is too brief and his sample size too small to substantiate his claim. Furthermore, as I show in subsequent chapters, the passages Meier cites contain historiographic features. Meier misses these and as a result misreads Plutarch and Suetonius.

⁹ Meier, *Marginal Jew*, 1:229–30.

¹⁰ Matt 2:1, 5–6, 8, 16; Luke 2:4, 15.

¹¹ Robert J. Miller, *Born Divine: The Births of Jesus and Other Sons of God* (Polebridge, 2003), 121–53, 175–87.

an unusual conception. Stories like these allow a god to physically father a child without the woman's realizing that a deity was involved or even suspecting that anything unusual occurred. This indicates that stories about divine paternity were purely interpretive, not informational. They were not based on knowledge about heroes' biological origins. They were created to account for the "superhuman" achievements of extraordinary men.[12]

Miller's conclusion is bold. But is it warranted? Let us reprise his argument in propositional form:

1. In some biographies, the god takes on the form of a woman's husband to have intercourse with her.
2. This is a "transparent admission that there was no information."
3. Therefore, stories about divine paternity in ancient biographies were "purely interpretive, not informational."

The flaws are not hard to spot. The move from premise 1 to premise 2 is anything but self-evident—what if the ancient author had sources for the claim in question? Miller then extrapolates from his dubious interpretation of a feature found in some Hellenistic birth narratives to a conclusion about all stories about divine paternity in ancient biographies.[13]

In his chapter "Are the Infancy Narratives Historical?" Miller provides four major reasons that the Gospel birth narratives are ahistorical. The first three of these are truth-oriented: (1) the birth narratives are "relatively late and isolated pieces of the New Testa-

---

[12] Miller, *Born Divine*, 134.

[13] Miller provides some excerpts of ancient birth stories with introduction and commentary. However, while he includes about a dozen stories (more than Meier), his sample size and discussion are not sufficient to substantiate his conclusion above that ancient birth narratives were "purely interpretive, not informational." In addition, even the birth stories he covers contain features that clearly contradict his thesis. For example, the first excerpt he includes is by Pausanias (*Description of Greece* 6.11.2–9), who attributes numerous details in his account to the Thasians ("The Thasians say . . ."). However, this is an instance of *distancing* (see below), which implies that Pausanias's account is information-based.

ment"; (2) "there are no plausible candidates for eyewitnesses to whom the material in the infancy narratives could be traced";[14] (3) the accounts of Matthew and Luke are "mutually contradictory and irreconcilable."[15] The fourth reason, however, is intent-oriented:

> The final reason for thinking that the infancy narratives do not record historical events is that, as best we can tell, their authors did not intend them to be historical accounts, nor did their audiences expect it. In Luke's hellenistic culture, biographies were expected to convey a plausible picture of the man's life and times and, more important, a true sense of the man's character. Stories of the man's birth and childhood were not evaluated on whether they preserved reliable memories from those who knew his early years. Instead, they were evaluated on how effectively they introduced the known abilities and character of the man by making them evident in the manner of his origin and in his childhood behavior.[16]

Having earlier determined that Hellenistic birth stories are intended to be ahistorical, Miller reasons that the Gospel birth narratives, too, are intended to be ahistorical. Note how this final argument is more potent than the first three combined. One might agree with Miller about the Gospel birth narratives' historical distance from the events they report, their lack of direct access to eyewitnesses, and their disagreement with each other and still hold that there might be significant historical information in one or both of them.[17] (Plutarch's *Lives*, for example,

---

[14] I take Miller here to mean that Matthew and Luke did not have direct access to eyewitnesses (or reliable access to their testimonies) for the information in their birth narratives. The other way to interpret this statement is that there are no eyewitnesses from whom these traditions might have been passed down. The latter is a much bolder claim and, if proven, might merit dismissing the Gospel birth narratives as historical sources. However, it seems unlikely that this is what Miller means, because it is quite plausible that Mary, Joseph, or other eyewitnesses could have passed down these traditions to others and that Matthew and Luke received them second- or thirdhand.

[15] Miller, *Born Divine*, 175–76.

[16] Miller, *Born Divine*, 177.

[17] Brown, for example, notes eleven points of agreement between Matt 1–2 and Luke 1–2 (*Birth*, 34–35). Why not use these as a starting point for historical investigation?

manifest the same sorts of issues, often to a greater extent, yet we do not disregard them as historical sources.)[18] However, Miller's final argument, if accepted, renders the Gospel birth narratives virtually useless for historical inquiry. Thus, while Miller displays skepticism of both truth and intent, it is the latter that does the heavy lifting.

Andrew Lincoln presents a similar perspective on the Gospel birth narratives in *Born of a Virgin? Reconceiving Jesus in the Bible, Tradition, and Theology*.[19] Lincoln argues that the Gospels are ancient biographies and should be interpreted as such. In discussing the expectations that ancient readers would have had for the birth stories of ancient biographies, Lincoln notes,

> Since most subjects only came to public attention as a result of their later careers, there was frequently very little authentic tradition for the early part of their lives and so the composition was particularly legendary as it attempted to show that the future life and career of subjects were already anticipated from the earliest days.[20]

Lincoln seems to be making a point here about ancient readers' expectations (and implicitly, the authors' intentions)—namely, that birth narratives were assumed to be legendary. He goes on to assert that in the birth stories of ancient biographies and particularly the Gospels, "ancestry, names and geographical and political setting may well have support from tradition, but much of the content, whether traditional or not, involves notions about the gods, fate, auguries, portents, divination and astrology that are legendary but nevertheless illustrate the significance that became attached to the subject's life."[21] Lincoln returns to this point about genre toward the end of the book:

---

[18] Donald Kagan, for example, uses Plutarch's *Pericles* as a major source for his own work on Pericles. See Donald Kagan, *Pericles of Athens and the Birth of Democracy* (Free Press, 1991), esp. xii.

[19] Andrew T. Lincoln, *Born of a Virgin? Reconceiving Jesus in the Bible, Tradition, and Theology* (Eerdmans, 2013).

[20] Lincoln, *Born of a Virgin?* 60.

[21] Lincoln, *Born of a Virgin?* 66.

On a critical reading the question of genre, then, turns out to be crucial not only for the discussion of historicity but also for reflection on scriptural truth. In their infancy narratives the Gospels tell the truth about what God is accomplishing in Jesus through one particular means of conveying such truth that was available to their writers. The content of scriptural truth depends on the type of literature through which it is mediated.... To this extent, and whether we employ the term legend or myth, we can agree with Spong's assertion, "To assign the birth narratives to mythology is not to dismiss them as untrue. It is rather to force us to see truth in dimensions larger than literal truth."[22]

Lincoln's argument, like those of Meier and Miller, depends on his claim about the ahistorical character of birth material in ancient biographies. However, the substantiation for this claim is again quite thin. Lincoln devotes about five pages to discussing Greco-Roman birth narratives and cites no scholars who provide more extensive evidence for his thesis.[23]

The three scholars above illustrate the extent to which the unique suspicion directed toward the Gospel birth narratives depends on skepticism of intent.[24] Skepticism of truth can generate

---

[22] Lincoln, *Born of a Virgin?* 249. Lincoln is quoting John S. Spong, *Born of a Woman: A Bishop Rethinks the Birth of Jesus* (HarperSanFrancisco, 1992), 45. Cf. Lincoln, *Born of a Virgin?* 243, 247–48.

[23] Lincoln, *Born of a Virgin?* 60–65. Lincoln (60n11) does cite Charles H. Talbert, "Miraculous Conceptions and Births in Mediterranean Antiquity," in *The Historical Jesus in Context*, ed. Amy-Jill Levine, Dale C. Allison Jr., and John Dominic Crossan, Princeton Readings in Religions (Princeton UP, 2006), 79–86. However, Talbert's discussion is barely longer than Lincoln's, and he does not argue that birth narratives were meant to be ahistorical.

[24] For other examples of skepticism of intent toward the Gospel birth narratives, see David Friedrich Strauss, *The Life of Jesus Critically Examined*, trans. George Eliot, 4th ed. (Sonnenschein, 1902), 107, 125, 140, 171–73, etc.; George M. Soares Prabhu, *The Formula Quotations in the Infancy Narrative of Matthew: An Enquiry into the Tradition History of Mt 1–2* (Pontifical Biblical Institute, 1976), 299–300; Herman Hendrickx, *The Infancy Narratives*, rev. ed., Studies in the Synoptic Gospels (Chapman, 1984), 20–21, 59; W. D. Davies and Dale C. Allison Jr., *The Gospel According to Saint Matthew*, 3 vols., ICC (T&T Clark, 1988–97), 1:221, 252; John Dominic Crossan, "The Infancy and Youth of the Messiah," in

some reasons for doubting the Gospel birth narratives (we noted the main ones above in our discussion of Miller). But even if one grants the validity of these concerns, they do not justify rejecting Matthew 1–2 and Luke 1–2 as historical sources altogether. Skepticism of intent, on the other hand, can silence the Gospel birth narratives entirely (perhaps excepting a few minimal details) simply by demonstrating that they are not meant to be historical. Meier, Miller, and Lincoln each take this route when they argue that ancient birth stories—and, by extension, the Gospel birth narratives—were largely legendary. However, all three scholars interestingly fail to demonstrate the legendary character of ancient birth narratives (the linchpin of their case) at length and seem unable to point to anyone who has done so.

I have focused on Meier, Miller, and Lincoln above because they explicitly discuss why they doubt the historical value of the Gospel birth narratives and thus allow us to distinguish between the different sorts of skepticism and how they function. However, not all skepticism of the Gospel birth narratives is so explicit or well developed. The attitude of suspicion that we observe in Meier, Miller, and Lincoln pervades historical Jesus scholarship, so much so that many recent studies of Jesus's life disregard the birth narratives and give little to no justification for this decision. What follows is a brief survey of this phenomenon in some of the major historical Jesus works of the last few decades.

In *Jesus the Jew* (1973), Géza Vermes briefly discusses Jesus's family background and birthplace and provides an excursus on Jesus as the son of God and the virgin birth. Beyond this, however, he does not treat Jesus's origins.[25] John Dominic Crossan admits the Gospel birth narratives as evidence for only two items in his construal of "the Jesus tradition" ("7 *Of David's Lineage*; 26 *Jesus Virginally Conceived*") in *The Historical Jesus* (1991).

The Search for Jesus: Modern Scholarship Looks at the Gospels, ed. Hershel Shanks (Biblical Archaeology Society, 1994), 59–81, esp. 71–73, 77; Edwin D. Freed, *The Stories of Jesus' Birth: A Critical Introduction* (Sheffield Academic, 2001), 16–17.

[25] Géza Vermes, *Jesus the Jew: A Historian's Reading of the Gospels* (Fortress, 1981), 20–21, 213–22.

Both items are attested by other sources (i.e., Crossan does not include them based on the witness of Matthew and Luke alone), and Crossan contends that "neither . . . gives us any biographical information about the historical Jesus."[26] In *The Historical Figure of Jesus* (1993), E. P. Sanders discusses the date of Jesus's birth and says that he grew up in Nazareth,[27] but he rejects most of what Matthew and Luke say about Jesus's origins, primarily because of intent-oriented concerns.[28] N. T. Wright gives only two sentences on Jesus's early life in *Jesus and the Victory of God* (1996), mentioning the date of Jesus's birth (4 BC) and the town where he grew up (Nazareth).[29] Gerd Theissen and Annette Merz discuss only the date and location of Jesus's birth in *The Historical Jesus: A Comprehensive Guide* (1998), interestingly asserting against Matthew and Luke that Jesus was born in Nazareth.[30] Similarly, James D. G. Dunn in *Jesus Remembered* refuses to include the birth narratives in his account of the historical Jesus, beginning instead at Jesus's baptism.[31] Marcus Borg does discuss the birth narratives in *Jesus: Uncovering the Life, Teachings, and Relevance*

---

[26] John Dominic Crossan, *The Historical Jesus: The Life of a Mediterranean Jewish Peasant* (HarperSanFrancisco, 1991), 371, 435–36. Crossan marks both of these items with the sign ±, which "means that the action or happening did not occur as an event at one moment in time or place (hence -) but that it represents a dramatic historicization of something that took place over a much longer period (hence +)" (434).

[27] E. P. Sanders, *The Historical Figure of Jesus* (Penguin, 1993), 10–12.

[28] Sanders, *Historical Figure*, 85–88. Sanders asserts that the Gospel writers invented stories about Jesus based on the Old Testament and says, "The clearest cases of invention are in the birth narratives" (85). He goes on to discuss a few truth-oriented concerns regarding the birth narratives but returns to the intent-oriented ones toward the end of his discussion, saying, "The birth narratives constitute an extreme case. . . . There is no other substantial part of the gospels that depends so heavily on the theory that information about David and Moses may simply be transferred to the story of Jesus. But we note that the early Christians regarded this as perfectly legitimate" (88).

[29] N. T. Wright, *Jesus and the Victory of God*, Christian Origins and the Question of God 2 (Fortress, 1996), 147.

[30] Gerd Theissen and Annette Merz, *The Historical Jesus: A Comprehensive Guide*, trans. John S. Bowden (SCM, 1998), 152–55, 164–65.

[31] James D. G. Dunn, *Jesus Remembered*, Christianity in the Making 1 (Eerdmans, 2003), 340–48.

of a Religious Revolutionary (2006).³² However, he dismisses them as "metaphorical narratives" because they involve supernatural elements and devotes the majority of his discussion to exploring their metaphorical significance.³³ Finally, Craig Keener does not seem to include any discussion of Jesus's birth and childhood in *The Historical Jesus of the Gospels* (2009).³⁴

The scholars and works above represent a diverse sampling of historical Jesus scholarship over the last few decades. Yet all seem to agree that it is acceptable to omit the Gospel birth narratives almost entirely from consideration of the historical Jesus. To be fair, the motives for this omission and the degree to which an author may regard it as "acceptable" may vary. Some scholars may dismiss the Gospel birth narratives because they believe them to be ahistorical or untrue.³⁵ Others may hold that Matthew 1–2

---

³² Marcus J. Borg, *Jesus: Uncovering the Life, Teachings, and Relevance of a Religious Revolutionary* (HarperSanFrancisco, 2006), 60–69.

³³ Borg notes that "the vast majority of mainstream biblical scholars see these stories [the birth narratives] as metaphorical narratives rather than as history remembered" (*Jesus*, 61). He provides three reasons for this judgment: (1) the birth narratives are late, and earlier sources such as the Gospel of Mark and Paul do not mention Jesus's special birth; (2) "what happens in the stories—the plot line—is quite different"; (3) "these stories look like they belong to the literary genre of metaphorical or symbolic narrative" (*Jesus*, 61–62). Of these points, the only one that directly relates to the genre of the birth narratives is (3), and this is largely a restatement of the conclusion it is meant to support. The only support Borg provides for (3) is that the birth narratives contain supernatural elements (angels, Matthew's star, divine conception, etc.). He contends that "when we find features like these in a story, we commonly conclude that its literary genre is not a literal-factual report, but a metaphorical or symbolic narrative" (*Jesus*, 62). Borg's only argument for the ahistorical nature of the birth narratives therefore seems to be that they contain supernatural elements.

³⁴ Craig S. Keener, *The Historical Jesus of the Gospels* (Eerdmans, 2009). Keener does refer to Matt 1–2 and Luke 1–2 multiple times (see his Scripture index), but there is no substantive discussion of these chapters or their subject matter in the body of the book.

³⁵ It is also possible that some of the scholars above omit the Gospel birth narratives because of space constraints. However, in my view, all the works noted above are long enough that this is not a compelling explanation.

and Luke 1–2 contain substantial historical information, but they choose to concede the point because they have other goals and do not wish to die on this hill at present (I think particularly here of Wright and Keener).[36] But whether one omits the Gospel birth narratives voluntarily or under duress, the point is that one can safely disregard this material without offering any sort of justification for doing so. And conversely, it seems that a scholar must exclude this material if they wish their work to be taken seriously. In short, historical Jesus scholarship has come to regard Matthew 1–2 and Luke 1–2 as guilty until proven innocent.

To sum up: Modern scholarship generally views the Gospel birth narratives as substantially less historically reliable than the rest of the Gospels. To omit the birth narratives from historical inquiry requires no justification, and to include them is at best unfashionable. And yet when we do find scholars explaining the reasons for their skepticism (Meier, Miller, Lincoln), the rationale seems quite thin. As we saw above in our discussion of Miller, it is difficult to produce truth-oriented reasons that warrant the near-complete disregard of the Gospel birth narratives in modern historical scholarship. And while the intent-oriented concerns might in theory justify dismissing Matthew 1–2 and Luke 1–2 as largely legendary, it does not appear that anyone has presented compelling evidence that ancient birth narratives were intended to be ahistorical. The unique skepticism that scholars have directed toward the Gospel birth narratives therefore appears to be a house of cards that stands or falls on the claim that ancient birth narratives—and, by extension, the Gospel birth narratives—were meant to be legendary.

THE CONTRIBUTION OF THIS BOOK

In this book, I challenge the skepticism of intent that lies at the root of the unique mistrust of the Gospel birth narratives in modern historical scholarship. In other words, I do not so much argue

---

[36] Keener, for example, defends the historiographic intent and reliability of Matt 1:18–2:23 in Craig S. Keener, *A Commentary on the Gospel of Matthew* (Eerdmans, 1999), 81–83.

that the Gospel birth narratives *are* historically true as that they *are meant to be* historically true. My basic argument is as follows:

1. The Gospels are ancient biographies.
2. Birth material in ancient biographies was not meant to be legendary but historical.
3. Therefore, the Gospel birth narratives are not meant to be legendary but historical.

I will discuss the rationale for premise 1 and outline my method for demonstrating premise 2 below. However, it is worth noting that while my primary argument is intent-oriented, it does have implications for the truth of the Gospel birth narratives in two ways: First, if the Gospel birth narratives are meant to be historical, then any skepticism about their truth will have to stand on its own two feet and either present sufficient reasons for its doubt or moderate its claims. As noted above, the truth-oriented reasons for doubting the Gospel birth narratives that are presently given cannot sustain the near-complete disregard for this material in modern historical scholarship. Second, comparing the Gospel birth narratives to birth material from other ancient biographies may yield reasons for thinking that the Gospel birth narratives are true. For example, if we were to find that the birth narratives of ancient biographies were generally based on sources, this would suggest that the Gospel birth narratives, too, are based on sources. And if we were to discover that the Gospel birth narratives were composed much closer to the events that they recount than most ancient birth narratives were, this might suggest that they are more reliable than most other ancient birth narratives. I will develop these truth-oriented implications in part 2, but I stress here that such issues are secondary for this book. As noted above, my primary argument is that ancient biographers—including Matthew and Luke—composed their birth material with historiographic intent.[37]

---

[37] For an argument that affirms this basic point but differs significantly regarding its implications, see M. David Litwa, *How the Gospels Became History: Jesus and Mediterranean Myths* (Yale UP, 2019). Litwa

THE STARTING POINT: ANCIENT BIOGRAPHY

I begin with what I regard as a fixed point: the Gospels are ancient biographies. This point, however, was not always so certain. In the mid-twentieth century, for example, it was common to view the Gospels as folk literature. Since the 1990s, however, there has been a growing consensus that the Gospels are ancient biographies. The primary impetus for this shift in opinion was the publication of Richard Burridge's *What Are the Gospels? A Comparison with Graeco-Roman Biography* (1st ed., 1992).[38] In this book, Burridge identified the generic features of ancient biography and demonstrated that the Gospels exhibit these features and therefore are best understood as ancient biographies. Subsequent scholarship has confirmed Burridge's basic point and sought to develop its implications.[39] Keener sums up the state of the question in current scholarship well: "Most Gospels scholars today view the Gospels as belonging to the genre of

---

argues that the Gospels (including the birth narratives) were meant to be read as historiography (*Gospels*, 3, 19, 108, 112–13, 118, 120–21, 209). However, he contends that "by modern standards . . . the gospels cannot be classified as historiography" because "post-Enlightenment registers of plausibility have shifted" (210). To respond to this argument in full would take us beyond the bounds of this project, but two points are important to note. First, Litwa seems to assume that miracle claims are necessarily off-limits for the modern historian. However, there are good reasons to doubt this—e.g., Craig S. Keener, *Miracles: The Credibility of the New Testament Accounts*, 2 vols. (Baker Academic, 2011); Michael R. Licona, "Historians and Miracle Claims," *JSHJ* 12 (2014): 106–29; Craig S. Keener, *Christobiography: Memory, History, and the Reliability of the Gospels* (Eerdmans, 2019), 331–45. Second, even if Litwa is correct, the Gospel birth narratives are no less relevant to the modern historian than the rest of the Gospels.

[38] Richard A. Burridge, *What Are the Gospels? A Comparison with Graeco-Roman Biography*, 2nd ed. (Eerdmans, 2004).

[39] E.g., Craig S. Keener and Edward T. Wright, eds., *Biographies and Jesus: What Does It Mean for the Gospels to Be Biographies?* (Emeth, 2016); Michael R. Licona, *Why Are There Differences in the Gospels? What We Can Learn from Ancient Biography* (Oxford UP, 2017); Keener, *Christobiography*; Helen K. Bond, *The First Biography of Jesus: Genre and Meaning in Mark's Gospel* (Eerdmans, 2020).

ancient biography. Both supporters and detractors now recognize this general consensus."[40]

If the Gospels are ancient biographies, then the birth material of ancient biographies should be our starting point for determining whether ancient authors (including Matthew and Luke) intended such material to be historically true. It is important to note that Meier, Miller, Lincoln, and most other scholars who question the historiographic intent of the Gospel birth narratives agree with me on this point.[41] Where I disagree with these scholars is their assertion that birth narratives in ancient biographies were meant to be legendary. Below I will discuss why I think ancient biographers generally intended their birth narratives to be historical, but first let us define "legendary" and "historical" more closely.

Ancient biography was a subtype of ancient historiography, or historical writing.[42] Ancient biographers, like ancient historians, wrote their accounts based on historical information. What distinguished ancient biography from ancient historiography was not the interest in historical truth but the focus: ancient biographers sought to display a single subject's character through their words and actions.[43] Ancient biographers, however, did not operate with the same historiographic standards as modern biographers. "The conventions of ancient biography," says Keener, "permitted considerable freedom in how biographers recounted their information."[44] Michael Licona, drawing on research by

[40] Keener, *Christobiography*, 27. Keener cites extensive bibliography for both claims.

[41] Meier and Miller also emphasize the importance of Jewish birth stories. However, in my estimation birth stories from ancient biographies prove to be more significant for their arguments.

[42] Christopher Pelling, "Truth and Fiction in Plutarch's Lives," in *Plutarch and History: Eighteen Studies* (Classical Press of Wales, 2002), 143–70; Keener, *Christobiography*, 151–220; Sean A. Adams, "What Are *Bioi/Vitae*? Generic Self-Consciousness in Ancient Biography," in *The Oxford Handbook of Ancient Biography*, ed. Koen De Temmerman (Oxford UP, 2020), 24–28.

[43] Plutarch, *Alex*. 1.1–3; Licona, *Differences*, 4–5; Keener, *Christobiography*, 134–38.

[44] Keener, *Christobiography*, 303.

classicists J. L. Moles and Christopher Pelling, notes a number of ways in which Plutarch adapts his sources:

- *Transferal*: attributing the words or deeds of one person to another.
- *Displacement*: moving an event from one context to another.
- *Conflation*: combining elements from two or more events or people.
- *Compression*: portraying events as occurring over a shorter period of time than they actually happened.
- *Spotlighting*: focusing on a single person and not mentioning others present.
- *Simplification*: omitting details.
- *Expansion of narrative details*: adding plausible details.
- *Paraphrase*: using different words to convey a similar idea.[45]

Similar adaptations occur elsewhere in ancient biography and in ancient historiography more broadly.[46]

The range of flexibility that we observe in ancient biography and historiography informs what counts as "historical" and "legendary" when it comes to the intent of ancient biographers. Ancient biography aimed to tell the truth about the subject's life within an accepted range of flexibility. Legends, by contrast, were not concerned with historical truth. To say that a biographer intends material to be historical (or is operating with historiographic intent), then, means that he aims to tell the truth within the conventions of ancient biography. To say that a biographer intends material to be legendary means that he is not concerned with historical truth and accordingly goes beyond the normal range of flexibility in ancient biography (e.g., making up events

---

[45] The list above is adapted from Licona, *Differences*, 19–21. Cf. J. L. Moles, introduction to *The Life of Cicero*, by Plutarch, ed. and trans. J. L. Moles (Aris & Phillips, 1988), 36–39; Christopher Pelling, "Plutarch's Adaptation of His Source-Material," in *Plutarch and History: Eighteen Studies* (Classical Press of Wales, 2002), 91–115.

[46] Moles, introduction to *Life of Cicero*, 40; Keener, *Christobiography*, 303–27.

with no sources). It will not do, then, to say that because a biographer compresses timelines, omits material, or adds plausible details, he intends the material in question to be legendary, for these all fall within the conventions of ancient biography.[47]

HISTORIOGRAPHIC FEATURES IN ANCIENT BIOGRAPHY

How do we know whether a source is intended to be historically true? This is the central methodological question that underlies the whole discussion of the Gospel birth narratives and historiography, and yet the answer to it is more presupposed than discussed. Meier, Miller, and Lincoln seem to assume that the presence of certain supernatural elements in ancient birth narratives (dreams, portents, divine paternity, etc.) indicates that these stories are meant to be ahistorical. But this is hardly a necessary conclusion. Ancient authors, for example, might well have had sources for these claims and intended to convey that the events in question really occurred. Or, they may have had ways of recounting these elements without asserting that they actually happened.

---

[47] Some scholars argue that ancient biographers regularly engaged in "fictionalization." Whether this is true obviously depends on how one defines the term. In the opening essay of a recent book on ancient biographies and fictionalization, Koen De Temmerman defines "fictionalization" as "the use of narrative techniques that interrogate, destabilize or challenge, if only for a minute, the narrative's intention to be believed or its claim to be truthful" ("Ancient Biography and Formalities of Fiction," in *Writing Biography in Greece and Rome: Narrative Technique and Fictionalization*, ed. Koen De Temmerman and Kristoffel Demoen [Cambridge UP, 2016], 14). Such techniques include characterization through speech (14), the representation of characters' thoughts (17), and the association of characters with paradigms (21). I do not dispute that ancient biographers do such things, but "fictionalization" is an unhelpful way of describing them, since in such cases ancient biographers are often recounting information they regard as plausible, whereas fiction is "untruth that is intended *not* to be believed as truth but rather to be acknowledged as untruth" (De Temmerman, "Ancient Biography," 6, emphasis original). Christopher Pelling argues compellingly that in such situations Plutarch is not engaging in fiction or invention but "creative reconstruction," recounting what "must have been true" ("Truth and Fiction," 154). See further Keener, *Christobiography*, 60–66.

Yet if such elements cannot in themselves indicate that a source is meant to be legendary, how might one go about determining that a source is meant to be historically true?

I suggest that four features of ancient biography can serve as indicators of historiographic intent.[48]

1. *Sources*: the author indicates that they have one or more sources for their narrative. Ancient biographers frequently note the sources for their narratives. The sources in question may be specific (e.g., Thucydides) or general (e.g., "the poets" or "the most reliable authorities"). An author may also mention their sources explicitly or implicitly. For example, Plutarch explicitly cites Didymus the grammarian and Heracleides Ponticus in his discussion of Solon's parents (*Sol.* 1.1–2). And Suetonius implies that he has sources when he says in his life of Augustus, "This is all that I have been able to learn about the paternal ancestors of Augustus" (*Aug.* 2.3 [Rolfe, LCL]). The fact that authors name or allude to sources suggests that they recognize a need for their account to be information-based rather than made up. *Sources* are the most basic of the four features and are implied by the other three features below, so they should be inferred wherever the others occur.

2. *Transparency*: the author notes disagreement among their sources. Ancient biographers sometimes mention that their sources disagree regarding certain events or details. For example, an author might note that there are two or three mutually incompatible accounts of a particular event. I call this "transparency" because the author is allowing the reader to look behind the curtain of their narrative to glimpse a conflict among their sources. *Transparency* indicates that the author (1) recognizes such differences as significant and (2) does not feel free to relate only one of the available accounts as if no others existed or to fabricate their own story.

---

[48] These four features are based on my own study of ancient historiography, but others have noted them as well. See, e.g., Keener, *Miracles*, 1:92–93; Keener, *Christobiography*, 211–20; Litwa, *Gospels*, 8.

3. *Evaluation*: **the author evaluates the historical reliability of an account.** Ancient authors often go beyond *transparency* to adjudicate between the available accounts and determine what is most historically probable. *Evaluation* can also occur without *transparency*. For example, an author might express skepticism about the truth of a claim without mentioning any alternative accounts. Of the four historiographic features, *evaluation* is the strongest indicator of historiographic intent because here the author explicitly expresses an opinion on the veracity of an account, showing that they are interested in telling a true story, not merely an interesting one.

4. *Distancing*: **the author distances their authorial reputation from a claim.** When recounting a miraculous or extraordinary event, ancient biographers often introduce the story with passive ("it is said") or third person ("she said," "they say") constructions rather than presenting the account as straightforward fact. I refer to this as *distancing* because the author is effectively placing distance between the account and their authorial reputation.[49] (Consider, for example, the difference between the statements, "Zeus slept with [the subject's] mother," and "*It is said* that Zeus slept with [the subject's] mother.") *Distancing* can also take place in other ways. For example, an author might admit at the outset that their sources are of dubious reliability and ask the reader to indulge them as they seek to separate fable from fact (e.g., Plutarch, *Thes.* 1.1–3). When an author employs *distancing*, this does not necessarily mean that they believe that the account is untrue; they simply do not want to take direct responsibility for its truth—as Herodotus says, "I cannot vouch for the truth of this story; I am simply recording what is said" (*Hist.* 4.195).[50]

---

[49] It can be difficult to choose between *sources* and *distancing* in some cases. Yet whichever of these one opts for in a given instance, the key point is that both are historiographic features.

[50] Unless otherwise noted, translations of Herodotus are from Herodotus, *The Histories*, trans. Robin Waterfield (Oxford UP, 1998). H. D. Westlake says that for Herodotus, λέγεται ("it is said") phrases "do not necessarily indicate disbelief but rather claim that, while he cannot

Distancing is an important historiographic indicator because it allows an author to include legendary/ahistorical elements in their account without necessarily affirming that these events happened (and while demonstrating a concern for historical truth). Many of the supernatural elements that scholars have used to argue for the legendary character of ancient birth narratives are actually elements from which the authors distance themselves. In such cases, it may be fair to say that the narrative contains elements that the biographer does not believe occurred, but it is manifestly unfair to conclude that the whole narrative is intended to be legendary, for in the act of *distancing*, the author has indicated a concern for historical truth.[51]

The four features above appear throughout ancient biographies—not only in birth material (see appendixes B–F). They also occur throughout ancient historiography more broadly (see appendix A). It therefore seems reasonable to think that they serve as reliable indicators of historiographic intent. One can, of course, imagine fringe cases where an author might utilize these features without intending to tell a true story. Cervantes, for example, mentions sources in *Don Quixote* to create a fictional façade

---

vouch for the trustworthiness of his information from personal knowledge or observation, at least it has the authority of some source, oral or written, which he has consulted" ("ΛΕΓΕΤΑΙ in Thucydides," *Mnemosyne* 30 [1977]: 362). Brad L. Cook rightly cautions against assuming that Plutarch uses λέγεται phrases to signal doubt, suspicion, or skepticism, noting that when Plutarch disagrees with a source, he tends to do so explicitly ("Plutarch's Use of λέγεται: Narrative Design and Source in Alexander," *Greek, Roman, and Byzantine Studies* 42 [2001]: 329–60). Cook argues positively that Plutarch uses λέγεται phrases "to tie the information to the great tradition that has been handed down" (359). I agree with Cook that λέγεται phrases (in Plutarch and elsewhere) may signal *sources*, but in my view, they often indicate *distancing*. See further the discussions in part 1 and J. L. Moles, commentary to *The Life of Cicero*, by Plutarch, ed. and trans. J. L. Moles (Aris & Phillips, 1988), 147.

[51] Lucian advises would-be historians: "If a myth comes along you must tell it but not believe it entirely; no, make it known for your audience to make of it what they will—you run no risk and lean to neither side" (*How to Write History* 60 [Kilburn, LCL]). I owe this reference to Keener, *Miracles*, 1:89.

of writing history.⁵² Few readers, however, have had difficulty recognizing the tongue-in-cheek nature of such references or the satirical character of the work as a whole. An author might also utilize the four features above with an intent to deceive, attempting to dupe the reader into thinking that an ahistorical story was historical. However, such cases highlight the extent to which the genre and character of a work impact how one should interpret the four features above. Once one has determined that a given work is not satirical or deceptive, the four features above become indicators of historiographic intent on a commonsense reading. Thus, where one finds these features in an ancient biography, one should conclude that the passage in question is intended to be historiographic unless there is substantial evidence to the contrary. Historiographic features, in other words, place the burden of proof on the one who asserts that a source is meant to be ahistorical.

Yet if these four features are sufficient indicators of historiographic intent in ancient biography, they are not necessary indicators of historiographic intent. A source, in other words, might lack these features but still be historiographic in nature. Any judgment about the historiographic character of a source must consider the genre as a whole and the conventions of the author in question. For example, if Plutarch employs historiographic features in many of his biographies, then it stands to reason that even if he does not use those features in a particular biography (or part thereof), the work is still historiographic.

THE PLAN OF THIS BOOK

The body of this book is divided into two parts. In part 1, "Ancient Birth Narratives and Historiography," I argue that birth narratives in ancient biographies were not intended to be legendary but historical. To demonstrate this thesis, I examine birth material in a representative sample of ancient biographies, focusing each chapter on the work of a particular biographer. The four biographers that I discuss are:

---

⁵² Such references occur frequently at the beginning of chapters in part 2 of *Don Quixote*.

- Cornelius Nepos
- Philo of Alexandria
- Plutarch
- Suetonius

I have selected these biographers for three main reasons: (1) they wrote within roughly a century of the Gospels; (2) they contain birth material; (3) Cornelius Nepos, Suetonius, and Plutarch all have numerous extant biographies that allow us to make significant conclusions about the nature of their birth material. I include Philo because his *Life of Moses* is our only extant Jewish biography, and many scholars have cited him in discussing the nature of the Gospel birth narratives.

In each chapter of part 1, I begin by introducing the biographer in question and their works. I then discuss historiographic features in their birth material and go on to consider some other issues that bear on the historiographic intent of this material and its relationship to the Gospel birth narratives. Due to space constraints, I do not attempt to discuss birth material in all the biographies of Nepos, Plutarch, and Suetonius but instead focus on representative examples. To demonstrate that the historiographic features that I note are not unique to the birth material I discuss, I provide a summary chart for each biographer that details historiographic features and other elements for all their extant biographies (see appendixes B–E). These summary charts focus on the birth material but also include examples of the historiographic features in the rest of each biography. A final chapter in part 1 summarizes my conclusions on ancient birth narratives and historiography.

In part 2, "Gospel Birth Narratives and Historiography," I turn to the Gospel birth narratives to consider how the historiographic nature of birth material in ancient biographies should shape our reading of Matthew and Luke. Following the author-centered approach of part 1, I treat the birth narratives of Matthew and Luke in separate chapters. A concluding chapter draws together my conclusions about the historiographic intent of the Gospel birth narratives and outlines some implications for the truth of the Gospel birth narratives and their use in future scholarship on the historical Jesus.

CONCLUSION

I noted at the beginning of this chapter that modern scholarship regards the Gospel birth narratives as substantially less reliable than the rest of the Gospels. As we have seen above, this distrust of the Gospel birth narratives and the resulting disuse of them in historical Jesus scholarship largely depends on a skepticism of intent that asserts that ancient birth narratives—and, by extension, the Gospel birth narratives—were intended to be legendary. However, the evidence that scholars have offered for the legendary character of ancient birth narratives is in reality quite thin. The present book challenges this skepticism of intent by demonstrating that in ancient biographies (including the Gospels) birth material was not meant to be legendary but historical. We turn now to ancient birth narratives themselves to examine their historiographic character.

I
Ancient Birth Narratives and Historiography

1
CORNELIUS NEPOS

Cornelius Nepos (ca. 110–24 BC) is the author of our earliest extant Latin biographies.[1] He was born in Cisalpine Gaul but lived much of his life in Rome and became acquainted with Cicero, Atticus, and Catullus.[2] Nepos published numerous works, including:

- *De viris illustribus* (*On Famous Men*), short biographies of Romans and foreigners grouped by categories (e.g., generals, historians) and comprising at least sixteen books
- *Chronica*, a history of the world in three books
- *Exempla*, moral anecdotes in at least five books

---

[1] Here and below I draw on John C. Rolfe, introduction to *On Great Generals. On Historians*, by Cornelius Nepos, trans. John C. Rolfe, LCL 467 (Harvard UP, 1929), vii–xiii; John C. Rolfe, Gavin B. Townend, and Antony Spawforth, "Cornelius Nepos," *OCD* 380; Michael von Albrecht, *A History of Roman Literature: From Livius Andronicus to Boethius: With Special Regard to Its Influence on World Literature*, rev. ed., 2 vols., Mnemosyne: Bibliotheca Classica Batavia 165 (Brill, 1997), 1:476–78.

[2] Nepos corresponded with Cicero, addresses his *De viris illustribus* to Atticus (pref. 1.1), and had a book of poems dedicated to him by Catullus. See Rolfe, introduction to *On Great Generals. On Historians*, vii–viii. Quotations of Cornelius Nepos below are from this volume unless otherwise noted.

- Biographies of Cato the Elder and Cicero
- A work on geography

Of these, only twenty-four lives from *De viris illustribus* have survived: twenty-two from a book on foreign generals (*De excellentibus ducibus exterarum gentium*), and two from a book on Roman historians (*De historicis latinis*).[3] The first edition of *De viris illustribus* is generally dated to around 34 BC, and a second edition appeared sometime before 27 BC.[4] It is unclear precisely what changes were made in the second edition, but it seems to have added the short section *On Kings* (not a biography), lives of Datames, Hamilcar, and Hannibal, and some material in the life of Atticus.[5] Here I will assume a date of 28 BC for the lives of Datames, Hamilcar, and Hannibal and 34 BC for the rest of the lives.

Cornelius Nepos presents an interesting case for our study for at least two reasons. First, his birth material is strikingly mundane. Where Nepos includes birth material, he typically limits

---

[3] Here I follow the LCL edition in counting *Hamilcar* and *Hannibal* as standalone lives in the book on foreign generals. For the view that the material on Hamilcar and Hannibal is an appendix to this book, see Albrecht, *History*, 1:478.

[4] Rolfe, introduction to *On Great Generals. On Historians*, xi; Nicholas Horsfall, "Life of Atticus," in *Cornelius Nepos: A Selection, Including the Lives of Cato and Atticus*, Clarendon Ancient History Series (Clarendon, 1989), 8–9; Albrecht, *History*, 1:478; Rolfe, Townend, and Spawforth, "Cornelius Nepos," 380. Nepos addresses Atticus as if he is alive (pref. 1.1), and Atticus died in 32 BC. Nepos seems to imply the publication of a second edition in *Atticus* 19.1. On the date of 27 BC, Rolfe notes that "Octavian is everywhere referred to as Caesar, never with the title Augustus, conferred on him in 27 B.C." (introduction to *On Great Generals. On Historians*, xi, n1). For some helpful cautions regarding the second edition, see John Alexander Lobur, *Cornelius Nepos: A Study in the Evidence and Influence* (University of Michigan Press, 2021), 86.

[5] Rolfe, introduction to *On Great Generals. On Historians*, xi. Cf. Nicholas Horsfall, "Prose and Mime," in *Latin Literature*, ed. E. J. Kenney and W. V. Clausen, vol. 2 of *The Cambridge History of Classical Literature* (Cambridge UP, 1982), 292. In the LCL edition, *De regibus* appears after the lives of the foreign generals and before the lives of the Roman historians. However, I do not count it as one of the lives because it is not a biography of a single figure but a collection of brief biographical information about multiple figures.

himself to brief comments on his subject's lineage and perhaps some information about his place of birth or childhood. Even from a modern perspective, it is difficult to find any claims that strain credulity or suggest an ahistorical intent.[6] Second, scholars who assert that ancient birth narratives were intended to be ahistorical generally do not discuss Cornelius Nepos.[7] This omission may simply be an oversight, but if so, it is a significant one.

In what follows, I begin by examining a representative sample of birth material from *De viris illustribus*. While Nepos uses all four historiographic devices (*sources, transparency, evaluation,* and *distancing*), he typically does so outside of birth material.[8] There are two ways to interpret this datum: (1) Nepos does not intend his birth material to be historical; (2) Nepos intends his birth material to be historical but does not find it necessary to use historiographic features. As we will see below, the latter view is by far the more likely. In the latter part of the chapter, I consider three other issues that bear on the historiographic character of Nepos's birth material: (1) the absence of birth material from some of Nepos's lives; (2) Nepos's attitude toward omens and supernatural events; (3) the time elapsed between the subjects' births and Nepos's writing.

BIRTH MATERIAL IN *DE VIRIS ILLUSTRIBUS*
Alcibiades

Cornelius Nepos opens his life of Alcibiades as follows:

> Alcibiades, the Athenian, son of Clinias. In this man Nature seems to have tried to see what she could accomplish; for it is

---

[6] One might attribute the sober character of Nepos's birth material to the brevity of his biographies, but length is not necessary to indicate legendary intent. One can, for example, insert a divine parent into a genealogy just as easily as a human parent.

[7] Meier does not mention Nepos in his discussion of ancient birth narratives (*A Marginal Jew: Rethinking the Historical Jesus*, 5 vols., ABRL [Doubleday, 1991–2016], 1:208–9, 234–35). Nepos does not appear in the indexes of Robert J. Miller, *Born Divine: The Births of Jesus and Other Sons of God* (Polebridge, 2003); Andrew T. Lincoln, *Born of a Virgin? Reconceiving Jesus in the Bible, Tradition, and Theology* (Eerdmans, 2013).

[8] See appendix B.

agreed by all who have written his biography that he was never excelled either in faults or in virtues. Born in the most famous of cities of a very noble family, he was by far the handsomest man of his time. (*Alc.* 1.1–2)[9]

Here Nepos provides three pieces of information about Alcibiades's birth and childhood: his father (Clinias), his place of birth ("the most famous of cities"—presumably Athens), and the fact that he was from "a very noble family." None of these seem to be legendary. Nepos also suggests that he has *sources* when he says, "It is agreed by all who have written his biography that he was never excelled in faults or in virtues" (1.1). To be sure, the specific point for which Nepos cites these sources is Alcibiades's remarkable ability to manifest both virtues and vices—a point about his adult character, as the rest of the paragraph makes clear (1.2–4). Yet the fact that Nepos mentions these biographies implies that he is drawing on them for other information as well, likely including the very basic details he provides about Alcibiades's origins in the surrounding sentences. Indeed, as we will see below, Nepos later confirms that he has sources for his birth material.

After summarizing the adult abilities and character of Alcibiades (1.2–4), Nepos returns to Alcibiades's childhood (2.1). He says that Alcibiades "was brought up in the home of Pericles (for he is said to have been his step-son)" and that Socrates was his teacher (2.1). Nepos employs *distancing* when he notes that Alcibiades "is said" (*dicitur*) to have been the stepson of Pericles.

---

[9] Unless otherwise noted, translations of Cornelius Nepos are from Rolfe, trans., *On Great Generals. On Historians*. Rolfe's translation "by far the handsomest *man* of his time" (emphasis added; *omnium aetatis suae multo formosissimus*) suggests that the claim applies to Alcibiades's adulthood. The Latin, however, is ambiguous; one might translate the phrase as "the handsomest of his time," in which case it would apply to Alcibiades's life in general. Even if one opts for the latter interpretation, however, this would not mean that Nepos intends the claim (as it pertains to Alcibiades's early life) to be ahistorical. Alcibiades was well known for his good looks, and we have no reason to think that they began only at adolescence. For ancient references to Alcibiades's good looks, see John L. Jackson, "A Commentary on Nepos' Life of Alcibiades" (MA thesis, Rhodes University, 1982), 22–23.

There is some question of whether Alcibiades was actually the stepson of Pericles.[10] However, this is an issue of truth, not intent. Precisely by distancing himself from this claim (which supports a key point regarding his subject's childhood), Nepos indicates his historiographic intent.

Nepos goes on to discuss Alcibiades's "early youth" (2.2). He focuses, however, on Alcibiades's romantic relationships with many "after the Greek fashion, including Socrates," referring to Plato's *Symposium* (2.2). The clear reference to pederasty suggests that the period in view is Alcibiades's teenage years, not his childhood. The birth material, then, seems to be limited to the three points noted above (1.1–2) and the additional datum that Alcibiades was raised in the home of Pericles (2.1). Throughout this material, Nepos exhibits historiographic restraint. While he clearly believes that as an adult Alcibiades was a paradoxical mix of virtue and vice, he does not attempt to retroject this character into his subject's childhood. Similarly, while Nepos knows of the potential stepson/stepfather relationship between Alcibiades and Pericles, he limits himself to this datum rather than portraying Alcibiades as the biological son of Pericles. If Nepos were simply trying to write an ahistorical origin story for Alcibiades, one would expect him to make Alcibiades the son of the great hero Pericles rather than the lesser-known Clinias.

Nepos notes some of his sources toward the end of *Alcibiades*:

> Although his reputation has been assailed by many writers, Alcibiades has been highly praised by three authoritative historians: Thucydides, who belonged to the same period, Theopompus, who was born somewhat later than he, and Timaeus. These last two, who are strongly inclined to abuse, somehow agree in praising that one man. For it is they that are my authority for what I have previously written about him, as well as for the following appraisement. (11.1–2)

It is unclear what Nepos means when he says that Theopompus and Timaeus are his authority for what he has written

---

[10] John C. Rolfe, the editor of the LCL edition of *De viris illustribus*, comments in a footnote, "The relationship was not so close as that." See further Jackson, "Commentary on Nepos' Life of Alcibiades," 34–36.

"previously" (*supra*) about Alcibiades. The Latin *supra* seems to refer to material within the present work, as opposed to content in an earlier work. But is Nepos referring to all the preceding material in *Alcibiades* or some subset of it? Unfortunately, Nepos does not clarify, and the works of Theopompus and Timaeus have largely been lost, so we cannot examine them to be sure. However, we must remain open to the possibility that Nepos used these historians as sources for his birth material.[11] And whatever we make of Theopompus and Timaeus, it seems that Nepos does draw on Thucydides for at least some of his birth material. When Thucydides introduces Alcibiades in *Peloponnesian War*, he notes that Alcibiades was an Athenian, that he was the son of Clinias, and that his family was noble (*Pel. War* 5.43)—essentially the same three points that Nepos makes in *Alcibiades* 1.1–2.[12] Thucydides nowhere portrays Alcibiades as being raised in the house of Pericles or being the stepson of Pericles, so it seems that he was not Nepos's source for this information. However, the fact that Nepos seems to use Thucydides as a source for three of the four points he provides about his subject's origins suggests that he had sources for his discussion of Alcibiades and Pericles as well.[13]

---

[11] In a footnote in the LCL edition, Rolfe identifies the previously (*supra*) written material as being "in chapters 1 and 2." Unfortunately, he does not explain his reasoning.

[12] Thucydides does not explicitly say that Alcibiades was born in Athens, but one might easily infer this from his account. Diodorus Siculus (*Library of History* 12.84.1; 13.37.2) also notes that Alcibiades came from a noble family.

[13] In the Platonic (or pseudo-Platonic) dialogue the *Greater Alcibiades*, Socrates addresses Alcibiades as the "son of Cleinias" (παῖ Κλεινίου; 103A). Plutarch likewise identifies Cleinias as the father of Alcibiades and says that he "was reared as the ward of Pericles and Ariphron, the sons of Xanthippus, his near kinsmen" (*Alc.* 1.1). Two factors suggest that Plutarch is not simply drawing on Nepos for this information: (1) Plutarch differs slightly with Nepos regarding Alcibiades's childhood, mentioning Ariphron and portraying Pericles as his kinsman rather than his stepfather (though, as noted, Nepos distances himself from this datum); (2) Plutarch goes on to provide information about Alcibiades's childhood beyond what Nepos mentions, citing sources (*Alc.* 1.2). The

In *Alcibiades*, Cornelius Nepos provides a simple and plausible account of his subject's birth and childhood, indicating his historiographic intent by noting his *sources* and *distancing* himself from one claim. There is nothing to suggest that Nepos regarded his birth material for Alcibiades as being ahistorical. On the contrary, Nepos abstains from fabricating material or bending facts at several points where it would have been convenient to do so if he only wished to forecast the adult character of Alcibiades.

Epaminondas

Nepos notes at the outset of *Epaminondas* that his subject was a Theban and the son of Polymnis (*Epam.* 1.1). After discussing some other introductory matters (1.1–4), Nepos goes on to describe Epaminondas's family and education:

> His family was an honourable one, but had been in moderate circumstances for some time; yet in spite of that he received as good an education as any Theban. Thus he was taught to play the lyre, and to sing with an instrumental accompaniment, by Dionysius . . . He learned to play the pipes from Olympiodorus and to dance from Calliphron. In philosophy he had as his master Lysis of Tarentum, the Pythagorean, and to him he was so attached that in his youth he was more intimate with that grave and austere old man than with any of the young people of his own age; and he would not allow his teacher to leave him until he so far surpassed his fellow-students in learning, that it could readily be understood that in a similar way he would surpass all men in all other accomplishments. (2.1–2)

Nepos's account is anything but fantastic. Epaminondas comes from a family that is honorable but not at the height of its powers. He receives an education that is good but within the range of what is normal for Thebes. Epaminondas excels in learning, but Nepos seems to credit his academic success to the amount of time he spent with his philosophy teacher rather than to him being a child prodigy. Nepos does connect Epaminondas's childhood to his adulthood by saying, "He so far surpassed his fellow-students

---

overall picture that emerges, then, is that Nepos is drawing on sources for his claims about Alcibiades's origins.

in learning, that it could readily be understood that in a similar way he would surpass all men in all other accomplishments" (2.2). However, Nepos's comment does not seem to suggest an ahistorical intent. Note that Nepos gives one example of Epaminondas's scholastic success and forecasts from it that he would "surpass all men in all other accomplishments." Here we see a historiographic restraint in play. While Nepos knows that Epaminondas will go on to excel in areas besides learning, he does not fabricate additional childhood stories to anticipate this. Rather, Nepos writes what he knows about his subject's childhood and connects this to his adulthood.

Nepos does not use historiographic features in *Epaminondas*, but it is not hard to see why. The account is eminently plausible, so *distancing* is unnecessary. While Nepos could certainly note his *sources*, this is not necessary for historiographic intent, and some of the information he provides may have been common knowledge. And if Nepos is unaware of alternate accounts (or does not think them worth mentioning), then there is no need for *transparency* or *evaluation*. A close reading of *Epaminondas* therefore suggests that Nepos has composed his birth material with historiographic intent. As we will see below, Nepos's other lives confirm this hypothesis.

Agesilaus

Nepos gives a nod to his *sources* at the beginning of *Agesilaus*, saying, "Agesilaus the Lacedaemonian was praised, not only by all other historians, but in particular by Xenophon, the disciple of Socrates, whose intimate friend he was" (*Ag.* 1.1). Nepos does not discuss Agesilaus's birth or childhood directly, but he does mention his lineage indirectly:

> [Agesilaus] began by having a dispute about the throne with Leotychides, his brother's son; for it was the custom of the Lacedaemonians, handed down from their forefathers, always to have two kings . . . from the families of Procles and Eurysthenes, who were descendants of Hercules and the first kings at Sparta. (1.2)

Here Nepos seems to trace the ancestry of Agesilaus (and other kings of Sparta) back to Hercules. One might be tempted to see this as an instance of legendary embellishment. However, two factors suggest that Nepos intends this claim to be not legendary but historical. First, many people in antiquity—including historians and biographers—regarded Hercules as a real person.[14] So while many people today may view Hercules as a legendary figure, we should not assume that Nepos did the same. Second, Nepos seems to have had a *source* for this claim. As noted above, Nepos explicitly mentions Xenophon at the beginning of *Agesilaus*, saying that he praised Agesilaus and was his friend (1.1). Nepos is presumably referring to Xenophon's own work about Agesilaus (also titled *Agesilaus*). Here Xenophon says of Agesilaus, "Even to-day the line of his descent from Heracles is traced through the roll of his ancestors" (*Ag.* 1.2).[15] It seems, then, that Nepos has not fabricated his claim that Agesilaus descended from Hercules but has drawn it from Xenophon.[16]

Hannibal

Nepos introduces Hannibal as "the Carthaginian, son of Hamilcar" (*Han.* 1.1). After giving an overview of Hannibal's adult life, Nepos relates a speech by Hannibal to King Antiochus about an event that happened when he was around nine years old.[17]

> My father Hamilcar, when I was a small boy not more than nine years old, just as he was setting out from Carthage to Spain as commander-in-chief, offered up victims to Jupiter, Greatest and Best of gods. While this ceremony was being performed, he asked me if I would like to go with him on the campaign. I eagerly

[14] E.g., Herodotus, *Hist.* 1.7; 2.44, 146; 7.204; 8.131; Xenophon, *Hell.* 3.3.3; 6.3.6; *Ag.* 1.2; 8.7; Diodorus Siculus, *Library of History* 4.8–39, esp. 4.8; Plutarch, *Ag.* 3.5; *Alex.* 2.1; *Lyc.* 1.3–4; *Pel.* 16.5.

[15] Translation from Xenophon, *Scripta Minora*, trans. E. C. Marchant and G. W. Bowersock, LCL 183 (Harvard UP, 1925). Xenophon elsewhere describes how descent from Heracles played a pivotal role in the Spartans choosing Agesilaus to be their king (*Hell.* 3.3.3).

[16] James R. Bradley, *The Sources of Cornelius Nepos: Selected Lives*, Harvard Dissertations in Classics (Garland, 1991), 122.

[17] The king in view seems to be Antiochus III.

accepted and began to beg him not to hesitate to take me with him. Thereupon he said: "I will do it, provided you will give me the pledge that I ask." With that he led me to the altar on which he had begun his sacrifice, and having dismissed all the others, he bade me lay hold of the altar and swear that I would never be a friend to the Romans. For my part, up to my present time of life, I have kept the oath which I swore to my father so faithfully, that no one ought to doubt that in the future I shall be of the same mind. Therefore, if you have any kindly intentions with regard to the Roman people, you will be wise to hide them from me; but when you prepare war, you will go counter to your own interests if you do not make me the leader in that enterprise. (2.3–6)

Nepos picks up the narrative here saying, "Accordingly, at the age which I have named, Hannibal went with his father to Spain" (3.1). This concludes the childhood material of *Hannibal*.

Nepos's treatment of Hannibal's childhood is fascinating for at least two reasons. First, the information that Nepos provides directly is remarkably restrained: Hannibal was a Carthaginian (1.1), the son of Hamilcar (1.1), and went with his father to Spain around age nine (3.1). Second, the sole story about Hannibal's childhood occurs in a speech on the lips of Hannibal himself (2.3–6). Hannibal, then, becomes the *source* of the information within Nepos's narrative. And Nepos seems to regard the story Hannibal tells as historically true (not merely a tall tale), for when he resumes his narrative, he says, "Accordingly..." and goes on to assume that both Hannibal's age indicated in the story and the reason it provides for why Hannibal went with his father to Spain are true (3.1).

One might protest, however, that Nepos could not have had a source for this story and that he puts it on the adult Hannibal's lips to distance himself from the report. Perhaps. But even if this is true, *distancing* would still indicate Nepos's historiographic intent. More importantly, though, there is good reason to think that Nepos did have a source for this claim. Toward the end of *Hannibal*, Nepos mentions a number of sources:

> Thus that bravest of men, after having performed many and varied labours, entered into rest in his seventieth year. Under what consuls he died is disputed. For Atticus has recorded in his

Annals that he died in the consulate of Marcus Claudius Marcellus and Quintus Fabius Labeo; Polybius, under Lucius Aemilius Paulus and Gnaeus Baebius Tamphilus; and Sulpicius Blitho, in the time of Publius Cornelius Cethegus and Marcus Baebius Tamphilus. And that great man, although busied with such great wars, devoted some time to letters; for there are several books of his, written in Greek, among them one, addressed to the Rhodians, on the deeds of Gnaeus Manlius Volso in Asia. Hannibal's deeds of arms have been recorded by many writers, among them two men who were with him in camp and lived with him so long as fortune allowed, Silenus and Sosylus of Lacedaemon. (13.1–3)

Most of the sources that Nepos refers to are lost. Polybius, however, has survived fragmentarily and records the speech that Nepos mentions.

> He [Hannibal] said that he was there, by the altar, aged nine, when his father was about to launch his campaign in Iberia with his army and was sacrificing to Zeus. After obtaining a favorable result—and once he had poured a libation to the gods and performed the customary rites—Hamilcar asked everyone else who was present at the sacrifice to stand back a bit, and then he called Hannibal over and asked him kindly if he would like to join him on the expedition. Hannibal eagerly said yes, and was even a bit insistent about it, as boys will be. So his father led him by the right hand up to the altar, and told him to place his hand on the victim and swear unremitting hatred for the Romans. (*Hist.* 3.11)[18]

There are, of course, minor differences between the versions of Polybius and Nepos. The core of the story, however, is the same—even regarding details like Hannibal's age. The close parallels between Polybius and Nepos suggest that Nepos drew on Polybius for Hannibal's speech and the information it provides about Hannibal's childhood.

Nepos therefore exhibits historiographic intent in the birth material of *Hannibal*. He limits the information he directly reports to basic details that are beyond dispute, and he credits the one

---

[18] Polybius, *The Histories*, trans. Robin Waterfield, Oxford World's Classics (Oxford UP, 2010), 140. Polybius also mentions earlier that Hamilcar took Hannibal to Iberia when Hannibal was nine (*Hist.* 2.1).

childhood story that he relates to Hannibal himself—probably based on the witness of Polybius.

Cato

Nepos begins his life of Cato as follows:

> Marcus Cato, born in the town of Tusculum, in his early youth, before entering on an official career, lived in the land of the Sabines, since he had there an hereditary property, left him by his father. (*Cat.* 1.1)

From here Nepos moves quickly to the beginning of Cato's public career, picking up a few lines later at his first campaign at age seventeen. Nepos provides two more pieces of information about Cato's youth in passing comments later in the biography. Nepos notes, "For about eighty years, from youth to the end of his life, he never ceased to incur enmity through his devotion to his country" (2.4). And in discussing Cato's literary achievements, he says, "From early youth he composed speeches" (3.1). However, Nepos provides no anecdotes to illustrate either claim. We can therefore sum up the information that Nepos provides about Cato's childhood in four points: (1) he was born in the town of Tusculum (1.1), (2) he lived in the land of the Sabines (1.1), (3) throughout his life (including his youth) he incurred enmity through devotion to his country, and (4) he composed speeches.

Nepos does not employ historiographic indicators in the birth material of *Cato*. Yet, as with *Epaminondas* above, to do so would be superfluous. The information Nepos provides about Cato's childhood is simple and restrained. While someone might question whether Cato exhibited patriotism or composed speeches at a young age, these claims seem plausible, and Nepos gives no reason to think that this information is ahistorical. Indeed, the fact that these two claims occur in material about Cato's adulthood makes it very difficult to argue that the claims about Cato's youth are intended to be less historiographic than the surrounding discourse.

It is also important to note that while Nepos does not cite sources in the birth material of *Cato*, he almost certainly had a source. At the end of *Cato*, Nepos says,

> Concerning this man's life and character I have given fuller details in the separate book which I devoted to his biography at the urgent request of Titus Pomponius Atticus. Therefore I may refer those who are interested in Cato to that volume. (3.5)

The *Cato* that we have, then, seems to be an extract of a much longer *Cato* that has not survived. Nepos's longer *Cato*, that is, functioned as a source for the shorter *Cato*. Of course, we do not know what sources Nepos drew on for the longer *Cato*, but his practice elsewhere (including *Han.* 13.1–3) suggests that he did have sources.

Atticus

Atticus provides an interesting change of pace from Nepos's normal mode of operation. As we have seen above, Nepos often gives just a few sentences on his subject's early life. In *Atticus*, however, he gives a full paragraph:

> Titus Pomponius Atticus, descended from the most ancient Roman stock, never abandoned the equestrian rank which he had inherited from his ancestors. His father was attentive to business and rich for those days. He was besides particularly interested in literature, and because of his own love of letters, trained his son in all the studies essential for the education of the young. Moreover, the boy had, in addition to a capacity for learning, a most agreeable enunciation and quality of voice, so that he not only quickly learned passages that were set, but also declaimed them admirably. Hence in childhood he was conspicuous among those of his own age, and showed greater superiority than his high-born schoolfellows could accept with indifference. Consequently, he inspired them all with a spirit of rivalry; and among them were Lucius Torquatus, the younger Gaius Marius, and Marcus Cicero, with all of whom he became so intimate that as long as he lived no one was dearer to them. (*Att.* 1.1–3)[19]

Overall, Nepos's account seems quite plausible. Atticus comes from "the most ancient Roman stock." His father is "rich for those days" but no god. The most ambitious claims that Nepos makes have to do with his subject's educational prowess. Atticus not only

---

[19] Nepos goes on to relate some events from Atticus's youth (2–4), but these seem to be from his teenage years.

received a good education; he "was conspicuous among those of his own age" and "inspired them all with a spirit of rivalry." Such a claim certainly goes beyond Nepos's norm. Does Nepos, then, tip his hand here, revealing a legendary intent?

The rest of *Atticus* suggests that the answer is "No." Nepos knew Atticus personally, addresses him in *De viris illustribus* (pref. 1.1), and appeals to his own eyewitness status at several points in *Atticus* (13.7; 17.1). He cites Cicero—both his published works and sixteen volumes of letters written to Atticus—to support a claim about Atticus (16.3). And Nepos also refers to several works by Atticus: a history of Rome (cf. *Han*. 13.1), other books that treat Roman genealogies, poetic works on great Roman men, and a book in Greek on Cicero's consulship (*Att*. 18.1–6). At the beginning of *Atticus* 19, Nepos says,

> Here ends what I wrote during the lifetime of Atticus. Now, since it was Fortune's decree that I should survive him, I will finish the account, and so far as I can, will show my readers by examples that as a rule—as I indicated above—it is the character of every man that determines his fortune. (19.1)

Nepos, in other words, composed *Atticus* 1–18 during his subject's lifetime and added chapters 19–20 for the second edition.[20]

What all of this means is that Nepos drew on an incredible wealth of information for *Atticus* and that Atticus himself would have had the opportunity to correct any errors before the second edition (the only one extant) appeared. We do not know precisely what sources Nepos drew on for the birth material, but his comments on sources elsewhere suggest that he had sources—quite possibly Atticus's own testimony. Therefore, the biography in which Nepos makes the most ambitious claims about his subject's childhood is also the one for which he has the best sources.

Summary

The six lives from Nepos's *De viris illustribus* that we have explored above demonstrate that Nepos composed his birth

---

[20] See Rolfe's footnote in the LCL edition; Horsfall, "Life of Atticus," 102.

material with historiographic intent. Although Nepos uses historiographic indicators only rarely, this is understandable given the limited birth material he provides. One hardly needs to employ *sources, distancing, transparency,* or *evaluation*, for example, to state that Hannibal was "the Carthaginian, son of Hamilcar" (*Han.* 1.1). It is also worth noting that Nepos utilizes historiographic indicators infrequently in adult material as well (see appendix B). We have seen that Nepos sometimes includes blanket source-notes for the life as a whole and that these often pertain to the birth material. In particular, we have discovered three cases where Nepos seems to draw on known historians (or similar sources) for his birth material and uses these sources responsibly.[21] Cornelius Nepos therefore poses a significant problem for the idea that ancient birth material was intended to be legendary. In what follows, we will explore some further facets of Nepos's birth material to sharpen our understanding of its historiographic character.

ABSENCE OF BIRTH MATERIAL

We must consider the absence of birth material in *De viris illustribus* on two levels: (1) partial absence and (2) complete absence. As we have seen above, Nepos provides minimal birth material for many of his subjects. The childhoods of Epaminondas, Hannibal, and Atticus get perhaps a paragraph (if one includes Hannibal's speech), but those of Alcibiades and Cato receive far less and are perhaps closer to the norm for Nepos. Indeed, in many lives Nepos notes only his subject's city (or nation) of origin and father. The brevity of the birth material in *Thrasybulus* is particularly interesting. Nepos clearly regards Thrasybulus as his favorite subject, saying,

> If merit were to be estimated absolutely, without reference to fortune, I rather think that I should rank this man first of all. Thus much is certain: I put no one above him in sense of honour, in steadfastness, in greatness of soul and in love of country. (*Thras.* 1.1)

---

[21] See above on *Alc.* 1.1–2 (cf. Thucydides, *Pel. War* 5.43); *Ag.* 1.2 (cf. Xenophon, *Ag.* 1.2); *Han.* 2.3–6 (cf. Polybius, *Hist.* 3.11).

Yet Nepos says nothing about Thrasybulus's origins beyond that he was an "Athenian, son of Lycus" (1.1). As Chris Alfred notes, "If Nepos were to have felt an urge toward persuasive embellishment, certainly it would have manifested when portraying a subject for whom he has professed such pleasant thoughts."[22] Here and elsewhere, the limited information that Nepos provides about his subjects' early lives suggests that he is restricting himself to the information in his sources, not fabricating birth material.[23]

In other cases, Nepos provides no birth material at all. Of the twenty-four extant lives from *De viris illustribus*, eight (33.33 percent) lack any birth material whatsoever.[24] And this is a very modest reckoning. If one were to include lives where Nepos mentions only his subject's city (or nation) of origin and father, the number of lives with no birth material would be much higher.

It is difficult to explain the absence of birth material if one assumes that Nepos regards birth material simply as an ahistorical anticipation of his subject's adult life. Yet if one grants that Nepos has composed his birth material with historiographic intent, a simple explanation emerges: Nepos does not include more birth material because (1) he lacked sources or (2) the information in his sources was not interesting or relevant enough to include. The absence of birth material (in part or whole) therefore suggests that Nepos's birth material is *information-based*.

---

[22] Chris Alfred, "Source Valuation in Greek and Roman Biography: From Xenophon to Suetonius," in *Biographies and Jesus: What Does It Mean for the Gospels to Be Biographies?* ed. Craig S. Keener and Edward T. Wright (Emeth, 2016), 99. Cf. Craig S. Keener, *Christobiography: Memory, History, and the Reliability of the Gospels* (Eerdmans, 2019), 171.

[23] The brevity of the birth material may be due in part to the fact that Nepos's biographies are short compared to those of Plutarch and other authors (cf. *Epam.* 4.6). However, even Nepos's longer biographies devote little space to the subject's early life.

[24] See appendix B.

SUPERNATURAL ELEMENTS

Scholars who hold that ancient birth narratives were legendary often point to supernatural elements in these stories to support their view. The elements are generally of two basic types:

1. Omens: events that are interpreted as signs regarding the significance of a person or event.[25] I include in this category portents, prophecies, oracles, and dreams where the author does not explicitly affirm supernatural causation.
2. Miracles: events that fall outside of normal human experience and natural causation.[26]

Cornelius Nepos, however, problematizes such an argument, for he includes no supernatural elements (omens or miracles) in his birth material. (See appendix B, which summarizes the supernatural elements that Nepos affirms.)[27] The few omens that Nepos recounts all occur in adult material (*Milt.* 1.2–3; *Them.* 2.6–7; *Paus.* 5.5). It is possible that Nepos puts no supernatural elements in his birth material (and few in his lives as a whole) because of space constraints: he wanted to write many short lives rather than fewer long ones (like Plutarch) and therefore had no room for supernatural trimmings. But the fact remains that Nepos fails to include the supernatural elements that one would expect if he were writing legends.

---

[25] The phenomena that ancient biographers describe as omens are generally things that moderns would describe as coincidences—a baby's birth coinciding with a catastrophe or victory, an eagle flying overhead, etc. It is the interpretation that transforms an event into an omen. And since many in the Greco-Roman world believed that omens did occur, it is not surprising that ancients often interpreted what we might call coincidences as omens or that ancient biographers report such events and their interpretation(s).

[26] On the definition of "miracle" see Craig S. Keener, *Miracles: The Credibility of the New Testament Accounts*, 2 vols. (Baker Academic, 2011), 1:109–13.

[27] Appendixes C–F likewise include only supernatural elements that the biographers affirm—i.e., not those qualified by *transparency*, negative *evaluation*, or *distancing*.

TIME ELAPSED

One factor that has not received sufficient attention in the discussion of ancient birth narratives and historiography is the time elapsed between the subject's birth and the biographer's writing. The time elapsed does not necessarily impact a biographer's historiographic intent, but it may significantly affect how well he can carry out that intent and the historiographic features he employs along the way. For example, a biographer writing seventy years after his subject's birth will often have access to better sources than a biographer writing seven hundred years after it. A biographer writing at a significant remove from the events may also have more occasion to employ *transparency, evaluation,* and *distancing* than a biographer who is close to the events.

Since this is the first chapter where I discuss time elapsed, I wish to note a few caveats that apply both to this chapter and to subsequent chapters. First, the time elapsed between the event and writing is not the only (or even the most important) chronological factor. Far more important is the time elapsed between the event and the biographer's sources. However, Nepos, Philo, Plutarch, and Suetonius rarely name specific, datable sources for their birth material, so it is impossible to calculate the time elapsed between event and sources with any sort of consistency. The time elapsed between event and writing therefore has its limitations, but it is often the best we can do. Second, here I use the publication date as the date of composition. Our biographers, of course, wrote their lives before they published them, but in most cases we simply do not know the date of composition apart from the date of publication. Third, to calculate the date of birth for ancient figures with any sort of accuracy is incredibly difficult. Here I follow the *Oxford Classical Dictionary* wherever possible for dates of birth.[28] If it does not provide a date of birth, I have consulted other sources and have sometimes had to make an educated guess. When the date of birth is ambiguous, I generally opt for a later date to allow our biographers to compare as favorably

---

[28] Simon Hornblower, Antony Spawforth, and Esther Eidinow, eds., *The Oxford Classical Dictionary*, 4th ed. (Oxford UP, 2012).

as possible with Matthew and Luke. I also use earlier dates of composition where possible for the same reason. The dates provided here are therefore approximate and must be used as such. Approximate dates, however, will be sufficient for our purposes; the insights I derive from the data do not depend on a few years in either direction.

With these caveats in hand, then, we turn to the time elapsed for Nepos. As noted above, I am assuming a date of 28 BC for the composition of *Datames*, *Hamilcar*, and *Hannibal*, and a date of 34 BC for the rest of the lives. The time elapsed for each of Nepos's lives appears in appendix B. Analysis of this data yields the following results:

Average	375.08 years
Median	380.5 years[29]
Maximum	521 years
Minimum	76 years

The major insight that emerges from these numbers is that *Nepos is writing at a significant historical distance from the births of almost all his subjects*. Atticus, Nepos's closest subject, was born approximately 76 years before Nepos wrote his life. Cato, the next closest, was born about 200 years before Nepos penned his biography. The average and median, however, are much higher—both over 375 years. The significant time elapsed between Nepos and his subjects' births gives rise to three related insights.

First, Nepos would have had direct access to eyewitness sources for the birth material of only one (at most) of his extant lives: *Atticus*. As noted above, Nepos and Atticus were contemporaries (both born around 110 BC) who knew each other personally. Atticus himself may have been one of Nepos's sources for the birth material. (Recall that Nepos focuses on Atticus's lineage and educational prowess—matters that Atticus would have known about.) Nepos may also have had the opportunity to interview other eyewitnesses of Atticus's early life; we do not know. What we do know is that Nepos did not have the opportunity to interview

---

[29] Because there are twenty-four of Nepos's lives, the median is the average of the middle two numbers.

eyewitnesses for his other extant biographies, though he may have had access to literary sources by eyewitnesses in some cases.

Second, the significant time elapsed further emphasizes the historiographic character of Nepos's birth material. Despite writing an average of 375 years after his subjects' births, Nepos includes no supernatural elements in his birth material, and he makes few (if any) claims that are remarkable, even from a modern perspective.

Third, while the historiographic intent with which Nepos has composed his birth material is helpful for understanding how Matthew and Luke might have approached the writing of their birth narratives, the level of accuracy he achieves (i.e., his ability to carry out his historiographic intent) is not a good gauge of what Matthew and Luke might have achieved. Among Nepos's lives, only *Atticus* approximates the access to sources that Matthew and Luke would likely have had.

CONCLUSION

Cornelius Nepos poses a significant challenge to the idea that ancient birth material was intended to be legendary. Nepos exhibits historiographic restraint throughout his birth material, uses historiographic features occasionally, and in at least three cases draws on known historians (or similar sources) that he uses responsibly. Nepos does not provide birth material for a third of his extant lives, which suggests that his birth material is information-based. He includes no omens or miracles in his birth material. And the significant time elapsed between the births of Nepos's subjects and his own writing further emphasizes the historiographic character of Nepos's birth material. Nepos therefore gives us significant reason to question the thesis that ancient birth material was ahistorical. And as we will see in the following chapters, Nepos is not alone.

2
PHILO

Philo of Alexandria (ca. 20 BC–AD 50) is one of the most significant Jewish authors from the Second Temple period.[1] Little is known about Philo's life directly beyond the fact that he participated in an embassy to the emperor Gaius around AD 39/40. It is clear, however, that he received both a Jewish and a Greek education and was heavily influenced by Platonic philosophy. Philo composed numerous works that may be divided into three groups: biblical commentaries, philosophical treatises, and apologetic treatises.[2]

The work of Philo that concerns us here is *On the Life of Moses*. Philo's extant works include three treatises on the lives of biblical figures: *On the Life of Abraham*, *On the Life of Joseph*, and *On the Life of Moses*.[3] Scholars generally do not regard *Abraham* and *Joseph* as ancient biographies; as Keener notes, Philo's

---

[1] Here and throughout this paragraph I draw on Gregory E. Sterling, "Philo of Alexandria," in *The Eerdmans Dictionary of Early Judaism* (Eerdmans, 2010), 1063–70; Tessa Rajak, "Philon (4), 'Philo'," *OCD*, 1134.

[2] Sterling, "Philo," 1065–67. For an early catalogue of Philo's works, see Eusebius, *Hist. eccl.* 2.18.1–9.

[3] Philo seems to have also written works on the lives of Isaac and Jacob, but if so, they have been lost. Cf. Philo, *Joseph* 1; Sterling, "Philo," 1067.

"philosophic penchant for allegorizing Pentateuchal narratives somewhat limits the analogy for mainstream biographies."[4] *Moses*, however, contains far less allegory, and numerous scholars regard it as an ancient biography.[5] Philo's *Moses* is important for our present investigation for two reasons: (1) as a Jewish biography, *Moses* provides an interesting comparison to Matthew and Luke, which both exhibit a significant knowledge of Israel's Scriptures and some acquaintance with contemporary Judaism; (2) many scholars have cited the birth narrative of *Moses* in arguing that the Gospel birth narratives are meant to be ahistorical.[6]

Our study here will follow a pattern similar to the preceding chapter, with a few adjustments. I begin by surveying historiographic features in the birth material of *Moses*. Philo's statements about his sources, however, make clear that he is drawing on Israel's Scriptures—a specific, extant source that we can compare to Philo's narrative. I will therefore also provide a more extensive discussion of how Philo is using his sources. In the latter part

---

[4] Craig S. Keener, *Christobiography: Memory, History, and the Reliability of the Gospels* (Eerdmans, 2019), 80. *Abraham* and *Joseph* also do not contain birth material, so they are not relevant to the present study.

[5] Charles H. Talbert, *What Is a Gospel? The Genre of the Canonical Gospels* (Fortress, 1977), 97; Klaus Berger, "Hellenistische Gattungen im Neuen Testament," *ANRW* 2.25.2:1234; David E. Aune, *The New Testament in Its Literary Environment*, Library of Early Christianity 8 (Westminster, 1987), 27; Richard A. Burridge, *What Are the Gospels? A Comparison with Graeco-Roman Biography*, 2nd ed. (Eerdmans, 2004), 128; Brian McGing, "Philo's Adaptation of the Bible in His *Life of Moses*," in *The Limits of Ancient Biography*, ed. Brian McGing and Judith Mossman (Classical Press of Wales, 2006), 217–19; Esteban Hidalgo, "A Redaction-Critical Study on Philo's *On the Life of Moses*, Book One," in *Biographies and Jesus: What Does It Mean for the Gospels to Be Biographies?* ed. Craig S. Keener and Edward T. Wright (Emeth, 2016), 277–301; Keener, *Christobiography*, 80–83.

[6] E.g., John P. Meier, *A Marginal Jew: Rethinking the Historical Jesus*, 5 vols., ABRL (Doubleday, 1991–2016), 1:208–9; Robert J. Miller, *Born Divine: The Births of Jesus and Other Sons of God* (Polebridge, 2003), 69; Roger David Aus, *Matthew 1–2 and the Virginal Conception: In Light of Palestinian and Hellenistic Judaic Traditions on the Birth of Israel's First Redeemer, Moses*, Studies in Judaism (UP of America, 2004), 4, 82–83; Andrew T. Lincoln, *Born of a Virgin? Reconceiving Jesus in the Bible, Tradition, and Theology* (Eerdmans, 2013), 65.

of the chapter, we will consider two further issues: (1) Philo's attitude toward omens and supernatural events and (2) the time elapsed between Moses's birth and Philo's writing.[7]

BIRTH MATERIAL IN PHILO'S *MOSES*
Historiographic Features

Philo discusses his *sources* in the introduction to *Moses*:

> I will... tell the story of Moses as I have learned it, both from the sacred books, the wonderful monuments of wisdom which he has left behind him, and from some of the elders of the nation; for I always interwove what I was told with what I read, and thus believed myself to have a closer knowledge than others of his life's history. (1.4)[8]

The "sacred books" are, of course, the books of the Torah, which ancient Judaism attributed to Moses. Philo, however, also mentions a second source: "some of the elders of the nation." Since he goes on to juxtapose "what I was told" with "what I read," it seems that the elders are an oral source. Philo seems to regard both the written Torah and the oral tradition as trustworthy, for he says that he "always interwove" the two and therefore understood Moses's life better than others. To modern readers, this might seem like a questionable historiographic move. Our present task, however, is not to evaluate Philo's presuppositions but to understand his intent. And Philo clearly views both the written Torah and the traditions of the elders as reliable sources for his life of Moses.

Philo's discussion of his sources in *Moses* 1.4 is significant for at least three reasons. First, Philo places this discussion *before* the birth narrative, suggesting that the sources in question apply to the whole life, including the birth narrative. Therefore, with

---

[7] As noted above, *Moses* is Philo's only extant ancient biography, so it is not possible to discuss the absence of birth material for Philo as I do with Cornelius Nepos, Plutarch, and Suetonius.

[8] Unless otherwise noted, translations of Philo, *Moses* are from Philo, *On Abraham. On Joseph. On Moses*, trans. F. H. Colson, LCL 289 (Harvard UP, 1935).

respect to sources, Philo therefore seems to regard the birth narrative as being just as historiographic as the rest of the life. Second, because Philo cites the Torah (which is extant) as a source, it is possible to compare *Moses* to the Torah to see how Philo is using his sources. We can study, for example, whether Philo uses the Torah any differently in recounting Moses's birth and childhood than in describing his adulthood. Third, because Philo says he is also drawing on Jewish oral traditions, we cannot assume that simply because *Moses* differs from the Torah at a given point, Philo is fabricating material. It is quite possible that in such cases Philo is drawing on Jewish oral tradition, and comparison with Jewish literature may help to confirm this.[9]

Philo employs historiographic features twice in the birth narrative. After describing how Moses's parents disobeyed the king's command to kill their male baby, Philo says, "In fact *we are told that*, unknown to all but few, [Moses] was kept at home and fed from his mother's breast for three successive months" (1.9, emphasis added). One might interpret this as *distancing*. However, each element of the claim finds support in the biblical account (Exod 2:2, 7–9), and it does not particularly strain credulity, so it is hard to imagine why Philo would want to distance himself from it. It therefore seems better to understand this as a reminder of Philo's *sources*. A few sentences later, Philo states,

> The king of the country had but one cherished daughter, who, *we are told* [φασί], had been married for a considerable time but had never conceived a child, though she naturally desired one, particularly of the male sex, to succeed to the magnificent inheritance of her father's kingdom, which threatened to go to strangers if his daughter gave him no grandson. (*Moses* 1.13, emphasis added)

---

[9] Many of the Jewish sources discussed below postdate Philo. One must therefore consider the possibility that they depend on Philo and therefore do not bear witness to Jewish traditions independent of Philo. In my view, however, none of the sources discussed below exhibit enough similarity to Philo to suggest direct dependence on him, and so they provide helpful insight into the sorts of traditions to which Philo might have had access.

Here "we are told" seems to apply to the claim that though the king's daughter had been married for some time, she had never conceived. Exodus does not include this information, but other ancient sources mention the barrenness of the king's daughter,[10] so it seems likely that this is part of the oral tradition that Philo received. It is difficult to see why Philo would want to distance himself from this claim, since it seems plausible, and Philo regards the oral tradition as trustworthy (1.4). Therefore, it seems best to interpret this as *sources*.[11]

In sum, Philo discusses his *sources* in an introductory passage prior to the birth narrative of *Moses*, and he employs *sources* twice within the birth narrative. We therefore have good initial reason to think that Philo regards the birth narrative of *Moses* as historiographic. We now turn to Philo's use of sources to test this hypothesis.

Use of Sources

Philo begins his account of Moses's birth and childhood as follows:

> Moses was by race a Chaldean, but was born and reared in Egypt, as his ancestors had migrated thither to seek food with their whole households, in consequence of the long famine under which Babylon and the neighboring populations were suffering. (1.5)

The only surprise here, biblically speaking, is Philo's assertion that Moses was a Chaldean (Χαλδαῖος). Louis Feldman, however, notes that "in this treatise Philo uses the terms 'Chaldean' and 'Hebrew' interchangeably."[12] Philo's claim also has some biblical

---

[10] Artapanus in Eusebius, *Praep. ev.* 9.27.3; Josephus, *Ant.* 2.232.
[11] Cf. Hidalgo, "Redaction-Critical Study," 278–79.
[12] Louis H. Feldman, "Philo's View of Moses' Birth and Upbringing," *CBQ* 64 (2002): 261. Feldman suggests that Philo has two purposes in calling Moses a Chaldean: (1) "he is ascribing further antiquity to Moses, since the Chaldeans were more ancient than the Hebrews"; (2) "he is associating Moses with Chaldean astronomy, the greatest achievement of the Chaldeans . . . , in which the youthful Moses is said by Philo to have been instructed (*Moses* 1.5.23), and which the Greeks prized so

support, for according to Genesis God brings Abraham out of Ur of the Chaldeans (Gen 15:7).

In his account of Moses's lineage, Philo says that Moses's parents were "the best of their contemporaries," and that Moses was the seventh from Abraham (*Moses* 1.7). Regarding Moses's parents, Exodus simply says that they were both from the tribe of Levi (Exod 2:1). Josephus, however, says that Moses's father was "a Hebrew of noble birth" (*Ant.* 2.210). Josephus does not go as far as Philo does in extolling Moses's parents, but the fact that both authors supplement the biblical account in similar-yet-distinct ways suggests that Philo is drawing on Jewish tradition rather than fabricating material. With respect to Abraham, the genealogy of Moses in Exodus places him as the fourth generation from Levi, and hence implicitly the seventh from Abraham (Exod 6:16–20).[13] Philo, then, is simply making explicit what is implicit in the biblical account. And he is not alone in doing so. Feldman notes that Demetrius, Josephus, and the rabbis likewise list Moses as the seventh generation from Abraham.[14] So even in this minor difference, Philo seems to depend on Jewish tradition.

Philo differs from Exodus at several points regarding Moses's birth. The most significant of these is the narrative sequence: whereas Exodus narrates the enslavement of the Israelites before Moses's birth, Philo mentions it after Moses's adolescence (*Moses* 1.34–39). Why has Philo done this? One possibility is that he wishes to avoid the question of why the Egyptians would enslave the Israelites and then seek to decrease their number, "since a slave-owner's supreme interest is to increase the number of his slaves."[15] In my view, this explanation leaves something to be

---

highly." See further Chan-Kok Wong, "Philo's Use of *Chaldaioi*," *Studia Philonica Annual* 4 (1992): 1–14.

[13] Counting from the first ancestor: (1) Abraham, (2) Isaac, (3) Jacob, (4) Levi, (5) Kohath, (6) Amram, (7) Moses.

[14] Feldman, "Philo's View," 261–62. Feldman cites Demetrius in Eusebius, *Praep. ev.* 9.29.2; Josephus, *Ant.* 2.229; Gen. Rab. 19.7; Song Rab. 5:1; Pesiq. Rav Kah. 23.10.

[15] Jonathan Cohen, *The Origins and Evolution of the Moses Nativity Story*, Studies in the History of Religions 58 (Brill, 1993), 11. I owe this reference to Feldman, "Philo's View," 263.

desired, for the question has a simple answer: the Israelites had grown so numerous that the king was afraid he would no longer be able to keep them enslaved. In my view, it is more likely that Philo places the Israelites' enslavement later to emphasize how it drove a wedge between Moses and his Egyptian roots. Just before narrating the Israelites' enslavement, Philo says that Moses extended gratitude to his Egyptian parents and that "he would have continued to do so throughout had he not found the king adopting in the country a new and highly impious course of action" (1.33). After describing the Israelites' enslavement and suffering, Philo returns to Moses, saying, "All this continued to depress and anger Moses" (1.40). Moses's killing of the Egyptian overseer follows (1.44). Thus, by displacing the account of the Israelites' enslavement, Philo shows how it alienated Moses from the Egyptians.

Does Philo's reordering of the story indicate an ahistorical intent? I think not—for two reasons. First, other Jewish sources place the Israelites' enslavement after Moses's birth.[16] It therefore seems likely that Philo's reordering of the story is not his own invention but part of the oral tradition he received.[17] Second, the sort of displacement that we observe in the birth narrative of

---

[16] Pirqe R. El. 48. See also Dibre Yeme Moshe Rabbenu, where after the pharaoh decrees the murder of the Hebrew children, Balaam says, "Now, if you take my advice, you won't kill them by the sword, but only impose a multiplicity of hardships on them, so that they die out of their own accord." The document continues: "And his words pleased Pharaoh and his servants." I owe this reference and the translation to Cohen, *Origins*, 83. Feldman also notes Mekh. R. Sim. 1.1, saying that it "connects the murder of the sons with the enslavement: 'After drowning their sons in water, they also immured them in the construction work'" ("Philo's View," 262n13). W. David Nelson, however, translates the passage in a way that does not imply a murder-enslavement sequence: "after [the Egyptian taskmasters] drowned their sons in water, they would then embed them [into the walls of a] building." See W. David Nelson, *Mekhilta de-Rabbi Shimon Bar Yoḥai: Translated into English, with Critical Introduction and Annotation* (Jewish Publication Society, 2006), 2, brackets original.

[17] *Contra* Cohen, *Origins and Evolution*, 41.

Moses was a common literary technique in ancient biography.[18] Indeed, Philo himself employs displacement elsewhere in *Moses*.[19] Philo is therefore operating within the historiographic conventions of ancient biography.

Philo (like Exodus) says nothing about how Moses was born. He does note that from birth Moses "had an appearance of more than ordinary goodliness [ἀστειοτέραν ἢ κατ' ἰδιώτην], so that his parents as long as they could actually set at nought the proclamations of the despot" (*Moses* 1.9). At first glance, the idea that Moses's good looks led his parents to disobey the king might seem like a legendary embellishment. However, Philo is essentially paraphrasing the Greek version of Exodus, which says, "Now when they saw [the child] was handsome [ἀστεῖον], they sheltered it for three months" (Exod 2:2 NETS).[20] Philo does upgrade Moses from being merely "handsome" to more handsome than normal, but this may simply be his interpretation of Exodus—if Moses were only ordinarily handsome, why would Exodus comment on this or suggest that it led his parents to hide him? Furthermore, other Jewish sources also emphasize Moses's good looks as a baby (sometimes much more than Philo does).[21] So if Philo is going beyond Exodus, he is most likely

---

[18] Christopher Pelling, "Plutarch's Adaptation of His Source-Material," in *Plutarch and History: Eighteen Studies* (Classical Press of Wales, 2002), 92–93; John Jordan Henderson, "A Comparison of Josephus' *Life* and *Jewish War*: An Attempt at Establishing the Acceptable Outer Limits of Biographies' Historical Reliability," in Keener and Wright, *Biographies and Jesus*, 269, 272; Michael R. Licona, *Why Are There Differences in the Gospels? What We Can Learn from Ancient Biography* (Oxford UP, 2017), 20, 109; Youngju Kwon, "Reimagining the Jesus Tradition: Orality, Memory, and Ancient Biography" (PhD diss., Asbury Theological Seminary, 2018), 297–303; Keener, *Christobiography*, 316–17.

[19] McGing, "Philo's Adaptation," 125–26; Hidalgo, "Redaction-Critical Study," 286–87.

[20] The MT is similar but has only Moses's mother seeing and hiding him. Hebrews 11:23, like the LXX and Philo, attributes these actions to both parents.

[21] E.g., Josephus, *Ant.* 2.231–232; Pirqe R. El. 48; Exod. Rab. 1.26; Midr. Tanh. PV Exod. 1.7. Pirqe Rabbi Eliezer 48 says that Moses's "form was like that of an angel of God" (Gerald Friedlander, ed. and trans., *Pirḳê de Rabbi Eliezer*, 4th ed. [Sepher-Hermon, 1981], 378).

doing so because of the oral tradition he received, not because he is making things up.

Philo adds several details to the biblical account of how Moses came to be adopted by the king's daughter (Exod 2:3–10).[22] First, Philo explains that Moses's parents were forced to give him up because "there were persons prying into holes and corners, ever eager to carry some new report to the king" (*Moses* 1.10). This specific explanation does not appear in other Jewish sources, but other explanations do.[23] It therefore seems likely that this is a tradition Philo received from the elders. Second, Philo has both of Moses's parents (rather than just his mother) place him on the bank of the river. Josephus, however, mentions this as well (*Ant.* 2.221), so it again seems likely that it is part of the oral tradition Philo received. Third, Philo describes the self-pity and self-reproach of Moses's parents when giving him up (*Moses* 1.10–11). We do not find this precise detail in other Jewish literature, but Pseudo-Philo recounts the elders scolding Moses's father in a way similar to how Philo has Moses's parents reproach themselves (LAB 9.14). It seems likely that here Philo is filling out Exodus with a plausible inference or drawing on a Jewish tradition that has not survived elsewhere. Fourth, Philo says that the king's daughter (1) was his only daughter, (2) had been married for some time but had not conceived, and (3) desired a male child to give her father an heir (*Moses* 1.13). As noted above, Philo prefaces the latter two claims with "we are told," indicating that he is using *sources*. Artapanus and Josephus both depict the king's daughter as barren, and Josephus presents Moses as the heir apparent to the Egyptian throne.[24] It seems, then, that Philo is again drawing on Jewish oral tradition. Finally, whereas Exodus says that the king's daughter gave Moses (מֹשֶׁה) his name "'because,' she said, 'I drew him out [מְשִׁיתִהוּ] of the water'" (Exod 2:10 ESV), Philo

---

[22] I owe these to Feldman, "Philo's View," 265–68.
[23] LAB 9.12; b. Sotah 12a; Exod. Rab. 1.20.
[24] Artapanus in Eusebius, *Praep. ev.* 9.27.3; Josephus, *Ant.* 2.232. Josephus does not explicitly say that the king's daughter was his only daughter as Philo does, but by presenting Moses as the heir apparent Josephus implies that the king had no other male grandchildren.

says that she "called him Moses, for *Môu* is the Egyptian word for water" (*Moses* 1.17). Feldman suggests that Philo "apparently realized the unlikelihood that an Egyptian princess would give a child a name derived from Hebrew" and so provided an Egyptian etymology.[25] If Feldman is correct, it is interesting that Philo does not deny the explanation of Exodus; he simply reinterprets it in a way that he regards as more historically plausible by tying Moses's name not to "I drew him out" but to the Egyptian word for "water." Josephus similarly links Moses's name to the Egyptian word for "water," so it seems likely that Philo is once again depending on Jewish oral sources for this information.[26]

Philo goes on to describe Moses's growth and education (*Moses* 1.18–24). This material finds no parallel in Exodus, which cuts directly to Moses's killing of the Egyptian (Exod 2:11–12). To some, this might seem like proof that Philo is fabricating material. Philo, however, has already told us that he has two sources: the written Torah and the oral tradition. Our starting assumption, then, should be that if Philo is going beyond Exodus, it is because he is following the oral tradition. Our investigation above has provided initial confirmation for this hypothesis, for we have found numerous Jewish parallels for Philo's extrabiblical material. Jewish and early Christian literature also give us good reason to think that Philo is drawing on oral tradition for his account of Moses's growth and education. Jubilees (second century BC) says that Moses's father taught him to write (Jub. 47.9). Ezekiel the Tragedian (second century BC) states that the king's daughter provided Moses everything appropriate for "princely rearing and instruction [παιδεύμασιν]" (Ezek. Trag. 37).[27] In Acts 7:22, Stephen says that Moses "was instructed in all the wisdom of the Egyptians." These passages are brief—tantalizingly so—but they suggest that some early Jews augmented the biblical account with material about Moses's education. Josephus provides a more

---

[25] Feldman, "Philo's View," 268.
[26] Josephus, *Ant.* 2.228; *Ag. Ap.* 1.286. In *Ant.* 2.228, Josephus says that "the Egyptians call water *môu* and those who are saved *esês*; so they conferred on him this name compounded of both words."
[27] Translation by R. G. Robertson, *OTP* 2:809.

extensive discussion of Moses's growth and education (*Ant.* 2.230–237). And rabbinic literature contains various traditions about Moses's childhood development.[28] It therefore seems likely that the oral traditions that Philo received contained information about Moses's growth and education and that Philo is drawing on these traditions for his account.

One might object, however, that Philo's account is historically suspect because of the Greek elements he includes in Moses's education. Philo, for example, says that some of Moses's teachers came from Greece (*Moses* 1.21). He also mentions that Moses's education included "arithmetic, geometry, the lore of metre, rhythm and harmony, and the whole subject of music" (1.23). Feldman notes,

> Despite the fact that Philo here ascribes the education of Moses in these subjects to the Egyptians, it is surely striking that these are the very subjects, indeed in that very order, that Plato (*Resp.* 7.521C–531C) prescribes for the higher education of his philosopher-king.[29]

Let us first clarify the issue. Our concern is not with the truth of Philo's account but with the nature of his intent: Does Philo intend for this account to be historical, or not? I suggest that even at this point Philo is operating with historiographic intent. First, if Philo merely wanted to show that Moses was influenced by Greek philosophy or received the sort of education Plato prescribes for the philosopher-king, we might expect him to ascribe the relevant elements of his education to Greeks, not to Egyptians. He therefore seems to be operating with some level of historiographic restraint. Second, Philo likely regards his account of Moses's education as historically plausible.

---

[28] Pirqe R. El. 48; Exod. Rab. 1.26; Deut. Rab. 11.10.
[29] Feldman, "Philo's View," 273. In an accompanying footnote, Feldman qualifies his statement, saying, "In the *Republic* the order is arithmetic, geometry, astronomy, and music. Philo has omitted astronomy, which he says was taught to Moses by Chaldeans and the Egyptians" (27n47). Philo says that Moses "had the Greeks to teach him the rest of the regular school course."

F. H. Colson notes that

> Philo may have derived [his description of Moses's education] from his own knowledge of the scope of education in Egypt in the present and past, but perhaps also from Plato, *Laws* 656D, 759A, 819A, where mathematics, music, and dancing are said to be the subjects most stressed by the Egyptians.[30]

Colson's suggestion is compelling. It was common in ancient historiography to supplement one's sources with plausible inferences,[31] and Philo may well have filled out his account of Moses's education from what he knew about Egyptian education either directly or from Plato.[32] Indeed, Clement of Alexandria provides a description of Moses's education similar to (and perhaps dependent on) Philo,[33] which suggests he sees such an account as plausible. Third, it is quite possible that the Greek elements that Philo includes in Moses's education were part of the oral tradition he received. The thoroughly Hellenized Philo we know did not emerge from a vacuum but was born and raised in a Jewish community that was itself Hellenized.[34] The Jewish elders who taught Philo had likely been

---

[30] See the footnote to Philo, *Moses* 1.23 in the LCL edition.

[31] Christopher Pelling, *Literary Texts and the Greek Historian*, Approaching the Ancient World (Routledge, 2000), 8–9, 47–49; Cynthia Damon, "Rhetoric and Historiography," in *A Companion to Roman Rhetoric*, ed. William Dominik and Jon Hall, Blackwell Companions to the Ancient World (Blackwell, 2007), 439–50; Craig S. Keener, *Acts: An Exegetical Commentary*, 4 vols. (Baker Academic, 2012–15), 1:101; Keener, *Christobiography*, 158–59.

[32] Sterling lists *Laws* among the works of Plato that Philo seems to have known ("Philo," 1064).

[33] Clement of Alexandria, *Stromateis* 1.23. Louis Ginzberg suggests that Clement's account "is very likely taken from Philo" (*The Legends of the Jews*, 7 vols. [Jewish Publication Society, 1909–38], 5:402n67). I owe this reference to Feldman, "Philo's View," 274n51.

[34] The Alexandrian Jewish historian Artapanus (third to second century BC) shows that Hellenism had already begun to influence Jewish traditions about Moses well before Philo. Artapanus notes (1) that as an adult Moses was called Mousaeus by the Greeks, (2) that Moses was said to be the teacher of Orpheus, and (3) that Moses was named Hermes by the Egyptians (Eusebius, *Praep. ev.* 9.27). Moses Hadas and Morton Smith argue that "Philo's work is to be understood . . . as influenced by and in part a reaction against the extremes of this anecdotal, Hellenizing

influenced by the Greek tradition, so it would not be surprising if the traditions they passed on to Philo exhibited some Greek influence as well. Put differently, anyone who wishes to argue that Philo has fabricated the Greek elements of Moses's education must first demonstrate that Philo did *not* receive this information from the Jewish elders of Alexandria—a difficult task, to say the least.[35]

Philo's use of sources in the birth narrative of *Moses*, then, suggests that he intends this material to be historiographic. Philo generally follows the Exodus account, and where he differs from Exodus it is likely that he is drawing on the Jewish oral tradition that he explicitly cites (*Moses* 1.4). Indeed, it is difficult to produce any example where Philo transgresses ancient historiographic conventions and clearly fabricates birth material.

To this point, I have focused on Philo's use of sources in the birth material itself, but we can also observe Philo's historiographic intent from two other vantage points. First, Philo's use of sources elsewhere in *Moses* suggests that he is not operating with a different historiographic standard for the birth narrative. Two points here are key: (1) Philo's account of Moses's teenage years (*Moses* 25–33)—like his description of Moses's growth and education—has no parallel in Exodus. One therefore cannot argue that because Philo goes beyond Exodus in the birth narrative, he intends this material to be uniquely ahistorical, for he does the same thing in his account of Moses's teenage years. (2) Philo's use of sources in the birth narrative is typical of his use of sources throughout *Moses*. In his introduction to the LCL edition of *Abraham*, *Joseph*, and *Moses*, Colson draws attention to

> the essential fidelity with which Philo adheres to the narrative of Scripture. Though he professes to draw also from the Tradition of the Elders, there is little or none of the legendary accretions with which the Book of Jubilees, the so-called "Antiquities of

---

haggadah" (*Heroes and Gods: Spiritual Biographies in Antiquity*, Religious Perspectives 13 [Harper & Row, 1965], 131).

[35] Litwa asserts that Philo "transformed the story" regarding Moses's education (*Gospels*, 130). However, he fails to note that Philo explicitly says that he is drawing not only on the Torah but also on the traditions he received from the elders (*Moses* 1.4).

Philo" and even Josephus, to say nothing of later Rabbinical tradition, endeavour to embellish the history of the Patriarchs and of Moses. There is of course any amount of amplification: that is according to the practice of many if not most ancient historians, who consider it their business not merely to state but to interpret facts—to infer what the actors probably would have felt, said, or done in the given circumstances.[36]

As Colson observes, the amplification of sources is typical not only of *Moses* but also of ancient historiography. Brian McGing and Esteban Hidalgo have demonstrated in separate studies that throughout *Moses* Philo adapts and supplements his biblical sources in a variety of ways, including but not limited to the ones we have observed in the birth narrative.[37] These studies show that the ways in which Philo adapts and expands Exodus in the birth narrative of *Moses* are typical of the life as a whole.

Second, when we compare the birth narrative of *Moses* with other Jewish retellings of Moses's birth, what is striking is how restrained Philo's account is. Philo does not mention numerous

---

[36] F. H. Colson, general introduction to *On Abraham. On Joseph. On Moses*, xvii. The "Antiquities of Philo" here are presumably the Liber antiquitatum biblicarum of Pseudo-Philo. Colson does note that the closest Philo comes to legendary accretions is his account of Moses's education in *Moses* 1.21 and following, but he says that "even this is merely a statement of what an Egyptian prince would, in Philo's view, have naturally been taught."

[37] McGing, "Philo's Adaptation," 117–40; Hidalgo, "Redaction-Critical Study," 277–301. McGing categorizes Philo's adaptation of biblical sources under the following headings: (1) omission of biblical episodes, (2) close adaptation of the biblical text, (3) abridgement, (4) chronological displacement, (5) transfer of an item from one character to another, (6) expansion of material by explanatory or dramatic detail, (7) expansion by allegorical explanation, and (8) avoidance of proper names. Hidalgo argues that throughout book one of *Moses*, Philo generally follows the Pentateuch but does engage in (1) thematic arrangements, (2) interpretative adaptations, (3) descriptive expansions, and (4) psychological analysis that go beyond the Pentateuch, as well as (5) the expansion or creation of discourses. Philip L. Shuler similarly shows that Philo amplifies the Pentateuch throughout *Moses*, not just in the birth narrative ("Philo's Moses and Matthew's Jesus: A Comparative Study in Ancient Literature," *Studia Philonica Annual* 2 [1990]: 86–103).

nonbiblical elements that appear in other Jewish literature.[38] These include:

- A prophecy about Moses by the king's servant(s)[39]
- A dream about Moses by Moses's father[40]
- A dream or prophecy about Moses by Miriam[41]
- Moses's mother giving birth with little or no pain[42]
- Moses's mother being 130 years old at the time of his birth[43]
- Moses being born already circumcised[44]
- The whole house being filled with light when Moses was born[45]
- Moses being called Tov ("good") or Tobiah[46]
- Moses walking and talking with his parents at three days old[47]
- Moses not needing to be nursed by his mother[48]
- Moses prophesying at three months old[49]

---

[38] I owe some of the following points and their primary source references to Cohen, *Origins*, 29–135; Feldman, "Philo's View," 264–65. These examples and primary source references could be easily multiplied, especially if one appeals to later rabbinic literature; see Ginzberg, *Legends*, 2:245–72, 5:391–401; Cohen, *Origins*, 67–135.

[39] Josephus, *Ant.* 2.205–206; b. Sotah 12b; Exod. Rab. 1.18; Pirqe R. El. 48.

[40] Josephus, *Ant.* 2.212–216.

[41] LAB 9.10; b. Meg. 14a; b. Sotah 12b–13a; Mekh. R. Ish. Shir. 10.58–61; Mekh. R. Sim. 36.3.

[42] Josephus, *Ant.* 2.218; b. Sotah 12a, 13a; Exod. Rab. 1.20. Philo elsewhere indicates that Moses's mother gave birth without needing the help of a midwife's skill (*Migration* 142), but he says nothing about this in *Moses*.

[43] b. B. Bat. 120a; b. Sotah 12a; Exod. Rab. 1.19.

[44] LAB 9.13; b. Sotah 12a, 12b; Avot R. Nat. A 2.4; Exod. Rab. 1.20; Lev. Rab. 20.1; Deut. Rab. 11.10; Eccl. Rab. 4:9–12 §1; Eccl. Rab. 9:2 §1; Midr. Tanh. B Deut. 2.1; Midr. Tanh. PV Gen. 2.5; Midr. Pss. 9.7.

[45] b. Sotah 12a.

[46] b. Sotah 12a; Exod. Rab. 1.20; Lev. Rab. 1.3; Eccl. Rab. 4:9–12 §1; Pirqe R. El. 48. Exodus 2:2 says Moses's mother *saw* that he was good (טוב), but not that they called him good (טוב).

[47] Deut. Rab. 11.10.

[48] Deut. Rab. 11.10.

[49] Deut. Rab. 11.10.

- Moses remaining in the basket for seven days[50]
- The maidens of the king's daughter scolding her for wanting to rescue Moses and the angel Gabriel beating them to the ground[51]
- The king's daughter seeing the divine glory with Moses when she opened the basket[52]
- The angel Gabriel striking Moses so that he would cry and the king's daughter would pity him[53]
- The king's daughter being healed of leprosy when she touched Moses[54]
- The king's daughter unwittingly prophesying about Moses[55]
- Moses refusing to be nursed by Egyptian women[56]
- Moses experiencing abnormal physical growth[57]
- Moses wearing the king's crown and/or casting it to the ground[58]

It is impossible to know whether Philo was aware of such traditions, but even if he was not, they show that Philo did not embellish the biblical story as one could (and as other Jews did).

In sum, Philo's use of sources in the birth narrative of *Moses* confirms that he intends this material to be historiographic. In the birth narrative, Philo provides us with exactly what he has promised: an interweaving of the Torah with Jewish oral tradi-

---

[50] Jub. 47.4.
[51] b. Sotah 12b; Exod. Rab. 1.23. Both sources are careful to note that Gabriel spared one maid to fetch the basket (Exod 2:5).
[52] b. Sotah 12b; Exod. Rab. 1.24.
[53] Exod. Rab. 1.24.
[54] Pirqe R. El. 48.
[55] b. Sotah 12b.
[56] b. Sotah 12b.
[57] Josephus, *Ant.* 2.230; Exod. Rab. 1.26.
[58] Josephus, *Ant.* 2.233–237; Exod. Rab. 1.26; Midr. Tanh. PV Exod. 1.7. In Exodus Rabbah, Moses places the crown on his own head, and the king's magicians test him to see if he understands what he is doing by placing a gold vessel and a live coal before him. Moses almost reaches for the gold, but Gabriel intervenes and makes him take the coal. Moses thrusts the coal into his mouth, burning his tongue, and according to Exodus Rabbah this is why he became slow of speech.

tion. Modern historians may, of course, question the reliability of both these sources, but what matters for our investigation is that Philo regards them as trustworthy. Philo's use of sources in the birth narrative of *Moses* is also typical of his method in the life as a whole, and comparison with other Jewish retellings of Moses's birth underscores how restrained Philo's account is.

SUPERNATURAL ELEMENTS

Philo attributes three events in the birth narrative to divine causation. He notes that when Moses's parents left him on the banks of the river, his sister stayed and waited "to see what would happen, all this being brought about, in my opinion, by the providence of God watching over the child" (*Moses* 1.12).[59] When describing how the king's daughter hired Moses's mother to be his nurse, Philo also remarks that "by God's disposing, it was provided that the child's first nursing should come from the natural source" (1.17). Finally, Philo says that the king's daughter "artificially enlarged the figure of her womb to make [Moses] pass as her real and not a supposititious child" (1.19). Perhaps recognizing the difficulty of this feat, Philo remarks, "God makes all that He wills easy, however difficult be the accomplishment" (1.19).

Do the miracles that Philo recounts indicate that he intends the story to be ahistorical? Certainly not. First, it is likely that all three miracles appeared in Philo's sources. The first two events occur in Exodus, and while Philo has made the divine causation explicit, it is certainly implied in Exodus. The third event does not appear in Exodus, but Philo's own account of his sources (1.4) and our study above suggest that he derived it from Jewish oral tradition. Second, Philo narrates many miracles outside the birth narrative. For example:

- The burning bush account, including the signs of Moses's staff turning into a serpent and his hand turning leprous (1.65–84)

---

[59] It is possible that Philo here engages in *evaluation*. However, since he is expressing an opinion on the cause of the event rather than the event itself, I have chosen not to include it in the analysis of historiographic features above.

- Aaron's serpent (staff) swallowing those of the Egyptian magicians (1.91–95)
- The plagues (1.96–145)
- The pillar of cloud guiding Israel (1.165–166)
- Crossing of the Red Sea (1.176–179)
- Bitter water turned sweet (1.184–186)
- Provision of manna and quail (1.198–209)
- Water from the rock (1.210–211)

Exodus, of course, records all these events. However, Philo regularly goes beyond Exodus both in recounting the events and in asserting divine causation. For example, Exodus simply says that Aaron's staff-turned-serpent swallowed up those of the Egyptian magicians (Exod 7:12). Philo, however, says that it

> showed its great superiority by rising high, widening its chest and opening its mouth, when with the suction of its breath it swept the others in with irresistible force, like a whole draught of fishes encircled by the net, and, after swallowing them up, changed to its original nature, and became a staff. (*Moses* 1.93)

Philo goes on to note that the onlookers "now regarded these events . . . as brought about by some diviner power to which every feat is easy" (1.94)—a detail with no parallel in Exodus. He also attributes all the plagues to God and even asserts that God accomplished three of them himself, apart from any human agent (1.96, 130). After describing how God brings forth water from the rock, Philo says,

> If anyone disbelieves these things, he neither knows God nor has ever sought to know Him; for if he did he would at once have perceived—aye, perceived with a firm apprehension—that these extraordinary and seemingly incredible events are but child's-play to God. (1.212)

These examples (which could be easily multiplied) show that Philo affirms the reality of divine causation and emphasizes divine causation throughout *Moses* in ways that go beyond Exodus. The miracles that he includes in the birth narrative, then, do not indicate that he regards the birth narrative as less historiographic than the rest of the life.

TIME ELAPSED

To determine the time elapsed between Moses's birth and Philo's writing of *Moses* is no easy task. Some may question whether Moses existed at all, and even those who affirm a historical Moses differ significantly as to when he lived. Proposed dates for the exodus, for example, range from around 1470 BC to around 1150 BC.[60] For the purposes of this study, I will (1) assume that Moses was a real person and (2) opt for dates that lessen the time elapsed between Moses's birth and Philo's writing as much as possible. The latter move is meant to eliminate any potential bias on my part by allowing Philo to compare as favorably as possible to Matthew and Luke.

Let us assume, then, that the exodus occurred in 1150 BC. Exodus portrays Moses as being around eighty years old at the time of the exodus event (Exod 7:7). If we take these two dates as our starting points, then Moses would have been born around 1230 BC. As noted above, we know little about Philo's life beyond that he participated in an embassy to Gaius around AD 39/40, and Philo seems to have been an old man at this time (*Embassy* 1). Let us suppose that Philo composed *Moses* in AD 11 as a middle-aged man (just under thirty years before the embassy to Gaius). This gives us an elapsed time of approximately 1,240 years.

The historical distance between Philo and Moses's birth is significant, for it impacts the sorts of sources available to Philo and the level of accuracy he might have achieved. As noted above, Philo draws on both the written Torah and oral tradition and seems to view both as reliable (*Moses* 1.4). However, even if one accepts the historical reliability of Exodus (which many scholars do not), it is highly questionable whether Jewish oral tradition from the first century BC / first century AD constitutes reliable evidence for reconstructing Moses's life. Therefore, while Philo

---

[60] John H. Walton, "Exodus, Date of," in *Dictionary of the Old Testament: Pentateuch*, ed. T. Desmond Alexander and David W. Baker (IVP, 2003), 259–60.

provides valuable insight into how a first-century AD biographer steeped in Israel's Scriptures (like Matthew or Luke) would have approached the writing of a birth narrative, the time elapsed between Moses's birth, at least some of Philo's sources, and Philo's writing suggests Philo does not provide a useful analogy to the sort of accuracy that Matthew and Luke might have achieved.

CONCLUSION

Philo presents the birth narrative of *Moses* with historiographic intent. At the outset, he promises the reader an interweaving of his two sources: the Torah and Jewish oral tradition. Philo delivers on this promise in the birth narrative, generally following Exodus but also going beyond it, likely based on Jewish oral traditions or his own logical inferences. The use of sources that we observe in the birth narrative is not exceptional but is typical of the rest of the life. Philo includes only three miracles in the birth narrative, all of which likely appeared in his sources, and the rest of *Moses* makes clear that he not only affirms but also emphasizes divine causation. Philo's use of miracles in the birth narrative, then, is—again—typical of the rest of the life. Philo and at least some of his sources also stand at a significant remove from Moses's birth. Therefore, while Philo provides valuable insight into how Matthew and Luke might have approached the writing of their birth narratives, the level of accuracy that we find in Philo is likely not comparable to what Matthew and Luke might have achieved.

3
PLUTARCH

Plutarch was born around AD 46 in the Greek town of Chaeronea and died at some point after AD 120.[1] He studied at Athens under the philosopher Ammonius and spent most of his life in Greece, but he also journeyed to Rome and even received Roman citizenship. Plutarch was a prolific writer; according to the fourth-century "Catalog of Lamprias," he produced 227 works. Many of these have been lost, but the 128 that survive are generally divided into two groups: (1) *Lives*, biographies of great Greek and Roman men, and (2) *Moralia*, essays on a variety of topics ranging from ethics to politics and medicine. Plutarch's *Lives* constitute some of our most important sources for understanding the nature of ancient biography.

Plutarch wrote numerous biographies, but only fifty have survived. Forty-six of these are parallel lives in which Plutarch pairs the life of a great Greek with that of a great Roman, often providing a brief comparison of the two at the end.[2] Plutarch

---

[1] Here and below I draw on J. R. Hamilton, *Plutarch: Alexander. A Commentary* (Clarendon, 1969), xiii–xvi; Henri D. Saffrey, "Plutarchus," BNP 11:410–27; D. A. Russell, "Plutarch," *OCD*, 1165–66.

[2] Four of the *Parallel Lives* (those of Agis, Cleomenes, Tiberius Gracchus, and Caius Gracchus) form a compound pair (*Agis et Cleomenes*; *Tiberius et Caius Gracchus*), so there are actually twenty-two pairs

seems to have composed the *Lives* between AD 90 and 120, and the parallel lives probably date to after AD 96.[3] However, beyond these broad parameters it is difficult to determine precisely when Plutarch penned each life. For the sake of simplicity, I will here assume an approximate date of AD 100 for Plutarch's *Lives*.

The amount of information that Plutarch provides about his subject's birth and childhood varies widely from one life to the next. In some cases, he provides no information at all; in others, he provides significant details and sometimes even a narrative. Here we will begin by examining six of Plutarch's *Lives* that do contain birth material (*Theseus, Romulus, Alexander, Lycurgus, Themistocles,* and *Cicero*) to see how Plutarch regards this material from a historiographic point of view. I have selected these six lives because scholars have cited them to demonstrate that ancient birth narratives were legendary rather than historiographic.[4] On the one hand, this should confirm that I have not merely selected a pool of data that is convenient for my thesis. On the other hand, if we find that Plutarch has composed the birth material of these lives with historiographic intent, then we will have strong evidence that he does not regard his birth material as legendary. (Readers may view a summary of historiographic features in all of Plutarch's *Lives* in the chart at the end of this chapter.) In the latter part of the chapter, we will consider three other issues that bear on the historiographic character of

---

instead of twenty-three. Plutarch provides comparison sections for nineteen of the twenty-two pairs. The four solo lives are *Aratus, Artaxerxes, Galba,* and *Otho*.

[3] C. P. Jones, "Towards a Chronology of Plutarch's Works," *Journal of Roman Studies* 56 (1966): 68–70; Saffrey, "Plutarchus," 11:11:412; Michael R. Licona, *Why Are There Differences in the Gospels? What We Can Learn from Ancient Biography* (Oxford UP, 2017), 16.

[4] John P. Meier, *A Marginal Jew: Rethinking the Historical Jesus*, 5 vols., ABRL (Doubleday, 1991–2016), 1:208, 234n14; Robert J. Miller, *Born Divine: The Births of Jesus and Other Sons of God* (Polebridge, 2003), 133–53, esp. 138–40; Andrew T. Lincoln, *Born of a Virgin? Reconceiving Jesus in the Bible, Tradition, and Theology* (Eerdmans, 2013), 57–67. Lincoln (61) cites *Lyc.* 5, which actually comes from Lycurgus's adulthood and thus is not relevant to Lincoln's point, but I will use this life nonetheless.

Plutarch's birth material: (1) the absence of birth material from many of Plutarch's *Lives*, (2) Plutarch's attitude toward supernatural events, and (3) the time elapsed between the subjects' births and Plutarch's writing.

BIRTH MATERIAL IN PLUTARCH'S *LIVES*

Theseus

Plutarch penned his life of Theseus (which he places in parallel with that of Romulus) around nine hundred years after his subject's birth. He therefore begins with a historiographic disclaimer:

> Just as geographers, O Socius Senecio, crowd on to the outer edges of their maps the parts of the earth which elude their knowledge, with explanatory notes that "What lies beyond is sandy desert without water and full of wild beasts," or "blind marsh," or "Scythian cold," or "frozen sea," so in the writing of my Parallel Lives, now that I have traversed those periods of time which are accessible to probable reasoning and which afford basis for a history dealing with facts, I might well say of the earlier periods: "What lies beyond is full of marvels and unreality, a land of poets and fabulists, of doubt and obscurity." But after publishing my account of Lycurgus the lawgiver and Numa the king, I thought I might not unreasonably go back still farther to Romulus, now that my history had brought me near to his times. (*Thes.* 1.1–2)[5]

Plutarch describes how he hit upon Theseus as a fitting parallel to Romulus and then says,

> May I therefore succeed in purifying Fable, making her submit to reason and take on the semblance of History. But where she obstinately disdains to make herself credible, and refuses to admit any element of probability, I shall pray for kindly readers, and such as receive with indulgence the tales of antiquity. (1.3)

By introducing his life of Theseus in this way, Plutarch demonstrates that he is well aware of the historiographic complexities involved in writing a biography of a figure from the distant past.

---

[5] Unless otherwise noted, translations of Plutarch's *Lives* are from Plutarch, *Lives*, trans. Bernadotte Perrin, 11 vols., LCL (Harvard UP, 1914–26).

His sources are poems and fables, "tales of antiquity" that he must tame and mold into something like history, and he asks his reader to indulge him as he does so. Samuel Byrskog rightly comments,

> Plutarch himself, as a biographer, is not against employing legendary material. But he is eager to distance it from the serious historical factuality of the past, hoping that the purifying process of reason will reduce this kind of material in his own writing to something like exact history.[6]

Two points about this introduction are important for our purposes. First, Plutarch places this historiographic disclaimer (a form of *distancing*)[7] at the very beginning of the life, which suggests that it pertains to the whole work, including the birth material. Second, Plutarch notes that he has sources (however historically dubious they may be) and plans to construct a story that is as historically reliable as possible. Plutarch therefore seems to view the birth material—like the rest of the life—as being information-based. To be sure, the sources that Plutarch is working with are fables that need "purifying," but he promises to separate the wheat from the chaff to the best of his ability and clearly does not think that he can simply fabricate the birth material from whole cloth.

Before launching into the birth material proper, Plutarch notes a number of similarities that led him to pair Theseus with Romulus. The first of these is that "both were of uncertain and obscure parentage, and got the reputation of descent from gods" (2.1). Here we find two historiographic indicators: (1) *transparency*—Plutarch notes that his subjects' parentage is "uncertain and obscure," suggesting ambiguity in his sources; (2) *distancing*—Plutarch does not directly claim that Theseus was descended from the gods but only that he "got the reputation" of divine descent.

---

[6] Samuel Byrskog, *Story as History—History as Story: The Gospel Tradition in the Context of Ancient Oral History* (Brill Academic, 2002), 216.

[7] Byrskog and Pelling both use distancing language to describe this passage. See Byrskog, *Story as History*, 216; Christopher Pelling, "'Making Myth Look Like History': Plutarch's *Theseus-Romulus*," in *Plutarch and History: Eighteen Studies* (Classical Press of Wales, 2002), 171.

Plutarch utilizes several historiographic indicators in his account of Theseus's lineage. He notes that Theseus's grandfather Pittheus was known as a wise man, and he quotes a maxim from Hesiod's *Works and Days* that "they say"[8] (λέγουσι) belongs to Pittheus: "Payment pledged to a man who is dear must be ample and certain" (3.2).[9] Plutarch goes on: "At any rate, this is what Aristotle the philosopher says, and Euripides, when he has Hippolytus addressed as 'nursling of the pure and holy Pittheus,' shows what the world thought of Pittheus" (3.2).[10] Here we observe both *distancing* and *sources*. Plutarch forgoes directly asserting that Pittheus spoke this maxim ("they say"), but he does claim support for this notion from Aristotle and even quotes Euripides to substantiate that Pittheus was a wise man.

According to Plutarch, Theseus's birth came about as follows: Aegeus, king of Athens, wanted to have children and received an oracle at Delphi telling him not to have intercourse with a woman until he returned to Athens. However, the oracle was apparently ambiguous, and when Aegeus stopped at Troezen on his way to Athens, Pittheus convinced him to sleep with his daughter Aethra. Aegeus did so, but when he found out that Aethra was Pittheus's daughter and suspected that she was pregnant, he placed a sword and a pair of sandals under a large rock and told Aethra that if she had a son by him, she should send the son to him in secret with the sword and sandals once he was able to lift the rock. Aethra did bear a son by Aegeus and named him Theseus. When Theseus came of age he lifted the stone with ease, retrieved the tokens, traveled to Athens to meet Aegeus, and was acknowledged as his successor.

Some might contend that the above account constitutes a prime example of a legendary birth narrative. However, several factors suggest that Plutarch is here engaging in historiography to the best of his ability given the available sources. First, nothing suggests that Plutarch regards the elements he affirms as

---

[8] My translation.
[9] This saying appears in *Works and Days*, line 370.
[10] The LCL edition notes that Plutarch here refers to Aristotle, frag. 556 and Euripides, *Hippolytus* 11.

incredible. Yes, Theseus's birth is preceded by an oracle. However, there is nothing improbable in this (oracles were commonplace in antiquity), and here the oracle is actually disobeyed. Aegeus hiding a sword and sandals under a rock and Theseus recovering them may seem a little too perfect, but again, nothing suggests that Plutarch views this as implausible. Second, Plutarch indicates at numerous points that he is interested in telling a true story, not merely an interesting one. For example, he notes that there is a disagreement in his sources about the reason for Theseus's name (4.1; *transparency*). He also distances himself from a claim that Theseus was descended from the gods ("a report was spread abroad by Pittheus that he was begotten by Poseidon," 6.1) and instead affirms that Theseus had a normal conception with two human parents.[11]

In sum, in the birth material of Plutarch's *Theseus* we observe multiple instances of *sources*, *distancing*, and *transparency*. Plutarch does not feel at liberty to invent a legend but rather engages critically with his sources in an endeavor to provide a reliable account of Theseus's origins.

Romulus

Plutarch places his life of Theseus in parallel with that of Romulus, another figure from the distant past. Since Plutarch's introduction to *Theseus* functions as the introduction to *Romulus* as well (cf. *Thes.* 1.2), we have good reason to think that Plutarch composed Romulus's life—including the birth material—with a historiographic intent similar to what we have observed above with Theseus. And, as we will see below, Plutarch's account bears this out.

Plutarch begins his life of Romulus by noting that writers disagree about the origin of Rome's name (*Rom.* 1.1–2.1; *transparency*). "Moreover," he says, "even those writers who declare, in accordance with the most authentic tradition, that it was Romu-

---

[11] *Contra* Andrew T. Lincoln, "Luke and Jesus' Conception: A Case of Double Paternity?" *JBL* 132.3 (2013): 655. Lincoln misrepresents the evidence when he suggests that Plutarch merely juxtaposes the accounts of paternity and leaves it up to the reader to decide which to accept.

lus who gave his name to the city, do not agree about his lineage" (2.1; *transparency*). Plutarch proceeds to survey the various views of Romulus's lineage (2.2–4.3). Several of these are quite commonplace, involving only human parents, albeit noteworthy ones (Aeneas and Dexithea, Roma and Latinus). However, "others" say that "Aemilia, the daughter of Aeneas and Lavinia bore [Romulus] to Mars" (i.e., the god; 2.3). However, Plutarch does not affirm this account; he simply relates it as an exercise in *transparency*, and he also seems to distance himself from the claim by attributing it to "others." Plutarch then goes on to relate an account that he regards as "altogether fabulous" (μυθώδη παντάπασι) (2.3; *evaluation*).[12] In this story, a phantom in the form of a phallus rises out of the hearth in the house of Tarchetius, king of the Albans, and remains there for some time. An oracle tells Tarchetius that a virgin must have intercourse with this phallus. The king orders his daughter to do so, but she disobeys and sends her handmaid to have intercourse with it instead. The handmaid conceives by the phantom phallus and gives birth to twins (Romulus and Remus). Tarchetius gives the babies to a servant to kill them, but the servant leaves them alive by a river. A she-wolf finds the babies and nurses them, and eventually a cowherd finds them, takes them home, and raises them. When the babies grow up, they overthrow Tarchetius.

The story of the phantom phallus might seem like exhibit A for the legendary character of ancient birth narratives. However, Plutarch explicitly rejects this story, describing it from the outset as "altogether fabulous." He also distances himself from the tale by crediting it at the beginning to "others" (2.3) and later to Promathion, "who compiled a history of Italy" (2.6). Plutarch thus recounts this story not because he regards it as true but because he wishes to be transparent about what his sources say.

Plutarch goes on to provide a fifth account that he regards as most reliable:

> But the story which has the widest credence and the greatest number of vouchers was first published among the Greeks, in

[12] Plutarch earlier described this period of history as "the land of poets and fabulists [μυθογράφοι]" (*Thes.* 1.1) and wishes for success in "purifying Fable [τὸ μυθῶδες]" (1.3).

its principal details, by Diocles of Peparethus, and Fabius Pictor follows him in most points. Here again there are variations in the story, but its general outline is as follows. (3.1)

In this introductory comment, we observe *transparency* ("there are variations") and *evaluation* ("widest credence . . . greatest number of vouchers").

Here is the essence of the story: Amulius, one of Aeneas's descendants, seized the kingdom of Alba from his brother Numitor. Wanting to make sure that Numitor's daughter did not bear children, Amulius "made her a priestess of Vesta, bound to live unwedded and a virgin all her days" (3.2).[13] However, the daughter conceived and gave birth to two boys. Amulius ordered a servant to kill the babies.[14] The servant put the babies in a trough and went to cast them into the river, but it was "swollen and violent" (3.4), so to keep from getting too close, he set the trough down near the bank. The river carried the trough to a smooth place, and a she-wolf nursed the babies with the help of a woodpecker. Plutarch pauses at this point to note that "these creatures are considered sacred to Mars," which is why "the mother was believed when she declared that Mars was the father of her babes" (4.2). "And yet," Plutarch notes, "it is said that she was deceived into doing this, and was really deflowered by Amulius himself, who came to her in armour and ravished her" (4.2). Plutarch distances himself from both claims ("she declared"; "it is said"), but he seems to prefer the latter, more mundane account.[15] He also provides a more commonplace alternative to the she-wolf:

> But some say that the name of the children's nurse, by its ambiguity, deflected the story into the realm of the fabulous [ἐπὶ τὸ μυθῶδες]. For the Latins not only called she-wolves "lupae," but also women of loose character, and such a woman was the wife of Faustulus, the foster-father of the infants, Acca Larentia by name. (4.3)

---

[13] Plutarch notes that different names are given for the daughter—Ilia, Rhea, or Silvia (3.3; *transparency*).

[14] Plutarch mentions that some call the servant Faustulus, but others give this name to the man who rescues the children (3.4; *transparency*).

[15] Lincoln conveniently neglects to mention the more mundane account ("Luke and Jesus' Conception," 655).

The she-wolf, then, may simply be the woman who nursed the infants. Again, Plutarch distances himself from this claim ("some say"), so it is unclear which version he prefers, but he at least offers an option that is more mundane.

When Plutarch returns to his narrative, he recounts how Faustulus, one of Amulius's swineherds, found the babies and raised them, and "no man knew of it; or, as some say with a closer approach to probability, Numitor did know of it, and secretly aided the foster-parents in their task" (6.1). Here Plutarch engages in both *transparency* and *evaluation*, noting different accounts and commending one as more probable. Plutarch also distances himself from several details regarding the boys' education and naming (6.1–2). He does note that "the noble size and beauty of their bodies, even when they were infants, betokened their natural disposition; and when they grew up, they were both of them courageous and manly" (6.2). While some might view this as an instance of backward development (Romulus and Remus's adult courage and virility have been projected back onto their childhood), there is nothing inherently implausible about a healthy baby boy growing up to be a virile man, and Plutarch's historiographic indicators throughout suggest that he does not feel at liberty to fabricate material.

At this point Plutarch skips over Romulus and Remus's childhood and recounts a number of their deeds as young adults, climaxing with their victory over Amulius (8.6). He concludes this section with the following note:

> Although most of these particulars are related by Fabius and Diocles of Peparethus, who seems to have been the first to publish a "Founding of Rome," some are suspicious of their fictitious and fabulous quality; but we should not be incredulous when we see what a poet fortune sometimes is, and when we reflect that the Roman state would not have attained to its present power, had it not been of a divine origin, and one which was attended by great marvels. (8.7)

This comment is interesting for several reasons. First, Fabius and Diocles are the same sources that Plutarch mentions in 3.1 when he introduces the account of Romulus's origins that he regards as most probable. Plutarch therefore seems to regard at least 3.1–8.6—which contains material regarding Romulus's birth, childhood, and young adulthood—as a unit, both from a narrative and historiographic perspective. This implies that Plutarch does not place what we might call a "birth narrative" on a different historiographic plane from the rest of the life. Birth material, like any other material, requires sources and is subject to historiographic scrutiny. Second, Plutarch acknowledges that "some are suspicious" of the "fictitious and fabulous quality" of the story he has related. On the one hand, this suggests that "fictitious and fabulous" were undesirable traits for birth material in an ancient biography; if "fictitious and fabulous" were the norm, Plutarch's comment would be unnecessary. On the other hand, Plutarch also exhorts the reader to recognize "what a poet fortune sometimes is" and to be open to the miraculous in light of Rome's clear divine origins.[16] Whatever we may think of the legitimacy of this plea, it alerts us to an important insight: Plutarch is not doing history within a naturalistic framework. Thus, while the modern historian may regard the idea that Romulus and Remus's trough floated downriver and lodged on a bank to be found by a swineherd as fanciful, we must recognize that *Plutarch* considered this to be quite plausible. Therefore, the appearance of supernatural events within Plutarch's stories does not necessarily indicate that those stories are intended to be ahistorical.

To sum up: The birth material of *Romulus* contains numerous instances of *sources, transparency, evaluation,* and *distancing,* all of which indicate Plutarch's historiographic intent. The account that Plutarch affirms is generally plausible, even from a modern perspective. At many of the more incredible points (Mars as father, the she-wolf nursing Romulus and Remus), Plutarch provides more mundane alternatives. The material surveyed above illustrates Plutarch's desire to "purify Fable" (*Thes.* 1.3).

---

[16] Christopher Pelling notes that Livy (*Hist.* pref. 6–7) makes a similar point ("Truth and Fiction in Plutarch's Lives," in *Plutarch and History*, 149).

Alexander

Plutarch wrote his life of Alexander the Great approximately 456 years after Alexander's birth (356 BC). After a preface (*Alex.* 1.1), Plutarch provides a brief lineage of Alexander, saying, "On his father's side he was a descendant of Heracles through Caranus, and on his mother's side a descendant of Aeacus through Neoptolemus; this is accepted without any question" (2.1; *evaluation*). He then launches into an account of Alexander's conception, saying, "And it is said [λέγεται] that . . ." (2.1).[17] Plutarch's phrasing here suggests that he has a source, but it also seems to be an instance of *distancing*, for in crediting the account to others Plutarch separates the story from his own authorial reputation. Alexander's father Philip apparently fell in love with a girl named Olympias when they were both young, and they were betrothed. The night before they consummated their marriage, "the bride dreamed that there was a peal of thunder and that a thunderbolt fell upon her womb, and that thereby much fire was kindled, which broke into flames that travelled all about, and then was extinguished" (2.2). After the marriage, "Philip dreamed that he was putting a seal upon his wife's womb; and the device of the seal, as he thought, was the figure of a lion" (2.2–3). Some of Philip's advisors interpreted this to mean that Philip needed to "put a closer watch on his marriage relations," but one named Aristander said it meant that Olympias was pregnant with "a son whose nature would be bold and lion-like" (2.3). Plutarch also reports that a serpent was seen lying by Olympias as she slept, and "they say"[18] (λέγουσιν) that this deterred Philip from sleeping with his wife often, either because he was worried that she might put a spell on him or because he believed that she was "the partner of a superior being" (2.4). However, Plutarch provides another story regarding Olympias's relation to snakes—namely, that Olympias was a passionate participant in Bacchic frenzies and would even "provide the reveling companies with great tame serpents" to use in their rituals (2.6; *transparency*). The implication seems to be

---

[17] My translation.
[18] My translation.

that the serpent seen with Olympias was not necessarily a god in disguise but may have simply been a mundane feature of her Bacchic devotion.

Plutarch notes that "they say"[19] (λέγουσι) that after his vision, Philip sent to Delphi and received an oracle from Apollo,

> who bade him sacrifice to Ammon and hold that god in greatest reverence, but told him he was to lose that one of his eyes which he had applied to the chink in the door when he espied the god, in the form of a serpent, sharing the couch of his wife. Moreover, Olympias, as Eratosthenes says, when she sent Alexander forth upon his great expedition, told him, and him alone, the secret of his begetting, and bade him have purposes worthy of his birth. Others, on the contrary, say that she repudiated the idea, and said: "Alexander must cease slandering me to Hera." (3.1–2)

Here we observe *distancing*, *sources*, and *transparency*. Plutarch does not affirm the story about the oracle from Apollo directly but rather *distances* himself from it by framing it as what "they say." He also cites Eratosthenes as a *source* for the story about Olympias telling Alexander the secret of his conception. And finally, he exhibits *transparency* in offering the alternative perspective that Olympias explicitly rejected the idea that Alexander was sired by a god.[20]

On the day that Alexander was born, the temple of Ephesian Artemis apparently burned down. Plutarch provides a number of perspectives on the significance of Alexander's birth. One Hegesias the Magnesian said that the temple burned because Artemis "was busy bringing Alexander into the world" (3.3). The magi at Ephesus said it meant that "a great calamity for Asia

---

[19] My translation.

[20] Litwa misrepresents the evidence when he says, "Plutarch himself narrated that Zeus impregnated Alexander's mother, Olympias; and Olympias supposedly acknowledged this point directly to the adult Alexander" (*How the Gospels Became History: Jesus and Mediterranean Myths* [Yale UP, 2019], 83–84, cf. 101). Plutarch says at the outset that Alexander was descended from Heracles on his father's side (*Alex.* 2.1), he nowhere affirms that Zeus impregnated Olympias, and it is misleading to note the tradition that Olympias acknowledged Zeus's paternity without also acknowledging the tradition that she denied it.

had that day been born" (3.4). On the same day, Philip won a battle and received messages that his general had won another battle, his horse had won a race, and that Alexander had been born, which his seers interpreted to mean that Alexander "would always be victorious" (3.5). These perspectives do not constitute *transparency* since they do not pertain to Plutarch's sources and are mutually compatible. Yet it is worth noting that there is nothing inherently legendary or far-fetched about what Plutarch affirms. A baby's birth will inevitably correspond with other events, and people may interpret these correspondences in different ways. Some of these will be forgotten because they did not come true, but others will be remembered because they did. One therefore cannot conclude that simply because an author includes an omen in a story, he intends the story to be ahistorical (more on this below).

Plutarch includes substantial information about Alexander's youth (4.4–8.4). Space does not allow us to summarize all this material here, so we will simply survey some key elements within it. One thing that bears mentioning, however, is that here (as elsewhere) Plutarch does not draw a clear line between his subject's birth and childhood and the rest of the life. For example, just after recounting Alexander's birth, Plutarch discusses his physical appearance and constitution (4.1–4), focusing more on his adulthood than childhood, before returning to Alexander's youth. And while it is clear that Alexander is sixteen years old by *Alexander* 9.1, his age throughout the preceding material is unclear, so it is not easy to tell where Plutarch transitions from the "birth narrative" to the rest of the life.

Plutarch repeatedly notes how Alexander's character manifested itself early in his life. For example, he notes that Alexander exhibited self-restraint against bodily pleasures early in life and possessed a gravitas beyond his years (4.4–5; cf. 21.4–23.6). Alexander also took an interest in state affairs and had political ambitions at an early age, complaining whenever he heard of one of his father's victories that nothing great would be left for him to do (5.1–2). Many scholars view such elements as the subject's adult character being read back into his early life, evidence of the legendary character of ancient birth narratives. However, such a conclusion is too hasty. It is not implausible that someone might manifest traits early in life that would become characteristic of him as an adult. Indeed, many parents make similar claims about their children on a regular basis. While such memories may be cemented more than others by the subject's later development, this does not mean that they are fabricated or false. For example, because my brother has become a worship director as an adult, my mother may be more likely to remember his early musical exploits than other things he did as a child that did not become a major part of his adult life, but it is not as if he became a worship director and she created a memory of him playing air drums as a toddler to match. The other reason that we should be wary of the backreading hypothesis is the historiographic care that we have observed in Plutarch's birth material. Historiographic features like *sources, transparency, evaluation,* and *distancing* do not make sense if Plutarch sees himself as simply fabricating a birth and childhood based on his subject's adult life. On this note, Plutarch actually cites Onesicritus to back up the claim that as a youth, Alexander kept a copy of Aristotle's recension of Homer's *Iliad* under his pillow because he regarded it as a compendium of military knowledge (8.2). Such authorial moves would be pointless if the standard of truth were simply to tell an interesting yet ahistorical tale.

In the birth material of Plutarch's *Alexander*, then, we observe numerous historiographic features including *sources, transparency, evaluation,* and *distancing*. Yes, Plutarch does relate some elements that modern historians might omit, such as dreams and omens. But he carefully distances himself from any claims that might be implausible and at several points he includes alternative accounts that are more historically sober (e.g., his discussion of Alexander's conception). The overarching impression that we are left with is that Plutarch desires to tell a true story, not merely an interesting one.

Lycurgus

Plutarch's *Lycurgus* likewise contains historiographic indicators in its birth material. Lycurgus, like Theseus and Romulus, was for

Plutarch a figure from the distant past. Plutarch therefore opens with a historiographic disclaimer:

> Concerning Lycurgus the lawgiver, in general, nothing can be said which is not disputed, since indeed there are different accounts of his birth, his travels, his death, and above all, of his work as law maker and statesman; and there is least agreement among historians as to the times in which the man lived. (*Lyc.* 1.1; *distancing, transparency*)

Note that Plutarch includes Lycurgus's "birth" (γένος) as one of the elements about which his sources disagree. This implies that Plutarch not only has sources for the birth material but also that he regards disagreement between these sources as significant—which is to say that here, as elsewhere in the life, he is interested in telling the truth.

After detailing the various perspectives on when Lycurgus lived (1.1–3), Plutarch declares,

> However, although the history of these times is such a maze, I shall try, in presenting my narrative, to follow those authors who are least contradicted, or who have the most notable witnesses for what they have written about the man. (1.3; *sources*)

Plutarch gives as an example the different genealogies of Lycurgus. Whereas Simonides the poet claims that Lycurgus was not the son but the brother of Eunomus, "most writers give a different genealogy" in which Lycurgus was the son of Eunomus (1.4; *transparency*). Plutarch affirms this latter, majority account and cites Dieutychidas as one of its *sources* (1.4). This passage is important, for here Plutarch illustrates his historical method by making a critical judgment concerning Lycurgus's genealogy based on the number and quality of his sources (*evaluation*).

Plutarch does not provide any further information about Lycurgus's conception or birth; he simply says that the kingdom of Sparta passed from Eunomus to Lycurgus's brother Polydectes and then to Lycurgus when his brother died (2.3–3.1). The fact that Plutarch presents a genealogy for Lycurgus but no further birth material suggests either that Plutarch lacked additional information in his sources or, if he did have information, that he did not regard it as relevant. What we can say with certainty is that Plutarch did not fabricate further birth material for Lycurgus that went beyond his sources.

Plutarch's account of Lycurgus's origins, while it is much briefer than the other accounts surveyed above, again demonstrates Plutarch's historiographic intent in composing birth material. Plutarch has sources, notes differences between them (*transparency*), and adjudicates between the varied accounts (*evaluation*) to construct an account that he regards as the most historically reliable given his sources.

Themistocles

Plutarch begins his life of Themistocles by noting that his subject's family "was too obscure to further his reputation" (*Them.* 1.1).[21] This claim is interesting, for it presses against the notion that ancient biographers inflated their subject's origins to correspond to their later greatness. In his discussion of Themistocles's parents, Plutarch cites the epitaph of Themistocles's mother to substantiate that she was an alien (*sources*):

> Abrotonon was I, and a woman of Thrace, yet I brought forth
> That great light of the Greeks,—know! 'twas Themistocles.
> (1.1)[22]

While the epitaph implies that Abrotonon was a Thracian, Plutarch says that Phanias "writes that the mother of Themistocles was not a Thracian, but a Carian woman, and that her name was not Abrotonon, but Euterpe. And Neanthes actually adds the name of her city in Caria,—Halicarnassus" (1.2; *transparency*). Plutarch does not explicitly take a side here, but it is significant that he notes the differences between the sources rather than simply selecting the one that is most convenient.

Plutarch says nothing about the conception or birth of Themistocles, cutting directly to his childhood. As a boy, Themistocles was "impetuous, by nature sagacious, and by election

---

[21] A footnote in the LCL edition states, "It is probable that one or more introductory paragraphs of this biography have been lost."

[22] The LCL edition cites "Athenaeus, xiii. p. 576."

enterprising and prone to public life" (2.1). When given the opportunity for leisure, he would compose and rehearse mock speeches instead of playing with the other boys. His teacher would often say to him, "My boy, thou wilt be nothing insignificant, but something great, of a surety, either for good or evil" (2.2). There is no doubt that Plutarch here foreshadows the kind of man that Themistocles will become, but this does not mean that he has fabricated the story. As noted above regarding Alexander the Great, such correspondences often do exist between a subject's character as a child and an adult, and Plutarch's historiographic intent elsewhere suggests that he is not fabricating material.

Indeed, Plutarch utilizes *transparency* and *evaluation* in his account of Themistocles's youth. He critiques Stesimbrotus for saying that Themistocles "was a pupil of Anaxagoras, and a disciple of Melissus the physicist," pointing out that both men were much younger than Themistocles (2.3). Better, Plutarch says, to follow "those who say that Themistocles was a disciple of Mnesiphilus the Phrearrhian" (2.4). Plutarch acknowledges that as a youth Themistocles was uneven and unstable, but he regards as false "what some story-makers add to this"—namely, that Themistocles's "father disinherited him, and his mother took her own life for very grief at her son's ill-fame" (2.6).[23] This last passage is particularly important, because here Plutarch clearly condemns those who invent stories regarding a subject's youth. It seems unlikely that Plutarch would have intentionally committed the same error for which he criticizes others.

---

[23] Plutarch's critique of "story-makers," of course, implies that he thinks some writers did fabricate material—in this case, regarding the subject's childhood. Two things must be said on this point. First, the fact that Plutarch believes other writers fabricated material does not necessarily mean that they did so. Cornelius Nepos, for example, says that Themistocles was disinherited by his father (*Them.* 1.3)—one of the claims that Plutarch condemns. Our earlier study of Nepos, however, has shown that it is improbable that he made this story up. Second, even if Plutarch is correct that some writers did fabricate childhood material, he clearly regards such fabrication as illegitimate within the genre of ancient biography.

In the birth material of *Themistocles*, Plutarch employs *sources*, *transparency*, and *evaluation*. Furthermore, everything that he affirms about Themistocles's origins is quite plausible. By all accounts, Plutarch seems to present his account as sincere historiography.

Cicero

Cicero was born in 106 BC, approximately 206 years before Plutarch penned his biography of Cicero. Of the subjects surveyed here, Cicero's birth thus falls closest to Plutarch's own time. It therefore provides an interesting comparison to some of the subjects from the more distant past discussed above.

Plutarch begins by discussing Cicero's parents:

> It is said of Helvia, the mother of Cicero, that she was well born and lived an honourable life; but of his father nothing can be learned that does not go to an extreme. For some say that he was born and reared in a fuller's shop, while others trace the origin of his family to Tullus Attius, an illustrious king of the Volscians, who waged war upon the Romans with great ability. (*Cic.* 1.1)

Here we observe *distancing* ("It is said"), *transparency* ("some say . . . others trace"), and *evaluation* in that Plutarch depicts both views he describes as "extreme" (he does not give a mediating view).

After discussing the origin of the family name "Cicero" (1.2–4), Plutarch turns to Cicero's birth:

> They say that Cicero was born, without travail or pain on the part of his mother, on the third day of the new Calends. . . . It would seem also that a phantom appeared to his nurse and foretold that her charge would be a great blessing to all the Romans. (2.1)[24]

The claim that Cicero's mother gave birth without pain should raise the suspicions of any good historian. Notice, however, that Plutarch distances himself from this datum, prefacing it with "They say." Similarly, he introduces the account of the phantom's prophecy with the phrase "It would seem." Plutarch does not directly assert that these events took place; he simply indicates

---

[24] LCL translation slightly modified.

that they appear in his sources. He also acknowledges the incredible nature of these accounts, saying, "And although these presages were thought to be mere dreams and idle fancies, [Cicero] soon showed them to be true prophecy" (2.2; *evaluation*). Plutarch recognizes that the accounts he has related are suspicious, but in this case, he seems to think that Cicero's development validates them. We may, of course, disagree, but we cannot accuse Plutarch of spinning a tall tale. He is simply not operating within a naturalist framework and is open to supernatural causation within history if there is sufficient evidence for it.[25]

Plutarch also mentions some of Cicero's boyhood exploits—namely, that he excelled in school (even to the point of making some parents of other students jealous) and was particularly good at writing poetry.[26] One might be tempted to view these claims as projecting Cicero's adulthood back onto his childhood. However, two factors suggest that this is not the case. First, Plutarch goes on to note that Cicero later "got the name of being not only the best orator, but also the best poet among the Romans" (2.3). Yet Plutarch says nothing specific about Cicero's young oratorical achievements, which one might expect if he were simply reading Cicero's adult accomplishments back onto his youth. Second, Plutarch backs up his claim about young Cicero writing poetry by noting that "a little poem which he wrote when a boy is still extant, called Pontius Glaucus, and composed in tetrameter verse" (2.3; *sources*). If Plutarch regarded childhood material as ahistorical, such a notice would be unnecessary.

Therefore, in *Cicero* as in the other lives above, Plutarch engages in historiography in recounting his subject's birth and childhood. Here we find *sources, transparency, evaluation,* and

---

[25] J. L. Moles notes that in *Cicero* Plutarch "oscillates between acceptance (here, 14.4; 20.1–2, 32.4) and rejection (45.1) of portents and other supernatural events according to circumstances" (J. L. Moles, commentary to *The Life of Cicero*, by Plutarch, ed. and trans. J. L. Moles [Aris & Phillips, 1988], 149).

[26] Plutarch's claim about the breadth of Cicero's education may draw on Cicero, *Epistulae ad familiares* 4.4.4. See Moles, commentary to *Life of Cicero*, 149.

distancing. Once again, Plutarch seems to be telling a story that he intends to be true, not merely interesting.

Summary

In the birth material of the six lives surveyed above, we observe repeated instances of *sources, transparency, evaluation,* and *distancing*, all of which indicate that Plutarch composed these accounts with historiographic intent. The historiographic features that we find in these biographies are not unique to them. As noted above, I have selected lives that other scholars have cited as examples of the ahistorical character of ancient birth narratives, so if anything, the lives above should be some of the most difficult for my thesis. These same historiographic features appear throughout Plutarch's *Lives*, both in birth material and elsewhere. Appendix D summarizes historiographic features in all Plutarch's biographies, focusing on the birth material (if available) but also providing examples from the rest of each life.

ABSENCE OF BIRTH MATERIAL

The absence of birth material (or substantial birth material) from many of the *Lives* also suggests that Plutarch aims to report fact rather than fiction in his birth narratives. As we have seen above, Plutarch sometimes provides an extended narrative regarding his subject's origins. However, eight of Plutarch's fifty extant lives (16 percent) lack any birth material at all, and many others contain only minimal details.[27] As noted in our study of Cornelius Nepos, it is difficult to account for this phenomenon if one holds that birth narratives were merely legendary anticipations of a subject's later greatness. Plutarch clearly regards all his

---

[27] See appendix D. The lives that lack any birth material are *Numa, Camillus, Timoleon, Flamininus, Caesar, Phocion, Galba,* and *Otho*. The lives that contain minimal information are generally those in which the birth material comprises only one to two sections or less (e.g., *Marcellus*, in which the birth material is limited to 1.1). It is difficult in some cases to quantify the birth material, as Plutarch does not always provide a clear break between the birth material and the rest of the life (e.g., *Alex.* 4.4–8.4) and sometimes interjects adult material into the birth material (e.g., *Cic.* 1.3–4).

subjects as great men, so if he viewed his birth material merely as ahistorical anticipations of his subjects' adulthoods, why did he not give all of them substantial birth material? One might attempt to salvage the hypothesis that ancient birth narratives were legendary by arguing that the amount of birth material that a subject receives corresponds to his greatness. However, such a response fails, because one of the figures who receives no birth material is Julius Caesar, whom Plutarch clearly regards as one of his greatest subjects. The flaws of this hypothesis become even more evident when we recognize Caesar's Greek parallel is Alexander the Great, who receives an extended birth narrative that we discussed above. If birth material required little to no grounding in history, then why did Plutarch not provide Caesar with a birth narrative to parallel that of Alexander? Indeed, of the eight figures who do not receive birth material, six of them are parallel lives in which the subject's counterpart receives birth material.[28] By not including birth material for these figures, Plutarch therefore passed not only on an opportunity to forecast his subjects' greatness but also on an opportunity to create a similarity with the parallel figure.

It seems far more reasonable to think that Plutarch did not include birth material (or more birth material) in the lives noted above because (1) he lacked sources or (2) the information in his sources was not interesting or relevant enough to include. In either case, what this implies is that Plutarch did not fabricate information that was more suitable for his purposes.[29] Or, to formulate the insight positively: Plutarch's birth material seems to be information-based. Christopher Pelling sums up the matter well:

> [Plutarch's] reluctance to fabricate is particularly plain in his treatment of boyhood and youth. So many Lives have virtually nothing before adulthood: *Antony, Nicias, Camillus, Flamininus, Marcellus, Fabius, Timoleon,* and more. We could all make up a

---

[28] The two that are not parallel lives are *Galba* and *Otho*.
[29] For the general point, see Craig S. Keener, *Christobiography: Memory, History, and the Reliability of the Gospels* (Eerdmans, 2019), 171–73.

few good stories about a schoolboy Antony or Nicias; Plutarch does not.[30]

SUPERNATURAL ELEMENTS

Scholars sometimes cite supernatural elements in Plutarch's birth narratives to substantiate that these stories are legendary in nature.[31] However, several points suggest that the mere presence of supernatural elements in Plutarch's birth material does not constitute evidence that Plutarch intends this material to be ahistorical.

First, our study above has shown that Plutarch often recounts elements that he either does not affirm or explicitly denies as being true (see discussions of *transparency, evaluation,* and *distancing*). The question, then, is not whether Plutarch relates supernatural events in his birth material but whether he affirms those events as historically probable. If a modern biographer of George Washington related the story of young Washington cutting down a cherry tree and treated it as legendary, it would be foolish—not to mention unfair—to question the biographer's historiographic intent on the grounds that she included ahistorical elements. We should extend the same courtesy to Plutarch. Ironically, many of the supernatural elements that scholars use to argue for the legendary character of Plutarch's birth material are elements that Plutarch himself does not affirm.[32] When we

---

[30] Pelling, "Truth and Fiction," 153. Cf. Christopher Pelling, "Aspects of Plutarch's Characterization," in *Plutarch and History*, 283, 290; idem, "Childhood and Personality in Greek Biography," in *Plutarch and History*, 302, 307–8; Tomas Hägg, *The Art of Biography in Antiquity* (Cambridge UP, 2012), 254. Pelling does note that Plutarch sometimes engages in "routine generalization" in which he retrojects aspects of men's later careers into their childhood. However, Pelling argues that in such cases Plutarch is not fabricating but making the sort of plausible inferences that he also makes in adult material ("Truth and Fiction," 153–54; "Childhood and Personality," 308–9).

[31] E.g., Miller, *Born Divine*, 134–35; Lincoln, *Born of a Virgin?* 63.

[32] E.g., Lincoln, *Born of a Virgin?* 63, citing *Cic.* 2; *Rom.* 2.5; 4.2; *Thes.* 2; 6; 36; *Alex.* 3. For discussion of historiographic features in all these passages, see above.

reduce the supernatural elements under consideration to those that Plutarch does affirm, the pool of data shrinks considerably.

Second, we noted at several points above that Plutarch does not seem to be doing historiography within a naturalistic framework (e.g., *Cic.* 2.2; *Rom.* 8.7). Rather, he seems to be open to supernatural causation if there is sufficient evidence for it. Plutarch discusses his views on supernatural causation in *Coriolanus* while commenting on an instance during his subject's adulthood where a statue of a goddess supposedly spoke audibly (*Cor.* 37.3). Plutarch initially seems reluctant to accept the report, calling it "difficult of belief" and something that "probably never happened" (38.1). He notes that statues might appear to sweat, shed tears, etc., since such things can be related to natural processes and "there is nothing in the way of believing that the Deity uses these phenomena sometimes as signs and portents" (38.1). Plutarch is even willing to grant that "statues may emit a noise like a moan or a groan, by reason of a fracture or a rupture" (38.2). However, he regards it as impossible that a statue might speak articulately, "since not even the soul of man, or the Deity, without a body duly organized and fitted with vocal parts, has ever spoken or conversed" (38.2). Yet Plutarch goes on to say,

> But where history forces our assent with numerous and credible witnesses, we must conclude that an experience different from that of sensation arises in the imaginative part of the soul, and persuades men to think it sensation; as, for instance, in sleep, when we think we see and hear, although we neither see nor hear. However, those who cherish strong feelings of goodwill and affection for the Deity, and are therefore unable to reject or deny anything of this kind, have a strong argument for their faith in the wonderful and transcendent character of the divine power. For the Deity has no resemblance whatever to man, either in nature, activity, skill, or strength; nor, if He does something that we cannot do, or contrives something that we cannot contrive, is this contrary to reason; but rather, since He differs from us in all points, in His works most of all is He unlike us and far removed from us. (38.3–4)

Plutarch clearly regards supernatural causation as a legitimate aspect of history. The question is, What sort of supernatural causation is acceptable? Plutarch seems to view supernatural causation that utilizes natural processes and/or has historical precedent as quite possible. And while he regards it as improbable that a statue might speak articulately, he is willing to grant that a god might cause humans to imagine as much and perceive it as sensation. It is therefore illegitimate to assume that when Plutarch reports a supernatural event he regards the event or the surrounding narrative as ahistorical. Plutarch was not a naturalist, and we should not treat him as one.

Third, Plutarch includes supernatural elements throughout his *Lives*, not just in birth material. For example, in *Alexander* he reports numerous omens from his subject's adult life. Many of these are interpreted by a "seer" named Aristander (*Alex.* 14.5; 25.1, 3–4; 50.2–3; 52.1). As noted above, this same Aristander interprets a dream by Alexander's father in the birth material (2.3). Interestingly, while Plutarch distances himself from the supernatural elements in the birth material, he does not distance himself from all the omens interpreted by Aristander during Alexander's adult life. Similarly, in *Lucullus* he includes no supernatural elements in the birth material but mentions many omens during his account of the subject's adult life (*Luc.* 2.3; 12.1–2; 23.3–4; 24.6–7).

We therefore cannot assume that when Plutarch narrates a supernatural event in birth material, he regards the event or the surrounding account as ahistorical. Of course, we may choose to deny that the event in question occurred, but if we are after the ancient author's intention (the primary focus of this book), then we must recognize that in birth material (as elsewhere in the life) Plutarch regards the supernatural as possible if there is sufficient evidence for it.

TIME ELAPSED

Scholars generally hold that Plutarch wrote his *Lives* from AD 90 to 120 and the parallel lives after AD 96. To determine the date of composition for each life would be incredibly difficult, so for the purpose of this analysis, I have taken AD 101 as Plutarch's date of composition for all the *Lives* in determining the time elapsed. A true average date of composition would likely be somewhat later than this. However, I have opted for an earlier date to decrease the time elapsed and thereby allow Plutarch to compare as favorably as possible with Matthew and Luke. The added benefit of taking AD 101 as the date of composition is that one can simply add 100 to a BC date of birth and have the time elapsed. (There was no 0 BC, hence my reason for choosing AD 101 instead of AD 100.)

The time elapsed for each individual life appears in appendix D. The following results emerge from the data:

Average	434.56 years
Median	427.5 years[33]
Maximum	900 years
Minimum	69 years

As with Cornelius Nepos, the key insight that arises from these figures is that *Plutarch is writing long after the births of almost all his subjects*. The closest subject (Otho) was born approximately 69 years before Plutarch penned his life, and next (Galba) 103 years. And, of course, the average and median years elapsed are much higher—both well above 400 years. Once again, several related points arise from this basic insight.

First, Plutarch would have had access to eyewitness sources for the birth material of only one (at most) of his fifty *Lives*: Otho. Galba (born 3 BC) would have been 48 when Plutarch was born (AD 46), so any reliable witnesses to Galba's birth would have been long gone by the time Plutarch reached adulthood.

Second, given this significant historical distance and the quality of Plutarch's sources, it is actually surprising how few of the claims Plutarch makes about his subjects' births are implausible, even from a modern perspective.

Finally, while Plutarch's compositional practices (e.g., historiographic features and the intention that they point to) provide

---

[33] Because there are fifty of Plutarch's *Lives*, the median is the average of the middle two numbers.

helpful analogies for understanding the Gospels, the level of accuracy that he achieves (i.e., his ability to carry out his historiographic intent) is not a good gauge for what Matthew and Luke might have achieved in composing their birth narratives. Among Plutarch's *Lives*, only *Otho* provides a close analogy to the access to sources that Matthew and Luke would have had. However, the analogy is only one of chronology, for as members of early Christianity (a comparatively small group in the first century AD) Matthew and Luke would have presumably had much better access to Jesus's family of origin than Plutarch would have had to that of Otho.

CONCLUSION

Our study has revealed that Plutarch has composed his birth material with historiographic intent. The birth narratives that we examined in the first section of this chapter exhibit numerous historiographic features that suggest Plutarch is attempting to tell true stories, not interesting but ahistorical ones. To be sure, Plutarch includes certain elements that he does not regard as historically true, but in such cases he employs *transparency*, *evaluation*, or *distancing* to indicate to the reader that he is not presenting these elements as fact but the opinion of others. The absence of birth material (or substantial birth material) from many of Plutarch's *Lives* also suggests that Plutarch's birth material is information-based, not spun out of thin air. In addition, we have seen that Plutarch is open to supernatural causation within history. Thus, in the limited cases where Plutarch does affirm supernatural elements in his birth material, we cannot assume that he regards such elements as ahistorical. Finally, an analysis of the time elapsed between the births of Plutarch's subjects and his composition of their lives reveals that Plutarch is writing at a significant historical distance (on average, well over four hundred years) from the births of almost all his subjects. Thus, while Plutarch's demonstrable historiographic intent (which is not impacted by chronological distance) is helpful in understanding the Gospel birth narratives, the level of accuracy that Plutarch achieves is likely far less than what Matthew and Luke might have accomplished.

4
SUETONIUS

Suetonius was born around AD 70 and died sometime after AD 122.[1] He tells us that his father was Suetonius Laetus, a Roman of the equestrian order (*Otho* 10.1), but beyond this most of our information about him comes from the letters of his friend and patron Pliny the Younger. Suetonius apparently practiced law for a short time. Through Pliny's patronage, he received a military tribunate (which he transferred to a relative) and the *ius trium liberorum*, a right awarded to Roman men who had at least three children (though he had none). Suetonius served under Trajan and Hadrian in three major secretarial roles: *a studiis*, *a bibliothecis*, and *ab epistulis*. However, he was dismissed around AD 122, apparently for a breach of court etiquette. "Nothing more," says Keith Bradley, "is known of him afterwards."[2]

---

[1] Here and below I draw on Michael von Albrecht, *A History of Roman Literature: From Livius Andronicus to Boethius: With Special Regard to Its Influence on World Literature*, rev. ed., 2 vols., Mnemosyne: Bibliotheca Classica Batavia 165 (Brill, 1997), 2:1391–92; Keith R. Bradley, introduction to Suetonius, *Lives of the Caesars*, vol. 1, *Julius. Augustus. Tiberius. Gaius Caligula*, trans. John C. Rolfe, rev. ed., LCL 31 (Harvard UP, 1998), 2–9; Keith R. Bradley, "Suetonius," *OCD* 1409–10.

[2] Bradley, introduction to *Julius. Augustus. Tiberius. Gaius Caligula*, 5.

Suetonius wrote numerous books in the areas of biography, Roman culture, natural history, and grammar. Most of these have unfortunately been lost and are known only through ancient lists and quotations.³ Two collections of biographies, however, survive in part or whole: (1) *Lives of Illustrious Men* (*De viris illustribus*), biographies of Roman men organized into five categories (poets, orators, historians, philosophers, and grammarians/rhetoricians). Only a few lives from the first four categories are extant (six poets, one orator, and one historian), and these are known only through quotations in other works. However, the part on grammarians and rhetoricians has survived independently.⁴ (2) *Lives of the Caesars* (*De vita Caesarum*), biographies of the twelve Caesars from Julius to Domitian.

Suetonius includes birth material in many of his lives, but the amount of material varies significantly from one biography to another. Here we will first explore birth material in three lives that scholars have cited to show that ancient birth material was meant to be legendary rather than historiographic: *Augustus*, *Tiberius*, and *Vespasian*.⁵ As in the previous chapter, I begin with these both to demonstrate that I have not rigged the investigation and because if we find that Suetonius exhibits historiographic intent in this material, we will have strong evidence against the view that he intends his birth material to be legendary. After examin-

---

³ For a list, see Bradley, introduction to *Julius. Augustus. Tiberius. Gaius Caligula*, 5–6.

⁴ On *Lives of Illustrious Men* see John C. Rolfe and G. P. Goold, prefatory note to Suetonius, *Lives of the Caesars*, vol. 2, *Claudius. Nero. Galba. Otho. Vitellius. Vespasian. Titus. Domitian. Lives of Illustrious Men: Grammarians and Rhetoricians. Poets (Terence. Virgil. Horace. Tibullus. Persius. Lucan). Lives of Pliny the Elder and Passienus Crispus*, trans. John C. Rolfe, rev. ed., LCL 38 (Harvard UP, 1997), 368–73.

⁵ John P. Meier, *A Marginal Jew: Rethinking the Historical Jesus*, 5 vols., ABRL (Doubleday, 1991–2016), 1:208, 234n14; Robert J. Miller, *Born Divine: The Births of Jesus and Other Sons of God* (Polebridge, 2003), 142–45, cf. 134; Andrew T. Lincoln, *Born of a Virgin? Reconceiving Jesus in the Bible, Tradition, and Theology* (Eerdmans, 2013), 61–63, 109–10, 121. Meier, Miller, and Lincoln all discuss *Augustus*; Lincoln also discusses *Tiberius* and *Vespasian*.

ing birth material in several other lives, we will consider the three issues discussed in earlier chapters: (1) the absence of birth material, (2) supernatural elements, and (3) the time elapsed between the subjects' births and Suetonius's writing.

BIRTH MATERIAL IN SUETONIUS'S *LIVES*

Augustus

Suetonius begins his life of Augustus by describing his subject's paternal ancestors. "There are many indications," he writes, "that the Octavian family was in days of old a distinguished one at Velitrae" (*Aug.* 1).[6] Suetonius gives several lines of evidence for this claim: (1) a street in Velitrae long-named "Octavian," (2) an altar there "consecrated to an Octavius," and (3) a public decree on record that *mentions* the family (*sources*).[7] Suetonius goes on to recount the family's involvement in Roman politics and society, interestingly placing Augustus in the less noteworthy and politically involved branch of the family (2.1–2).

Suetonius concludes his account of Augustus's family as follows:

> This is the account given by others; Augustus himself merely writes that he came of an old and wealthy equestrian family, in which his own father was the first to become a senator. Marcus Antonius taunts him with his great-grandfather, saying that he was a freedman and a rope-maker from the country about Thurii, while his grandfather was a money-changer. This is all I have been able to learn about the paternal ancestors of Augustus. (2.3)

Suetonius here exhibits *transparency* by crediting the account to others and noting Augustus's own less detailed version (another

---

[6] Unless otherwise noted, translations of Suetonius are from Rolfe, trans., *Lives of the Caesars*, vols. 1 and 2.

[7] The imperfect tense verbs used in connection with these points may suggest that Suetonius did not obtain the information from his own eyewitness experience but from a literary source (such as Augustus's *Memoirs*). See D. Wardle, commentary to *Life of Augustus*, by Suetonius, ed. and trans. D. Wardle, Clarendon Ancient History Series (Oxford UP, 2014), 80. Yet regardless of how Suetonius acquired the information, the fact remains that he does cite sources.

source).[8] D. Wardle rightly comments, "Suet[onius]'s indication of a conflict in his sources at one level reassures his reader that the narrative is the product of genuine research."[9] Suetonius displays further *transparency* by noting information from Marcus Antonius that (if believed) would undermine the nobility of Augustus's family. Suetonius does not explicitly evaluate the claim, but he seems to prefer the accounts of the "others" and Augustus to that of Marcus Antonius.[10] Suetonius's final remark, "This is all I have been able to learn . . . ," again indicates his use of *sources* and emphasizes "his thoroughness and the plausibility of his account."[11]

Before arriving at Augustus's birth, Suetonius discusses Augustus's father, Gaius Octavius (3–4). He describes Gaius as "a man of wealth and repute," and goes on to say,

> I cannot but wonder that some have said he too was a money-changer, and was even employed to distribute bribes at the elections and perform other services in the Campus; for as a matter of fact, being brought up in affluence, he readily attained to high positions and filled them with distinction. (3.1)

Here we have *transparency* accompanied by *evaluation*. Suetonius clearly presents the claim that Gaius was a money-changer and bribe-distributer as spurious.[12] He does not fully explain his reasoning, but he does mention letters of Marcus Cicero that describe Gaius as a proconsul (3.2; *sources*).[13] After noting Gaius's sudden death, Suetonius discusses the lineage of Atia, Augustus's mother. He says that she came from "a family displaying many

---

[8] Suetonius describes Augustus's autobiography and other writings in *Aug.* 85. Only a few fragments of the autobiography have survived, and the passage in question is unfortunately not one of them. For the fragments, see Christopher Smith and Anton Powell, eds., *The Lost Memoirs of Augustus and the Development of Roman Autobiography* (Classical Press of Wales, 2009), 1–13.

[9] Wardle, commentary to *Life of Augustus*, 85.

[10] Suetonius later critiques those who disparage Augustus's lineage, including Marcus Antonius (*Aug.* 3.1; 4.2).

[11] Wardle, commentary to *Life of Augustus*, 87.

[12] Wardle, commentary to *Life of Augustus*, 88.

[13] Wardle argues that Suetonius refers to Cicero, *Quint. Fratr.* 1.2.7 (as opposed to 1.1.21, which also mentions Gaius Octavius).

senatorial portraits" (4.1).[14] However, he also notes that (Marcus) Antonius and Cassius of Parma attempt to disparage Augustus's maternal lineage (4.2). Suetonius does not explicitly say that Antonius and Cassius are wrong, but his tone toward them is clearly negative, so it seems best to regard this as both *transparency* and *evaluation*.[15]

Suetonius continues to exhibit historiographic intent in narrating Augustus's birth. He gives the precise date of Augustus's birth and says it occurred "at the Ox-Heads in the Palatine quarter, where [Augustus] now has a shrine, built shortly after his death" (5). Suetonius explains that senate proceedings record that a certain Gaius Laetorius, in begging for a reduced sentence for adultery, claimed to own the place where Augustus was born. The senate apparently believed Laetorius, and "it was decreed that part of his house should be consecrated" (5; *sources*). Wardle notes that here Suetonius "demonstrates his ability to use valuable official sources to make his point. Here the most prestigious records of the state establish beyond question that Aug[ustus] was born in Rome."[16] Suetonius also exhibits *transparency* by noting that others believe Augustus was born in a small room in his paternal grandfather's house near Velitrae (6).[17]

Suetonius also says that Augustus "was given the surname Thurinus," and he substantiates this claim with two *sources*. First, Suetonius says, "I once obtained a bronze statuette, representing

[14] The accompanying footnote in the LCL edition states, "*Imagines* were waxen masks of ancestors of noble (i.e., senatorial) rank, kept in the hall (*atrium*) of their descendants." Wardle questions Suetonius's accuracy on this point, but not his historiographic intent (commentary to *Life of Augustus*, 92).

[15] Wardle notes that both Antonius and Cassius "were renowned enemies of Aug[ustus]. Even a careless reader should be able to discount such testimony" (commentary to *Life of Augustus*, 86).

[16] Wardle, commentary to *Life of Augustus*, 98. Cf. John M. Carter, commentary to *Divus Augustus*, by Suetonius, ed. John M. Carter (Bristol Classical, 1982), 95.

[17] Suetonius does mention that some people had bizarre experiences in connection with this room (*Aug.* 6). However, these experiences seem to have taken place substantially after Augustus's childhood, so I will treat them as adult material.

him as a boy and inscribed with that name in letters of iron almost illegible from age" (7.1). Second, he notes that Augustus "is often called Thurinus in Mark Antony's letters by way of insult; to which Augustus merely replied that he was surprised that his former name was thrown in his face as a reproach" (7.1).[18] Suetonius concludes his birth material proper by noting that Augustus lost his father at age four and at age twelve gave a funeral oration for his grandmother Julia (8.1).[19]

In sum, Suetonius amply demonstrates his historiographic intent in *Augustus* 1.1–8.1. He cites a wide range of *sources*—including official senate proceedings—that suggest serious historical investigation. He repeatedly employs *transparency* and *evaluation*. And even from a modern perspective, Suetonius's account of Augustus's lineage, birth, and childhood seems quite plausible. Yet—we recall—*Augustus* is often cited as evidence that Suetonius's birth material is ahistorical. How can this be?

Put simply, scholars ignore this material. Meier, Miller, and Lincoln—all of whom cite *Augustus* as an example of legendary birth material—hardly discuss *Augustus* 1.1–8.1 at all. To be precise: Meier and Miller do not even mention it. Lincoln briefly comments on a few paragraphs (*Aug.* 2; 4; 7) but does not discuss any of the historiographic features.[20] All three scholars instead focus on *Augustus* 94, where Suetonius catalogs omens that occurred in connection with Augustus. Meier states, "In the exceptional cases of towering figures like Alexander the Great or the Emperor Octavian Augustus, some facts [regarding birth, infancy, and early years] were preserved, though even these were often interwoven with mythical or legendary motifs."[21]

---

[18] Wardle comments, "M. Antonius' correspondence is a rich source for Suet[onius] (cf. 16.2, 69.2–70.1), which he consulted directly. Whether in its entirety or in collected extracts, it was available to Tacitus (Tac. *Ann.* 4.34.5)" (commentary to *Life of Augustus*, 103).

[19] Nicolaus of Damascus (*Augustus* 3) and Quintilian (*Institutio oratoria* 12.6.1) also mention an oration the young Augustus gave, though Nicolaus says Augustus was around nine years old.

[20] Lincoln, *Born of a Virgin?* 62–63, 121; idem, "Luke and Jesus' Conception: A Case of Double Paternity?" *JBL* 132.3 (2013): 655.

[21] Meier, *Marginal Jew*, 1:208.

In the accompanying note, he says that in *Augustus* 94 "omens occur around the time of Augustus' birth; . . . a serpent glides by his mother; Augustus is considered the son of Apollo; dreams and portents show that Augustus will rule the world; he shows miraculous power even as a youth."[22] Miller includes *Augustus* 94.1–11 in a collection of passages that illustrate, among other things, his assertion that "stories about divine paternity were purely interpretive, not informational."[23] Lincoln cites *Augustus* 94 as an example of how "the composition" of birth stories in ancient biographies "was particularly legendary."[24]

Such claims are at best half-truths. In the first place, *Augustus* 1.1–8.1 constitutes the primary birth material in the biography, and to treat *Augustus* 94 in isolation from this heavily historiographic material is misleading. Second, *Augustus* 94 begins a long catalog of omens that occur before and throughout Augustus's life (94.1–97.3).[25] The omens in *Augustus* 94.1–9 pertain to Augustus's birth and childhood, but those in *Augustus* 94.10–96.2 occur during his adulthood, and Suetonius goes on to discuss omens surrounding Augustus's death (97.1–3). The presence of omens therefore cannot demonstrate that Suetonius intends his birth material to be less historical than the rest of the life. Third, as noted in our studies of Philo and Plutarch, the fact that an author recounts omens does not necessarily indicate an ahistorical intent. Fourth, Meier, Miller, and Lincoln fail to observe historiographic features that occur within *Augustus* 94.1–9. We will examine these in detail below.

Suetonius uses historiographic features to recount many of the omens related to Augustus's birth and childhood. Indeed, he goes no further than the second omen before citing a *source*. "According to Julius Marathus," he says, "a few months before Augustus was born a portent was generally observed at Rome" (94.3). Suetonius earlier describes Marathus as Augustus's "freedman and

---

[22] Meier, *Marginal Jew*, 1:234n14.
[23] Miller, *Born Divine*, 134, 142–45.
[24] Lincoln, *Born of a Virgin?* 60–61.
[25] Cf. the structural analysis in Wardle, commentary to *Life of Augustus*, 9–18, esp. 12, 14.

the keeper of his records" (79.2),[26] so he seems to be a significant historical *source*.

Suetonius also cites a source for some extraordinary information regarding Augustus's conception and birth:

> I have read the following story in the books of Asclepias of Mendes entitled *Theologumena*. When Atia had come in the middle of the night to the solemn service of Apollo, she had her litter set down in the temple and fell asleep, while the rest of the matrons also slept. On a sudden a serpent glided up to her and shortly went away. When she awoke, she purified herself, as if after the embraces of her husband, and at once there appeared on her body a mark in colours like a serpent ... In the tenth month after that Augustus was born and was therefore regarded as the son of Apollo. Atia too, before she gave him birth, dreamed that her vitals were born up to the stars and spread over the whole extent of land and sea, while Octavius dreamed that the sun rose from Atia's womb. (94.4)

At first glance, this passage might seem like evidence that birth narratives were meant to be legendary. Yet Suetonius cites a *source*—something that would be unnecessary if he were simply spinning a tale out of thin air. Suetonius also says nothing about such a conception in his account at the beginning of *Augustus*, so it seems likely that he is not only citing a source but also *distancing* himself from this story. And note how restrained even the distanced account is: Suetonius refrains from saying that the serpent was Apollo or that it had intercourse with Atia.[27] He simply provides the story and lets the reader decide if they wish to regard Augustus as the son of Apollo based on it (as others did). It is unclear whether Suetonius intends to cite Asclepias as the source for the story about Atia and Octavius's dreams as well, but even if he does not, there is nothing necessarily legendary or implausible about such dreams.

It is also worth noting that the historian Cassius Dio (ca. AD 164–after 229) records a very similar story:

---

[26] Wardle, commentary to *Life of Augustus*, 511.
[27] *Contra* Lincoln, *Born of a Virgin?* 63.

> For Caesar, being childless and basing great hopes upon [Augustus], loved and cherished him, intending to leave him as successor to his name, authority, and sovereignty. He was influenced largely by Attia's emphatic declaration that the youth had been engendered by Apollo; for while sleeping once in his temple, she said, she thought she had intercourse with a serpent, and it was this that caused her at the end of the allotted time to bear a son. Before he came to the light of day she saw in a dream her entrails lifted to the heavens and spreading out over all the earth; and the same night Octavius thought that the sun rose from her womb. (*Rom. Hist.* 45.1.2–3)[28]

Note that Dio utilizes *distancing* as well ("Attia's emphatic declaration . . . she said") but somewhat differently than Suetonius. Dio may be using Suetonius as a source.[29] But whether Dio is drawing on Suetonius or another source, the key point is that he seems to regard the information as historically relevant.

Suetonius continues to use historiographic features in narrating subsequent omens. He notes that on the day Augustus was born, "Publius Nigidius, as everyone knows, . . . declared that the ruler of the world had been born" (*Aug.* 94.5).[30] The phrase "as everyone knows" indicates that Suetonius has *sources* (oral, literary, or both) for this information.[31] Suetonius cites Gaius Drusus as a *source* for a story about Augustus escaping from his cradle (94.6). He also distances himself from another childhood story:

> As soon as he began to talk, it chanced that the frogs were making a great noise at his grandfather's country place; he bade them be silent, and *they say* that since then no frog has ever croaked there. (94.7, emphasis added)

---

[28] Unless otherwise noted, translations of Cassius Dio are from Cassius Dio, *Roman History*, trans. Earnest Cary and Herbert B. Foster, 9 vols., LCL (Harvard UP, 1914–27).
[29] Wardle, commentary to *Life of Augustus*, 512. Dio goes on to recount several other events recorded in *Augustus* 94.
[30] Cf. Cassius Dio, *Rom. Hist.* 45.1.3–5.
[31] Wardle notes that Suetonius "wrote a biography of Nigidius in *De viris illustribus*" (commentary to *Life of Augustus*, 518).

Note that Suetonius employs distancing precisely at the point where the story becomes implausible. Finally, he exhibits *transparency* in relating some dreams by Quintus Catulus (94.8).

In sum, Suetonius indicates his historiographic intent not only in the oft-ignored *Augustus* 1.1–8.1 but also in the oft-cited *Augustus* 94. In the birth material of Augustus, we find instances of *sources, transparency, evaluation,* and *distancing.* Suetonius does recount some events that modern historians might forgo. However, such instances are not limited to birth material and do not necessarily indicate an ahistorical intent.

Tiberius

Suetonius provides an extensive account of his subject's lineage at the beginning of *Tiberius* (*Tib.* 1–4). Suetonius occasionally reminds the reader of his historiographic intent throughout this material (2.1, 3; *sources*; 3.2; *distancing*), but he puts his abilities as a historian on full display when he reaches Tiberius's birth:

> Some have supposed that Tiberius was born at Fundi, on no better evidence than that his maternal grandmother was a native of that place, and that later a statue of Good Fortune was set up there by decree of the senate. But according to the most numerous and trustworthy authorities, he was born at Rome, on the Palatine, the sixteenth day before the Kalends of December, in the consulship of Marcus Aemilius Lepidus and Lucius Munatius Plancus (the former for the second time) while the war of Philippi was going on. In fact it is so recorded both in the calendar and in the public gazette. Yet in spite of this some write that he was born in the preceding year, . . . and others in the following year. (5)

Here Suetonius employs *transparency* and *evaluation,* not only acknowledging the different accounts but also adjudicating between them based on the number and reliability of the sources.[32] Suetonius says nothing about Tiberius's conception

---

[32] Hugh Lindsay notes other ancient sources that support the date Suetonius gives for Tiberius's birth, including Cassius Dio, *Rom. Hist.* 57.18.2. See Hugh Lindsay, commentary to *Tiberius,* by Suetonius, ed. Hugh Lindsay (Bristol Classical, 1995), 70. Lindsay also comments

or how he was born. He simply says that Tiberius "passed his infancy and his youth amid hardship and tribulation, since he was everywhere the companion of his parents in their flight" (6.1) following the Perusine War (4.2–3). After giving a few interesting but non-supernatural examples of these difficulties, Suetonius says, "The gifts which were given him in Sicily by Pompeia, sister of Sextus Pompeius, a cloak and clasp, as well as studs of gold, are still kept and exhibited at Baiae" (6.3). Suetonius seems to regard these artifacts and whatever traditions that connect them to Tiberius as *sources*. Suetonius goes on to report a eulogy Tiberius gave for his deceased father and a few other events from his early adolescence (6.4) before transitioning to his youth (7).

Suetonius therefore gives an initial account of Tiberius's origins that not only is demonstrably historiographic in intent but is also quite plausible, even from a modern perspective. Lincoln, however, cites *Tiberius* as evidence that birth material was "particularly legendary."[33] How so?

As with *Augustus*, the answer is that Lincoln has neglected the primary birth material in the biography—which is clearly historiographic—and has instead focused on a catalog of omens later in the life. In *Tiberius* 14, Suetonius discusses several omens that gave Tiberius a "strong and unwavering confidence in his destiny" (14.1). The catalog here is shorter than the one in *Augustus* 94.1–97.3, but like the earlier catalog it contains omens related both to Tiberius's birth/childhood and to his adulthood. The former are quite mundane:

> When Livia was with child with him, and was trying to divine by various omens whether she would bring forth a male, she took an egg from under a setting-hen, and when she had warmed it in her own hand and those of her attendants in turn,

---

that Suetonius's "insistence that some writers still made errors on this count shows how slowly the notion of using archival materials was grasped at Rome. Suetonius had reason to promote the value of this approach in view of his personal involvement in the secretariat, and his role as *a bybliothecis*" (70).

[33] Lincoln, *Born of a Virgin?* 60.

a cock with a fine crest was hatched. In his infancy the astrologer Scribonius promised him an illustrious career and even that he would one day be king, but without the crown of royalty; for at that time of course the rule of the Caesars was as yet unheard of. (*Tib.* 14.2)

Suffice it to say that a cock emerging from an egg (probability: fifty percent) and an astrologer making a prediction that turned out to be only somewhat correct (Tiberius did receive a crown) do not prove legendary intent. Lincoln, however, focuses on a different omen, saying, "Suetonius relates how an eagle landed on the roof of [Augustus's] house and underlines that he was confident of his destiny because of the predictions of astrologers (*Tib.* 14)."[34] The problem, though, is that the eagle incident occurs during Tiberius's adulthood. And while the plural "astrologers" may imply that Lincoln has in mind the prediction of Scribonius (14.2) and a later one by Thrasyllus (14.4), only the former pertains to Tiberius's childhood. Such features, then, cannot demonstrate that Suetonius regards birth material as uniquely legendary.

Suetonius also mentions Tiberius's childhood later in a discussion of his habitual cruelty, saying,

> His cruel and cold-blooded character was not completely hidden even in his boyhood [*in puero*]. His teacher of rhetoric, Theodorus of Gadara, seems first to have had the insight to detect it, and to have characterized it very aptly, since in taking him to task he would now and then call him πηλὸν αἵματι πεφυραμένον, that is to say, "mud kneaded with blood." But it grew still more noticeable after he became emperor. (57.1)

One might be tempted to see this as an example of legendary intent: Suetonius, one might argue, has fabricated childhood material to anticipate Tiberius's adult character. Yet several factors problematize such a reading. First, Suetonius cites Theodorus of Gadara as a *source* for the claim—something that would be unnecessary if historical truth were unimportant.[35] Second,

---

[34] Lincoln, *Born of a Virgin?* 62.
[35] A fragment of Cassius Dio notes that Tiberius was called πηλὸς αἵματι πεφυρμένος, though it is unclear who said this and when (*Rom.*

Suetonius exhibits historiographic restraint by acknowledging that Tiberius's cruelty "was not completely hidden" in childhood and had to be detected. This suggests that Suetonius is limiting his claims about Tiberius's childhood to what the data can support, not making up material to illustrate his adult character. Third, Suetonius goes on to recount an episode from Tiberius's early reign that foreshadows his later, more vehement cruelty (57.2). Precisely because Suetonius includes foreshadowing in both childhood and adult material, foreshadowing cannot indicate that birth material is uniquely ahistorical.

In *Tiberius*, then, Suetonius seems to compose his birth material with historiographic intent, employing *sources*, *transparency*, *evaluation*, and *distancing*. Suetonius does include omens and foreshadowing that some modern biographers might not, but these elements are not unique to the birth material and need not indicate an ahistorical intent.

Vespasian

As in *Augustus* and *Tiberius*, Suetonius begins *Vespasian* by discussing his subject's lineage. He notes at the outset that the Flavian family brought stability to the Roman Empire, which had been floundering after a quick succession of three emperors (i.e., Galba, Otho, Vitellius). He then comments, "This house was, it is true, obscure and without family portraits, yet it was one of which our country had no reason whatever to be ashamed" (*Vesp.* 1.1).[36] Note that Suetonius does not fabricate a stellar lineage for Vespasian; he simply acknowledges that the Flavians were humble yet decent. Suetonius continues to demonstrate his historiographic intent by employing numerous historiographic features in the material that follows. Regarding Vespasian's father Sabinus, Suetonius notes that "some say that he was an ex-centurion of the first grade, others that while still in command of a cohort he was retired because of ill-health, took no part in military life, but farmed the public tax

---

Hist. 58, frag. 1). I owe the reference to Lindsay, commentary to *Tiberius*, 162.

[36] On the "family portraits," see above on *Aug.* 4.1.

of a fortieth in Asia" (1.2; *transparency*).³⁷ Suetonius, however, says that "there existed for some time statues erected in his honour by the cities of Asia, inscribed 'To an honest tax-gatherer'" (1.2; *evaluation*). This is striking: Suetonius clearly knows of traditions that make Vespasian's father a military man (a convenient background for a general who became emperor), but he seems to reject these based on epigraphic evidence.³⁸ Suetonius notes that Vespasian's mother Vespasia Polla "was born of an honorable family at Nursia" (1.3). To support this claim, he says,

> There is moreover on the top of a mountain, near the sixth milestone on the road from Nursia to Spoletium, a place called Vespasiae, where many monuments of the Vespasii are to be seen, affording strong proof of the renown and antiquity of the house. (1.3; *sources*)

Suetonius concludes the lineage by noting that "some have bandied about the report" that Vespasian's paternal great-grandfather "came from the region beyond the Po and was a contractor" (1.4; *transparency*). Yet he says, "I have found no evidence whatever of this, in spite of rather careful investigation" (1.4; *evaluation*). A. W. Braithwaite comments, "The whole chapter, and especially this last sentence, is evidence of careful independent research by Suetonius."³⁹

Suetonius gives Vespasian an unremarkable birth, simply noting the place (a small village called Falacrina) and the precise date. Regarding Vespasian's childhood, Suetonius says, "He was brought up under the care of his paternal grandmother Tertulla

---

[37] Here the revised LCL edition by G. P. Goold differs somewhat from Rolfe's original LCL edition regarding what information Suetonius credits to others and what information he himself affirms. But regardless of which translation one follows, Suetonius clearly employs both *transparency* and *evaluation*.

[38] Suetonius does say that Vespasian's paternal grandfather was "a centurion or a volunteer veteran" in the civil war (*Vesp.* 1.2), so Vespasian apparently had some military background on the Flavian side. But this makes it even more surprising that Suetonius decides against Vespasian's father being in the military.

[39] A. W. Braithwaite, notes to C. Suetoni Tranquili, *Divus Vespasianus* (Clarendon, 1927), 22.

on her estates at Cosa" (2.1) and mentions that Vespasian visited this place even after he became emperor. After this, Suetonius cuts to Vespasian's young adulthood.

In the birth material of *Vespasian*, then, Suetonius repeatedly demonstrates his historiographic intent. It is difficult to see how anyone could examine this material closely and conclude that it is meant to be legendary. Yet—we recall—*Vespasian* is one of the lives that supposedly demonstrates the legendary character of birth material. How can this be?

Once again, such a judgment requires ignoring the primary birth material and focusing on a later omen list. Lincoln states, "[Suetonius's] account of Vespasian lists a number of portents of his future imperial dignity, including a prediction from Josephus and incidents involving a dog, an ox and eagles (*Vesp*. 5)."[40] All the omens Lincoln mentions, however, occur during Vespasian's adulthood.[41] Suetonius records only one omen related to Vespasian's birth: An oak sacred to Mars on the Flavian estate puts forth a branch when Vespasian's mother gives birth to each of her three children. The first is slender and withers quickly, and the child likewise dies within a year. The second is strong and long, and the third (corresponding to Vespasian) is "the image of a tree" (5.2). "Therefore" Suetonius recounts, "their father Sabinus, so they say, being further encouraged by an inspection of sacrificial victims, announced to his mother that a grandson had been born to her who would be a Caesar" (5.2). Note that Suetonius qualifies this claim with "so they say," *distancing* himself from the crucial interpretation of the branch. Suetonius, then, exhibits historiographic intent in recounting the sole omen related to Vespasian's childhood. Furthermore, he goes on to provide numerous omens from Vespasian's adulthood (5.3–7), which suggests that for Suetonius omens cannot indicate that birth material is uniquely legendary.

To sum up: Suetonius amply displays his historiographic intent in *Vespasian* 1.1–2.1, the primary birth material in the life, employing *sources*, *transparency*, and *evaluation*. He also uses *distancing* in narrating the sole omen related to Vespasian's

[40] Lincoln, *Born of a Virgin?* 62.
[41] See *Vesp*. 5.6 (Josephus), 4 (dog, ox), 7 (eagles).

birth (5.2), and he includes far more omens from Vespasian's adulthood. Only by ignoring all of this can one conclude that Suetonius intends his birth material to be legendary. Thus, *Augustus*, *Tiberius*, and *Vespasian*—the three lives that have been cited to show the legendary character of Suetonius's birth material—actually demonstrate quite the opposite.

Gaius Caligula

We now turn to some of Suetonius's other biographies. Suetonius begins *Gaius Caligula* with an extended account of his subject's lineage that focuses on Gaius's father Germanicus (*Cal.* 1–7). Here we find numerous instances of *distancing* (1.2; 2; 3.1; 4; 5). Suetonius, however, reserves his most significant historiographic discussion for Gaius's birth.

> Gaius Caesar was born the day before the Kalends of September in the consulship of his father and Gaius Fonteius Capito. Conflicting testimony makes his birthplace uncertain. Gnaeus Lentulus Gaetulicus writes that he was born at Tibur, Plinius Secundus among the Treveri, in a village called Ambitarvium above the Confluence. Pliny adds as proof that altars are shown there, inscribed, "For the Delivery of Agrippina." Verses which were in circulation soon after he became emperor indicate that he was begotten in the winter-quarters of the legions:
>
> He who was born in the camp and reared in the arms of
>   his country,
>   Gave at the outset a sign that he was fated to rule.
>
> I myself find in the gazette [*acta*] that he first saw the light at Antium. (8.1–2)[42]

---

[42] Donna Hurley comments, "The open records of state were variously the *acta publica* (Suet. *Tib.* 5) or *diurna* (Tac. *Ann.* 13.31.1) or *diurna populi Romani* (Tac. *Ann.* 16.22.3), often simply *acta*" (Donna W. Hurley, *An Historical and Historiographical Commentary on Suetonius' Life of C. Caligula*, American Philological Association American Classical Studies 32 [Scholars, 1993], 21, emphasis original). Cf. D. Wardle, *Suetonius' Life of Caligula: A Commentary*, Collection Latomus 225 (Latomus, 1994), 57–58, 131.

Suetonius here engages in some impressively thorough *transparency*, noting four different accounts of Gaius's birthplace.[43]

Suetonius goes on to *evaluate* the accounts. Gaetulicus, he contends, is wrong, for Pliny says he lied and did so "with the more assurance because Germanicus really did have a son born to him at Tibur, also called Gaius Caesar" (8.2). Pliny, however, "has erred in his chronology; for the historians of Augustus agree that Germanicus was not sent to Germany until the close of his consulship, when Gaius was already born" (8.3). Suetonius argues that the inscription Pliny mentions does not help his view since Gaius's mother "twice gave birth to daughters in that region, and any childbirth, regardless of sex, is called *puerperium*" (8.3). Suetonius also cites a letter from Augustus to Gaius's mother saying he had arranged for Gaius to be brought to his father when he was just under two years old. Suetonius concludes,

> I think it is clear enough that Gaius could not have been born in a place to which he was first taken from Rome when he was nearly two years old. This letter also weakens our confidence in the verses, the more so because they are anonymous. We must then accept the only remaining testimony, that of the public record, particularly since Gaius loved Antium as if it were his native soil. (8.5)

Throughout this discussion, Suetonius does not merely demonstrate his historiographic intent; he exhibits a historiographic rigor that scholars have praised as "a classic example of ancient source criticism,"[44] "a model of historical discussion,"[45] and "clear and vigorous argumentation."[46]

---

[43] The Latin makes it clear that "Pliny" refers to "Plinius Secundus."

[44] Wolf Steidle, *Sueton und die antike Biographie*, Zetemata 1 (Beck, 1951), 68. The German original is "mustergültiges Beispiel einer antiken Quellenkritik." The translation above is my own.

[45] Jacques Gascou, *Suétone historien*, Bibliothèque des écoles françaises d'Athènes et de Rome 255 (École française, 1984), 544. The French original is "un modèle de discussion historique." The translation above is my own.

[46] Andrew Wallace-Hadrill, *Suetonius: The Scholar and His Caesars* (Duckworth, 1983), 89. I owe this reference and the references to Steidle

In the birth material of *Gaius Caligula*, then, Suetonius employs *distancing, transparency,* and *evaluation*—the latter two in an exemplary manner. Suetonius's careful historiographic work here undermines the claim that he regards the birth material as legendary.

Nero

Suetonius uses numerous historiographic features in the birth material of *Nero*. He begins his discussion of Nero's lineage by noting two significant branches of the Domitian family—the Calvini and the Ahenobarbi ("bronze-beards"; 1.1). He explains,

> The latter have as the founder of their race and the origin of their surname Lucius Domitius, to whom, as he was returning from the country, there once appeared twin youths of more than mortal majesty, *so it is said*, and bade him carry to the senate and people the news of a victory, which was as yet unknown. And as a token of their divinity *it is said* that they stroked his cheeks and turned his black beard to a ruddy hue, like that of bronze. (1.1, emphasis added)

One might be tempted to see this passage as an example of legendary birth material. Note, however, that Suetonius employs *distancing* twice, precisely at the points where the story might seem implausible. Plutarch interestingly recounts a similar story with *distancing* in adult material (*Aem.* 25.1–2). It is difficult to tell whether Plutarch served as Suetonius's source or merely bears witness to a similar tradition, but he confirms that Suetonius is

---

and Gascou above to Wardle, *Suetonius'* Life of Caligula, 127. Wardle, following Barry Baldwin, is less impressed with Suetonius, commenting on the three quotes above, "This assessment can be questioned, whilst acknowledging that Suetonius' conclusion is correct" (127). Cf. Barry Baldwin, *Suetonius* (Hakkert, 1983), 158–60. Hugh Lindsay comments, "The trouble Suetonius takes to settle this debate is quite unusual not only by his own standards but also by the standards of ancient historiography. The suggestion which has been made with increasing confidence in recent years that he was responding to Tacitus is attractive." See Hugh Lindsay, commentary to *Caligula*, by Suetonius, ed. Hugh Lindsay (Bristol Classical, 1993), 64.

not simply making things up.[47] Suetonius also employs *distancing* for the somewhat surprising claim that all the early Ahenobarbi males were named either Gnaeus or Lucius: "The first, second, and third of the Ahenobarbi, *we are told*, were called Lucius, the next three in order Gnaeus, while all those that followed were called in turn first Lucius and then Gnaeus" (*Nero* 1.2, emphasis added). Suetonius then makes an interesting remark:

> It seems to me worth while to give an account of several members of this family, to show more clearly that though Nero degenerated from the good qualities of his ancestors, he yet reproduced the vices of each of them, as if transmitted to him by natural inheritance. (1.2)

Here Suetonius does connect Nero's origins to his adult character—a move that to some might suggest legendary intent. Yet Suetonius does not make this connection by fabricating a fanciful story about Nero's childhood but by showing that some of Nero's ancestors displayed vices that he later perfected (even citing a *source* in 2.2). Such a point might be less fashionable in modern Western biography, which tends to focus on the individual, but it is a valid line of historical inquiry, particularly from an ancient perspective.

Suetonius narrates Nero's birth as follows:

> Nero was born at Antium nine months after the death of Tiberius, on the eighteenth day before the Kalends of January, just as the sun rose, so that he was touched by its rays almost before he could be laid upon the ground. Many people at once made many direful predictions from his horoscope, and a remark of his father Domitius was also *regarded as* an omen; for while receiving the congratulations of his friends, he said that "nothing that was not abominable and a public bane could be born of Agrippina and himself." (6.1, emphasis added)

---

[47] Bradley notes that Suetonius differs from Plutarch regarding the location of this meeting. See Keith R. Bradley, *Suetonius'* Life of Nero: *An Historical Commentary*, Collection Latomus 157 (Latomus, 1978), 25. Bradley also compares Suetonius's story to Livy (*Hist.* 2.19–20; 2.42.5) and Dionysius of Halicarnassus (*Antiquitates romanae* 6.3).

B. H. Warmington notes that other sources confirm that Nero was born on this day and month. "The only doubt," he says, "arises about the year because of inexact statements about [Nero's] age . . . but there is no overwhelming reason to reject the date given here."[48] Suetonius's remark about Nero being born as the sun rose is interesting, but it is by no means ahistorical. Indeed, comparison with Cassius Dio demonstrates Suetonius's historiographic intent. Dio says, "At [Nero's] birth just before dawn rays not cast by any visible beam enveloped him" (*Rom. Hist.* 61.2.1). Dio not only corroborates the broad contours of Suetonius's testimony; he depicts the light as supernatural ("not cast by any visible beam"), showing that Suetonius has *not* appealed to supernatural causation at a point where he might have. Suetonius also employs *distancing* when he notes that Domitius's saying was "regarded as" an omen. Dio records a similar remark from Domitius, again corroborating Suetonius's testimony (*Rom. Hist.* 61.2.3). Suetonius also notes "another manifest indication of Nero's future unhappiness"— namely, that Gaius Caesar joked about naming Nero after the then-mocked Claudius (*Nero* 6.2). Suetonius clearly regards Gaius's joke as a forecast of Nero's destiny, yet nothing suggests that he has fabricated the story or would regard doing so as appropriate.

Suetonius also indicates his historiographic intent in narrating Nero's childhood. He *evaluates* a claim about a supposed assassination attempt:

> When [Nero's] mother was recalled from banishment and reinstated, he became so prominent through her influence that it leaked out that Messalina, wife of Claudius, had sent emissaries to strangle him as he was taking his noon-day nap, regarding him as a rival of Britannicus. An addition to this bit of gossip

---

[48] B. H. Warmington, commentary to *Nero*, by Suetonius, ed. B. H. Warmington, 2nd ed. (Bristol Classical, 1999), 26. Warmington refers to his comments on *Nero* 8 and 57.1 for examples of the imprecision regarding Nero's age. I owe the references to Cassius Dio and Tacitus below to Warmington.

> is, that the would-be assassins were frightened away by a snake which darted out from under his pillow. The only foundation for this tale was, that there was found in his bed near the pillow the slough of a serpent. (6.4)

Suetonius indicates that he regards the assassination story as spurious by describing it as "gossip," and he specifically questions the evidence for the snake claim.[49] Suetonius includes two final stories from Nero's boyhood:

> While he was still a young, half-grown boy he took part in the game of Troy at a performance in the Circus with great self-possession and success. In the eleventh year of his age he was adopted by Claudius and consigned to the training of Annaeus Seneca, who was then already a senator. *They say* that on the following night Seneca dreamed that he was teaching Gaius Caesar, and Nero soon proved the dream prophetic by revealing the cruelty of his disposition at the earliest possible opportunity. (7.1, emphasis added)

Nothing Suetonius says indicates a legendary intent, and Tacitus corroborates Suetonius's claims that Nero participated in these games and that Seneca served as Nero's tutor (*Ann.* 11.11.5; 12.8.3). Suetonius also indicates his historiographic intent by *distancing* himself from the story about Seneca's dream.

The primary birth material of *Nero* concludes at 7.1, but Suetonius does mention Nero's childhood in a few passages later in the biography. The most significant of these is *Nero* 52:[50]

> When a boy he took up almost all the liberal arts; but his mother turned him from philosophy, warning him that it was a drawback to one who was going to rule, while Seneca kept him from reading the early orators, to make his admiration for his teacher endure the longer. Turning therefore to poetry, he wrote verses with eagerness and without labour, and did not, as some think, publish the work of others as his own. I have had in my

---

[49] Tacitus *distances* himself from a similar story about serpents watching over Nero as an infant (*Ann.* 11.11.6). Dio notes that a serpent's skin was found around the infant Nero's neck and was interpreted as an omen (*Rom. Hist.* 61.2.4).

[50] See also *Nero* 20.1; 22.1.

possession note-books and papers with some well-known verses of his, written with his own hand and in such wise that it was perfectly evident that they were not copied or taken down from dictation, but worked out exactly as one writes when thinking and creating; so many instances were there of words erased or struck through and written above the lines. He likewise had no slight interest in painting and sculpture.

Suetonius claims that as a boy Nero wrote poetry "with eagerness and without labour." Has he fabricated this claim to anticipate Nero's adult character? I think not, for two reasons. First, Suetonius says little about Nero's adult poetic abilities. The most significant discussion is likely in the passage just quoted ("and did not . . . above the lines"), where Suetonius seems to digress from Nero's childhood to respond to allegations of plagiarism against Nero (presumably as an adult).[51] As a point of comparison, Suetonius says far more about the adult Nero's passion for singing (*Nero* 20–24) and does not credit Nero with any special childhood abilities in this area (20.1). So it seems unlikely that Suetonius would fabricate material to anticipate the adult poetic abilities of Nero that he hardly discusses at all. Second, Tacitus corroborates Suetonius's claim that Nero wrote poetry as a boy and even says his verses "showed that he had in him the rudiments of culture" (*Ann.* 13.3.5). Therefore, while Suetonius does ascribe poetic proficiency to young Nero, this does not seem to indicate an ahistorical intent.

In sum, Suetonius employs *sources, evaluation*, and *distancing* in the birth material of *Nero*. While Suetonius does mention Nero's boyhood poetic abilities, this does not seem to be a fabricated claim or to indicate ahistorical intent.

Vitellius

Suetonius opens the birth material of *Vitellius* with *transparency*:

Of the origin of the Vitellii different and widely varying accounts are given, some saying that the family was ancient and noble,

---

[51] On this interpretation, the notebooks and papers that Suetonius mentions are from Nero's adulthood. Another possibility is that the notebooks and papers are from Nero's childhood, in which case Suetonius would be citing a source for the childhood claim.

others that it was new and obscure, if not of mean extraction. I should believe that these came respectively from the flatterers and detractors of the emperor, were it not for a difference of opinion about the standing of the family at a considerably earlier date. (*Vit.* 1.1)

Suetonius provides further details on the differing accounts. A book by Quintus Elogius says "the Vitellii were sprung from Faunus, king of the Aborigines, and Vitellia, who was worshipped as a goddess in many places; and that they ruled in all Latium" (1.2). Note that Suetonius refrains from asserting that Vitellia—Vitellius's alleged ancestor—actually was a goddess; he credits the claim to Elogius and merely says she "was worshipped as" a goddess. "On the other hand," Suetonius says,

> Several have written that the founder of the family was a freedman, while Cassius Severus and others as well say further that he was a cobbler, and that his son, . . . fathered a child by a common woman, the daughter of one Antiochus who kept a bakery, and this son became a Roman knight. (2.1; *transparency*)

Suetonius refuses to take a side, saying, "But this difference of opinion may be left unsettled" (2.1). He does, however, declare that Vitellius's grandfather Publius was "unquestionably a Roman knight and a steward of Augustus's property" (2.2; *evaluation*).

Suetonius likewise employs *transparency* regarding Vitellius's date of birth, saying, "The emperor Aulus Vitellius . . . was born on the eighth day before the Kalends of October, or according to some, on the seventh day before the Ides of September, in the consulship of Drusus Caesar and Norbanus Flaccus" (3.2). Suetonius notes that Vitellius's parents were "aghast at his horoscope as announced by the astrologers" (3.2), but he does not say precisely what the horoscope was, and there is nothing necessarily ahistorical about the claim. He interestingly summarizes Vitellius's boyhood and youth together: "He spent his boyhood and early youth at Capreae among Tiberius' lewd entourage being branded for all time with the nickname Spintria and suspected of having been the cause of his father's first advancement at the expense of his own chastity" (3.2).

Suetonius is vague about the timeline for these potential sexual incidents, so it is possible that they occurred during both Vitellius's boyhood and his adolescence. Suetonius elsewhere details the sexual immorality that took place under Tiberius at Capreae and says it involved boys (*Tib.* 43–44), so it seems likely that the claim here is in earnest.[52] More importantly, however, Suetonius employs *distancing* for the claim about Vitellius's sexual activity: he does not say that the young Vitellius *was* sexually active, only that he "was suspected of" this (*Vit.* 3.2).

In *Vitellius*, then, Suetonius uses *transparency*, *evaluation*, and *distancing* to recount his subject's birth and childhood. The *transparency* and *distancing* regarding Vitellius's lineage are particularly significant, for they show that while Suetonius could have easily claimed that Vitellius's line was noble and that he was descended from a goddess, he refrained from doing so and opted for a more historiographic account.

Virgil

We now turn to consider two biographies from *Lives of Illustrious Men*.[53] Suetonius notes at the outset of *Virgil* that his subject

> had parents of humble origin, especially his father, who according to some was a potter, although the general opinion is that he was at first the hired man of a certain Magus, an attendant on the magistrates, later became his son-in-law because of his diligence, and greatly increased his little property by buying up woodlands and raising bees. (*Vir.* 1)

Far from fabricating a glorious origin story for Virgil, Suetonius explicitly notes his humble beginnings and employs *transparency*

---

[52] Tacitus (*Ann.* 6.1) corroborates Suetonius at this point, as does Cassius Dio (*Rom. Hist.* 58.22.1) to a lesser degree. I owe these references to Charles L. Murison, commentary to *Galba, Otho, Vitellius*, by Suetonius, ed. Charles L. Murison (Bristol Classical, 1992), 142.

[53] As noted above, the lives from *Lives of Illustrious Men* that have survived are known only from quotations in other works. However, scholars generally agree that *Terence*, *Virgil*, *Horace*, and *Lucan* are largely authentic (Rolfe and Goold, prefatory note to *Lives of the Caesars*, 2:370–71).

along the way. Suetonius notes the date and location of Virgil's birth and describes the circumstances as follows:

> When [his mother] was on the way to a neighbouring part of the country with her husband, she turned aside and gave birth to her child in a ditch beside the road. *They say* that the infant did not cry at its birth, and had such a gentle expression as even then to give assurance of an unusually happy destiny. (3–4, emphasis added)

Note that Suetonius *distances* himself from the remarkable claim about Virgil not crying and having a peaceful countenance. He goes on to recount a dream by Virgil's mother and an omen related to his birth (5), but both are unremarkable events that were interpreted as significant. And as we have seen above, omens for Suetonius do not necessarily indicate ahistorical intent.

Regarding Virgil's childhood, Suetonius initially says only that he "spent his early life at Cremona until he assumed the gown of manhood" (6). He returns to Virgil's childhood, however, when discussing his education:

> He made his first attempt at poetry when he was still a boy, composing the following couplet on a schoolmaster called Ballista, who was stoned to death because of his evil reputation for brigandage:
>
> "Under this mountain of stones Ballista is covered and buried;
> Wayfarer, now night and day follow your course without fear." (17)

While Suetonius does not say where he found this poem, he seems to be quoting a *source*. The modesty of the claim is also noteworthy. Suetonius does not retroject Virgil's later poetic prowess onto his childhood by, for example, having the young Virgil compose an epic in the vein of the *Aeneid*. Rather, he credits the boy Virgil with two modest lines. According to Suetonius, Virgil composed six more works, but not until the age of sixteen (17–18).

Suetonius therefore amply demonstrates his historiographic intent in the birth material of *Virgil*. Rather than trying to hide or replace Virgil's humble origins, he acknowledges two differing accounts of them (*transparency*). Suetonius also *distances* himself from the only claim in the birth narrative that seems extraordinary. And when he discusses Virgil's childhood poetic abilities—the precise point where one would most expect legendary elaboration—Suetonius cites a *source* that limits young Virgil's literary output to two lines.

Horace

Suetonius begins *Horace* with a brief account of his subject's origins:

> Quintus Horatius Flaccus of Venusia had for a father, *as he himself writes*, a freedman who was a collector of money at auctions; but *it is believed* that he was a dealer in salted provisions, for a certain man in a quarrel thus taunted Horace: "How often I have seen your father wiping his nose with his arm!" (1.1–5, emphasis added)[54]

Suetonius here cites Horace himself as a *source* for the first account. Suetonius is likely referring to *Satires*, where Horace repeatedly uses "son of a freedman father" in first-person self-reference (*Satires* 1.6.6, 45, 46), or possibly *Epistles* 1.20.20, where he describes himself as "a freedman's son."[55] Suetonius also exhibits *transparency* by noting an alternate account. He does not explicitly evaluate this claim, but he seems to favor Horace's own account.[56] It is also worth noting that both versions give Horace

---

[54] The LCL edition does not provide reference numbers for *Horace*, so here I cite the paragraph and line in the corresponding Latin text of the LCL edition.

[55] I owe the Horace references to Tristan Power, "Poetry and Fiction in Suetonius' *Illustrious Men*," in *Writing Biography in Greece and Rome: Narrative Technique and Fictionalization*, ed. Koen De Temmerman and Kristoffel Demoen (Cambridge UP, 2016), 220. Power notes that some scholars fault Suetonius for misinterpreting Horace on this point, but he argues that Suetonius's interpretation is more compelling than that of his critics (221). Regardless, the key point for the present study is that Suetonius does cite a source.

[56] Power argues that Suetonius does not regard the alternative account as true but may use it to allude to Horace's literary forebears Bion and Lucilius ("Poetry and Fiction," 221). He also claims that for Suetonius such stories "represented at times a middle ground between fact and

a humble beginning. Once again, Suetonius seems to be sticking close to his sources rather than fabricating material. From here, he moves directly to Horace's adulthood.

Horace, then—like the lives surveyed above—suggests that Suetonius has composed his birth material with historiographic intent. In just a few lines on Horace's early life, he uses *sources* and *transparency*, acknowledging his subject's lowly lineage rather than manufacturing a more glorious (but unfounded) origin story.

Summary

Suetonius employs the full range of historiographic features—*sources, transparency, evaluation,* and *distancing*—in his birth material. Indeed, it is in birth material that he exhibits some of his most impressive historiographic work (e.g., *Cal.* 8.1–5). Scholars who have cited Suetonius's *Augustus, Tiberius,* and *Vespasian* to support the legendary character of ancient birth material have only been able to do so by ignoring the primary birth material in each biography (which is obviously historiographic) and cherry-picking examples from omen lists later in the life (which are also historiographic). The five other lives that we have examined (*Gaius Caligula, Nero, Vitellius, Virgil,* and *Horace*) further confirm that Suetonius has composed his birth material with historiographic intent. Readers may examine historiographic features in other lives by Suetonius using appendix E.

ABSENCE OF BIRTH MATERIAL

Suetonius includes birth material in many—but not all—of his lives. As with Plutarch in the previous chapter, the absence of birth material (or substantial birth material) from some of the lives suggests that Suetonius intends to report history rather than fabricate legend.

---

fiction" (224). In my view, the allusion to Bion and Lucilius is speculative, but even if correct it does not demonstrate that Suetonius regarded this material as ahistorical (or partially so). Suetonius is simply recording a piece of information in his sources that he is not fully convinced of, but which must be historically true or false.

All the biographies in *Lives of the Caesars* contain birth material.⁵⁷ However, the amount of birth material can vary significantly (see appendix E). For example, whereas *Augustus*, *Tiberius*, *Gaius*, and *Nero* have 6–8 chapters of birth material, *Claudius*, *Otho*, and *Vespasian* have just over one chapter, and *Domitian* has only a few sentences. The fact that Suetonius provides varying amounts of birth material for the Caesars (all of whom he regards as noteworthy men) suggests that he is not simply fabricating interesting-but-ahistorical origin stories for them. If he were, we would expect them to receive birth narratives of roughly equal length (though perhaps shorter ones for Galba, Otho, and Vitellius due to their brief reigns). Similar to Plutarch in the previous chapter, it seems more reasonable to think that Suetonius provides more or less birth material based on the amount of information (or relevant information) in his sources.

The situation is more complex with *Lives of Illustrious Men*. Of the six lives that have been preserved in quotations by other authors, three lack birth material (*Tibullus*, *Pliny the Elder*, and *Passienus Crispus*). However, it is possible that the quotations do not include the whole life and that the original versions contained birth material. The lives in the part on grammarians and rhetoricians, though very short, rarely include birth material.⁵⁸ The absence of birth material again suggests that Suetonius is not making things up but is drawing on the relevant information in his sources.

SUPERNATURAL ELEMENTS

We have already observed above in our study of *Augustus*, *Tiberius*, and *Vespasian* that Suetonius does not regard omens as

---

[57] The only birth material in *Julius* is a brief description of Julius's boyhood writings (for which Suetonius employs *sources*). However, the beginning of the work (where Suetonius usually places the birth material) is lost, so it is possible that this life originally had more birth material.

[58] Of the twenty-three lives, only four contain birth material: those of Marcus Antonius Gnipho, Publius Valerius Cato, Lenaeus, and Quintus Remmius Palaemon. I do not include the lives from this part in appendix E due to their brevity.

ahistorical. Indeed, in the very passages where he records omens related to the childhoods of these subjects, Suetonius recounts far more omens related to their adulthoods. A similar phenomenon occurs throughout Suetonius's *Lives*: Suetonius chronicles far more omens related to his subjects' adulthoods than to their childhoods (see appendix E). In some cases, he notes no omens related to the birth/childhood but does record omens related to the adulthood (e.g., *Claudius, Vespasian, Titus, Domitian*). In other cases, he records an omen related to the childhood but records far more related to the adulthood. For example, Suetonius narrates several omens surrounding Nero's birth (*Nero* 6.1–2, discussed above), but includes far more for Nero's adulthood (19.1; 36.1; 40.1–3; 41.2; 46). Similarly, he mentions a horoscope that caused some consternation at Vitellius's birth (*Vit.* 3.2, discussed above), but he relates more that occurred when Vitellius was an adult (9; 14.5; 18). Omens therefore cannot indicate that Suetonius regards birth material as less historical than adult material.

What about miracles? Suetonius records very few, and all the ones I have observed are related to the subject's adulthood (*Jul.* 32; *Aug.* 6; *Cal.* 60). It is possible that Suetonius (like Plutarch) is open to supernatural causation in history. However, since he does not include any miracles in birth material, we may simply conclude that his use of miracles provides no basis for the idea that he regards his birth material as ahistorical.

TIME ELAPSED

Suetonius presents an interesting conundrum with respect to the time elapsed between the subjects' births and his writing. As noted above, Suetonius wrote two sets of biographies: *Lives of Illustrious Men* and *Lives of the Caesars*. Only a few lives from the former have survived—six poets, one historian, one orator, and a part on grammarians and rhetoricians. However, we know little about many of the subjects in the part on grammarians and rhetoricians, and this makes it even more difficult than usual to assign dates of birth to them with any kind of accuracy. Rather than arbitrarily assigning dates of birth or picking and choosing which grammarians and rhetoricians to include, I have limited my analysis to *Lives of the Caesars* and the eight lives from *Lives of Illustrious Men* outside the part on grammarians and rhetoricians.[59]

Suetonius likely completed *Lives of Illustrious Men* around AD 106–13 and *Lives of the Caesars* around AD 120–28.[60] Here I will assume a date of AD 106 for the former (to allow Suetonius to compare as favorably as possible to the Gospels) and AD 120 for the latter.

The time elapsed for each of the lives analyzed appears in appendix E. Analysis of this data yields the following results:

Average	129.1 years
Median	113 years[61]
Maximum	290 years
Minimum	67 years

Suetonius generally stands much closer to the births of his subjects than Nepos, Philo, and Plutarch do, but still at a significant remove from most of them.[62] Let us reflect briefly on the three matters raised in preceding chapters: access to eyewitnesses, relation to historiographic intent, and correspondence to the Gospel birth narratives.

First, Suetonius would have had direct access to eyewitness sources for the birth material of—at most—a few of the lives analyzed. The three lowest times elapsed are Lucan (sixty-seven

---

[59] Scholars question the authenticity of *Tibullus* and *Persius* (Rolfe and Goold, prefatory note to *Lives of the Caesars*, 2:371; Bradley, "Suetonius," 1409). I include these lives because—concerns about authenticity notwithstanding—they appear with the rest of Suetonius's lives in the LCL edition. However, they make a negligible impact on the time elapsed; if one removes them, the average time elapsed increases to 130.94 years and the other numbers remain unchanged.

[60] On the date of *Lives of Illustrious Men*, see Rolfe and Goold, prefatory note to *Lives of the Caesars*, 2:370. On the date of *Lives of the Caesars*, see Hugh Lindsay, introduction to *Caligula*, 3–6; Bradley, introduction to *Julius. Augustus. Tiberius. Gaius Caligula*, 25–26.

[61] Because twenty lives are included in the analysis, the median is the average of the middle two numbers.

[62] Only three lives (Lucan, Domitian, and Persius) have a time elapsed of less than eighty years. Only seven have a time elapsed of less than a hundred years.

years), Domitian (sixty-nine years), and Persius (seventy-two years). But it is questionable whether Suetonius would have been able to interview these subjects or other eyewitnesses directly. Suetonius's father served as a tribune under Otho and shared information about Otho as an adult with Suetonius (*Otho* 10.1),[63] but Suetonius gives no indication that he interviewed Otho about his childhood or even received secondhand information about this from his father. Yet while Suetonius would have had little (if any) direct access to eyewitnesses for his birth material, he would have had elite access to literary sources by virtue of his status as an imperial official. Our investigation above indicates that some of these contained information about the subject's birth and childhood, and it is possible that some of them came from eyewitnesses.

Second, the significant time elapsed makes it all the more striking that Suetonius does not affirm any miracles or engage in legendary development (so far as we can tell) in his birth material.

Third, while the historiographic intent that Suetonius exhibits in his birth material is helpful for understanding the Gospel birth narratives, the time elapsed suggests that in many cases he does not approximate the level of accuracy that Matthew and Luke might have achieved in writing their birth narratives.

CONCLUSION

Suetonius is often cited to support the legendary character of ancient birth narratives, but not for good reason. Suetonius repeatedly employs *sources, transparency, evaluation, distancing* in his birth material—sometimes in exemplary fashion. The absence of birth material (or substantive birth material) from some of his lives suggests that he intends to report history rather than spin tall tales. Suetonius's use of supernatural elements provides no basis for the idea that his birth material is uniquely

---

[63] I owe this point to Craig S. Keener, "Otho: A Targeted Comparison of Suetonius's Biography and Tacitus's History, with Implications for the Gospels' Historical Reliability," in *Biographies and Jesus: What Does It Mean for the Gospels to Be Biographies?* ed. Craig S. Keener and Edward T. Wright (Emeth, 2016), 169.

legendary, for he recounts omens related not only to his subjects' births and childhoods but also to their adulthoods, and he only affirms miracles in adult material. Finally, the time elapsed suggests that while Suetonius provides helpful insight into the intent with which Matthew and Luke would have composed their birth narratives, in many cases he does not approximate the accuracy they might have achieved.

5
ANCIENT BIRTH NARRATIVES AND HISTORIOGRAPHY: CONCLUSIONS

The preceding four chapters have presented detailed studies of birth material in the biographies of Cornelius Nepos, Philo, Plutarch, and Suetonius. In the present chapter, I summarize the overarching picture that emerges from these four biographers and reflect on its significance for the Gospel birth narratives—the subject of part 2. The discussion here draws on all the lives of our four biographers (not just the ones discussed in the preceding chapters), so I encourage readers to familiarize themselves with appendixes B–E, which summarize historiographic data for the biographies of each author, before continuing.

HISTORIOGRAPHIC FEATURES

Cornelius Nepos, Philo, Plutarch, and Suetonius all employ historiographic features in and with respect to their birth material. *Sources, transparency, evaluation,* and *distancing*—the same features that indicate historiographic intent in ancient histories and elsewhere in the biographies of these four authors—appear regularly in relation to material about the births and childhoods of their subjects.[1] We have also identified several instances where

---

[1] See appendix A for historiographic features in ancient historians. See appendixes B–E for examples of historiographic features elsewhere in the biographies of Nepos, Philo, Plutarch, and Suetonius.

these biographers draw on extant sources for their birth material, and in each case they seem to use their sources responsibly by the standards of ancient biography. Furthermore, the historiographic features discussed above constitute only a small portion of the relevant data. Readers will recall that we limited our study of Plutarch and (partially) Suetonius to biographies that scholars have cited to show that ancient birth narratives were legendary. Plutarch and Suetonius, however, also employ historiographic features in the birth material of many of their other biographies. Space does not permit us to discuss these, but I encourage readers to explore them using appendixes B–E.

The foregoing chapters of part 1 have focused on noting the presence of historiographic features in birth material. However, historiographic features are also absent from birth material in some of the biographies of Nepos, Plutarch, and Suetonius (see appendixes B, D, and E). What should we make of this? One might conclude that birth material without historiographic features is not meant to be historical. This, however, would be a mistake. As noted in the Introduction, historiographic features are sufficient indicators of historiographic intent (barring satire and intent to deceive), but they are not necessary indicators of historiographic intent. The fact that Nepos, Plutarch, and Suetonius employ historiographic features in the birth material of many of their biographies indicates that they intend their birth material to be historiographic. When we find birth material by one of these authors that lacks historiographic features, then, we should assume that it is historiographic unless they explicitly indicate otherwise.

The absence of historiographic features from adult material (and how we respond to that absence) proves the point. Let us take Nepos (appendix B) as an example: Appendix B indicates that I have found no historiographic features in the adult material of more than half the lives in *De viris illustribus*. It would be absurd to argue on this basis that Nepos intends this material to be ahistorical. Similarly, it would be foolish to think that the birth material where Nepos employs historiographic features is more historiographic than the adult material where he does not.

Historiographic features are therefore significant both in their presence and their absence. The fact that Nepos, Philo, Plutarch, and Suetonius often employ historiographic features in or with respect to their birth material indicates that they intend it to be historiographic rather than legendary. The fact that they sometimes forgo using historiographic features shows that ancient biographers could intend birth material (and adult material) to be historiographic without explicitly indicating their intent.

ABSENCE OF BIRTH MATERIAL

Cornelius Nepos, Plutarch, and Suetonius—our biographers with multiple extant lives—also indicate their historiographic intent by (1) omitting birth material from some lives or (2) providing substantially less birth material for some subjects than for others.[2] The partial or complete absence of birth material is sometimes quite shocking. We have seen, for example, that Nepos gives minimal birth material to Thrasybulus, one of his favorite subjects (*Thras.* 1.1). We have also observed that Plutarch gives Julius Caesar no birth material even though Caesar is one of his greatest subjects and Alexander the Great, the Greek whom Plutarch places in parallel with Caesar, receives an extended birth narrative. It seems reasonable to think that if Nepos, Plutarch, and Suetonius regarded birth material as legendary—an ahistorical anticipation of the subject's adult life—they would give birth material to all their subjects, perhaps varying the amount according to each subject's reputation. But this is not what we find. If, on the other hand, our biographers composed their birth material with historiographic intent (as their use of historiographic features would suggest), then the absence is easy to explain: our biographers do not include more birth material because (1) they lacked sources or (2) the information in their sources was not interesting or relevant enough to include.

SUPERNATURAL ELEMENTS

Our study has shown that the omens and miracles that appear in our biographers' birth material do not necessarily constitute

[2] See further appendixes B, D, and E.

evidence for legendary intent. Four points are key: First, our biographers often qualify supernatural elements with *transparency, evaluation,* or *distancing*. Scholars who treat supernatural elements as evidence of legendary intent tend to miss these historiographic features and therefore misinterpret the biographer's intent. What matters is not the supernatural elements a biographer *mentions*, but the ones he *affirms*.

Second, it is important to distinguish between omens and miracles. Omens, as I have defined them here, are events that are interpreted as signs regarding the significance of a person or event. To say that Plutarch affirms an omen, then, means only that he recounts an event that people interpreted as a sign, not that he affirms that the event involved supernatural causation (for then it would be a miracle). Many people in antiquity believed that the gods spoke through everyday events, so it should not surprise us to find ancient biographers (or historians) describing omens.

Third, our biographers affirm relatively few supernatural elements in their birth material. Nepos affirms no omens or miracles in birth material, though he does recount a few omens in adult material. Philo affirms divine causation at three points in his birth narrative, but all these were likely in his sources, and he affirms divine causation frequently in adult material. Plutarch and Suetonius affirm a few omens in birth material, but they affirm omens often and miracles occasionally in adult material.

Finally, our biographers who include supernatural elements in their birth material seem to regard supernatural causation as a legitimate aspect of history. Philo, Plutarch, and Suetonius all affirm miracles outside their birth material, and Philo and Plutarch explicitly express their openness to supernatural causation.

It is therefore time to put to rest the notion that supernatural elements necessarily indicate the legendary intent of ancient birth material. Such a view not only ignores the historiographic character of ancient birth narratives; it also assumes a methodological naturalism that is foreign to our biographers and to ancient historiography in general.

TIME ELAPSED

Our biographers generally wrote long after the births of their subjects. The preceding chapters have given the average, median, maximum, and minimum time elapsed for each biographer. Below are the same figures for all ninety-five lives (weighted equally) from the earlier analyses:

Average	363.71 years
Median	370 years
Maximum	1,240 years
Minimum	69 years

One must, of course, use these numbers carefully since they are approximate and do not tell us anything about the time elapsed between the subjects' births and the biographers' sources. Nonetheless, it is striking that, on average, our biographers are writing over 360 years after their subjects' births.[3] We have considered the significance of the time elapsed at length in the preceding chapters, so here I will simply reiterate three key points: First, our biographers generally would not have had the opportunity to interview eyewitness sources, though in limited cases they may have had access to literary sources by eyewitnesses. Second, the significant time elapsed emphasizes the historiographic character of our biographers' birth material. Despite writing an average of over 360 years after their subjects' births, our biographers affirm few miracles in their birth material and do not appear to engage in legendary development. Third, the time elapsed constitutes a stark point of contrast between our biographers and Matthew and Luke. Therefore, while the historiographic intent with which Nepos, Philo, Plutarch, and Suetonius have composed their birth material helps us to understand how Matthew and Luke would have approached the writing of their birth narratives, their accuracy is not a good gauge for what Matthew and Luke might have achieved.

---

[3] One might protest that Philo, *Moses* (the highest time elapsed at 1,240 years) has skewed the analysis. Yet even if one removes this life from consideration, the average time elapsed is still 354.38 years.

BIRTH MATERIAL: NOT A SPECIAL CASE

The historiographic features, absence of birth material, use of supernatural elements, and time elapsed that we observe in the birth narratives of Nepos, Philo, Plutarch, and Suetonius all point to a single conclusion: our biographers intend their birth material to be historiographic. The fact that they place their birth material in ancient biographies (a type of historiographic literature) might, of course, have suggested this conclusion. But the skepticism of intent that scholars have leveled at ancient birth narratives has required us to dig deeper into the birth material itself. We are now in a position to see the truth: birth material is not a special case with respect to historiographic intent.

The legendary intent hypothesis also proves unworkable as a reading strategy. Interpreters who hold that ancient birth material was meant to be legendary seem to assume a double historiographic standard: birth material is intended to be ahistorical, non-birth material historical (or at least more historical). Our biographers, however, problematize this assumption in a variety of ways. First, they are sometimes unclear about where their birth material is. Plutarch, for example, does not clearly indicate where he transitions from the birth narrative to the rest of the life in *Alexander*. How could Plutarch have expected his reader to apply a historiographic double standard here? Second, our biographers sometimes include birth material amid adult material and vice versa. Suetonius, for instance, lists omens related to his subjects' births and adulthoods together in *Augustus*, *Tiberius*, and *Vespasian*. Are we really to suppose that Suetonius expected his reader to switch from reading historically (adult material) to ahistorically (birth omens) and back (adult omens) in these cases? This seems unlikely. Conversely, Plutarch mentions Cicero's adulthood in the birth material (*Cic.* 1.3–4). Are we to think that Plutarch intended the reader to switch from reading ahistorically (birth material) to historically (adult material) and back (birth material)? Again, this seems improbable. Third, our biographers sometimes treat material regarding the subject's birth, childhood, and young adulthood as a single entity. Plutarch, for example, presents material regarding all three of these life stages as a literary and historiographic unit in *Romulus* 3.1–8.6. And Suetonius summarizes Vitellius's boyhood and youth together (*Vit.* 3.2). Why do Plutarch and Suetonius combine these life stages if they expect the reader to interpret them with different historiographic standards? Therefore, while the legendary intent hypothesis may sound plausible in the abstract, it runs aground on the very ancient biographies that it attempts to explain.

The birth material of Nepos, Philo, Plutarch, and Suetonius, then, does not constitute a special case with respect to historiographic intent. Our biographers appear to have composed their birth material with the same historiographic intent that they exhibit elsewhere in their biographies, and to read them otherwise requires special pleading at numerous points.

OTHER ANCIENT BIOGRAPHERS

As noted in the introduction, I have chosen to study Nepos, Philo, Plutarch, and Suetonius because they wrote within roughly a century of the Gospels, they have birth material to discuss, and most of them have numerous extant biographies. These biographers therefore provide the best insight into how Matthew and Luke would have approached the writing of their birth narratives. However, the historiographic intent that we observe in these four authors is not unique; an analysis of other ancient biographers would yield similar results. To demonstrate this fully would take us beyond the bounds of the current project, so I have opted to present some of the relevant data in summary form in appendix F. Here readers will find historiographic data for the following (in chronological order):

- Tacitus, *Agricola* (first century AD)
- Lucian, *Demonax* (second century AD)
- Diogenes Laertius, *Lives of Eminent Philosophers* 3 Plato; 10 Epicurus (third century AD)
- Porphyry, *Life of Pythagoras* (third century AD)
- Iamblichus, *On the Pythagorean Life* (fourth century AD)

The historiographic features in the birth material of these other biographies suggest that the historiographic intent that we observe in Nepos, Philo, Plutarch, and Suetonius is typical of ancient biographies. Are there exceptions? Possibly. But some of the birth narratives with the best claim to legendary intent (the Infancy Gospel of Thomas, the Protevangelium of James, or the *Life of Alexander* of Pseudo-Callisthenes) are not in ancient biographies.[4] And even if we were to find some examples of birth narratives with legendary intent in ancient biographies, the combined witness of Nepos, Philo, Plutarch, Suetonius, and the biographers in appendix F suggests that most ancient biographers intended their birth narratives to be historical. The burden of proof, then, rests firmly on those who argue that the birth narratives of ancient biographies (including the Gospels) were meant to be legendary.

CONCLUSION

I noted in the introduction that the distrust and disuse of the Gospel birth narratives among scholars is founded on a skepticism of intent that asserts that ancient birth narratives—including the Gospel birth narratives—were meant to be legendary. Part 1, however, has demonstrated quite the opposite: Ancient biographers composed their birth material with historiographic intent. Cornelius Nepos, Philo, Plutarch, and Suetonius all exhibit historiographic intent in their birth material, as do the biographers in appendix F. The evidence suggests that historiographic intent was the dominant trend for birth material in ancient biographies—particularly biographies written within a century or so of the Gospels. In part 2, we will consider how the Gospel birth narratives accord with this picture.

---

[4] On Pseudo-Callisthenes, *Life of Alexander* as fiction rather than biography see Christopher Pelling, "Truth and Fiction in Plutarch's Lives," in *Plutarch and History: Eighteen Studies* (Classical Press of Wales, 2002), 143–70, 162; Craig S. Keener, *Christobiography: Memory, History, and the Reliability of the Gospels* (Eerdmans, 2019), 48–49.

II
Gospel Birth Narratives and Historiography

6
MATTHEW

We come at last to the Gospel birth narratives, but now with fresh eyes. Apart from our study in part 1, it would be easy to assume that birth material in ancient biographies was meant to be legendary and that the burden of proof rests on anyone who argues that the Gospel birth narratives are meant to be historical. Part 1, however, has demonstrated quite the opposite: birth material in ancient biographies was meant to be historical. We should therefore assume that the Gospel birth narratives are intended to be historical unless Matthew and Luke give us good reason to think otherwise. In the present chapter and the one that follows, I will argue that Matthew and Luke not only fail to indicate that they intend their birth material to be legendary but also exhibit historiographic intent. Each chapter will begin by discussing historiographic features and then go on to address supernatural elements and the time elapsed.

Matthew 1–2 is a fitting place to begin, both because it comes first canonically and because scholars have been far more skeptical of its historiographic intent. Ulrich Luz, for example, comments on Matthew's genealogy, "Scholarship, probably in this case with finality, has recognized that it is a fiction."[1] Similarly, J. C. Fenton asserts

---

[1] Ulrich Luz, *Matthew 1–7: A Commentary*, rev. ed., Hermeneia (Fortress, 2007), 87.

that "when we examine Matthew 1, 2 we shall find that they are very largely made up out of reflections upon certain Old Testament passages read in light of Jewish expectations and Christian faith."[2] W. D. Davies and Dale Allison likewise say regarding the magi, the star, and other elements of Matthew 2:1–12,

> These are things to delight and enchant, to entertain and cause wonder. They are also vehicles of truths when contemplated within their literary context. . . . In our view, however, they are not the stuff out of which history is made. Rather do they supplement history as history's addendum. As the Haggadah fills up the voids in the OT text, so does Mt 2.1–12 close one of the gaps in the Jesus tradition.[3]

Such assessments, however, not only overlook the historiographic character of ancient birth narratives (part 1); they also miss numerous indications of historiographic intent within Matthew 1–2 itself.

SOURCES

I begin with an uncontroversial point: Matthew does not cite historiographic sources for his birth material. It would be a mistake, however, to conclude that Matthew has no sources for this material. Two insights from part 1 are relevant here. First, Cornelius Nepos, Philo, Plutarch, and Suetonius regularly cite sources for their birth material. This suggests that birth material—like ancient biographies in general—was information-based. Second, the absence of birth material from many of Nepos, Plutarch, and Suetonius's biographies shows that birth material was not a necessary part of an ancient biography. The absence of any birth narrative in Mark and John also confirms this. The natural conclusion, then, is that Matthew has included his birth material because (1) he had the requisite information and (2) he saw it as relevant.

Matthew, however, provides us with resources to press further. Even though Matthew does not cite sources for his birth material,

---

[2] J. C. Fenton, *Saint Matthew*, Westminster Pelican Commentaries (Westminster, 1963), 34.

[3] W. D. Davies and Dale C. Allison Jr., *The Gospel According to Saint Matthew*, 3 vols., ICC (T&T Clark, 1988–97), 1:252.

we can identify extant sources for some of it and examine how he has used those sources. Matthew also includes numerous Old Testament references that may speak to his historiographic intent. And since Matthew has likely used Mark as a source, we can compare his use of sources in the birth material to his use of Mark elsewhere. We will examine each of these areas below.

Genealogy

It will be helpful to consider at the outset what sorts of sources Matthew might have used to compose his genealogy. Matthew depends heavily on the Old Testament throughout his Gospel, quoting the Old Testament more than any other Gospel does and alluding to it many times as well.[4] It therefore seems reasonable to think that Matthew had access to genealogical information in the Old Testament.[5]

Matthew also goes beyond the Old Testament at points, which suggests that he had additional sources—as scholars of various stripes have concluded.[6] Jews of antiquity placed a high value

---

[4] On Matthew's use of the Old Testament, see Krister Stendahl, *The School of St. Matthew and Its Use of the Old Testament*, 2nd ed. (Fortress, 1968); Robert H. Gundry, *The Use of the Old Testament in St. Matthew's Gospel. With Special Reference to the Messianic Hope*, NovTSup 18 (Brill, 1967); George M. Soares Prabhu, *The Formula Quotations in the Infancy Narrative of Matthew: An Enquiry into the Tradition History of Mt 1–2* (Pontifical Biblical Institute, 1976); Craig L. Blomberg, "Matthew," in *Commentary on the New Testament Use of the Old Testament*, ed. G. K. Beale and D. A. Carson (Baker Academic, 2007); Richard B. Hays, *Echoes of Scripture in the Gospels* (Baylor UP, 2016), 105–90; Patrick Schreiner, *Matthew, Disciple and Scribe: The First Gospel and Its Portrait of Jesus* (Baker Academic, 2019).

[5] *Contra* Luz, *Matthew 1–7*, 81.

[6] E.g., Raymond E. Brown, *The Birth of the Messiah: A Commentary on the Infancy Narratives in the Gospels of Matthew and Luke*, rev. ed., ABRL (Doubleday, 1993), 69–70; D. A. Carson, *Matthew*, vol. 8 of *The Expositor's Bible Commentary* (Zondervan, 1984), 63; René Laurentin, *The Truth of Christmas Beyond the Myths: The Gospels of the Infancy of Christ*, trans. Michael J. Wrenn and associates, Studies in Scripture (St. Bede's, 1986), 352; Davies and Allison, *Matthew*, 1:165–66; Donald A. Hagner, *Matthew 1–13*, WBC 33A (Word, 1993), 8; Luz, *Matthew 1–7*, 81–82.

on lineage and kept genealogical records, so such information would likely have been available.[7] There is some question of how common such records were for non-priestly families.[8] Richard Bauckham, however, rightly notes,

> Whether or not there were ever public genealogical records of lay families and however common or uncommon it was for Jewish families to keep their own records, it is likely enough that a Davidic family would do so. Pride in their royal descent along with the traditional expectation of a Messiah ben David would be strong motives for doing so.[9]

It therefore seems likely that Matthew would have had access to sources beyond the Old Testament. The question is what these additional sources contained and how Matthew has used them. Raymond Brown, for example, argues that Matthew drew on two genealogical lists that already contained many of his differences with the Old Testament (e.g., the 3×14 pattern).[10] Brown's proposal is attractive because it allows one to credit many of Matthew's differences with the Old Testament to his sources. However, it seems unlikely that Matthew would have used nonbiblical genealogical

---

[7] 1 Chr 1–9; Ezra 2:59–63; Neh 7:61–65; Josephus, *Ag. Ap.* 1.28–36; *Life* 1–6; Eusebius, *Hist. eccl.* 1.7.13–14; 3.12; 3.19–20; 3.32.3–4; m. Yevam. 4.13; m. Qidd. 4.4–5; y. Ta'an. 4.2; b. Ketub. 62b; b. Pesah. 4a; b. Qidd. 76b; Gen. Rab. 98.8. See further Herman L. Strack and Paul Billerbeck, *A Commentary on the New Testament from the Talmud and Midrash*, ed. Jacob N. Cerone, trans. Andrew Bowden and Joseph Longarino, 4 vols. (Lexham, 2022), 1:4–7; Joachim Jeremias, *Jerusalem in the Time of Jesus: An Investigation into Economic and Social Conditions During the New Testament Period*, trans. F. H. Cave and C. H. Cave (Fortress, 1969), 275–302; Gerard Mussies, "Parallels to Matthew's Version of the Pedigree of Jesus," *NovT* 28.1 (1986): 35–36; Richard Bauckham, *Jude and the Relatives of Jesus in the Early Church* (T&T Clark, 1990), 340–41, 360–61.

[8] Marshall D. Johnson, *The Purpose of the Biblical Genealogies with Special Reference to the Setting of the Genealogies of Jesus*, SNTSMS 8 (Cambridge UP, 1969), 99–108.

[9] Bauckham, *Jude and the Relatives of Jesus*, 360.

[10] Brown, *Birth of the Messiah*, 69–70. Luz similarly argues that Matthew is using a nonbiblical genealogy and perhaps making minor additions to it (*Matthew 1–7*, 81–82). For critiques of Brown that also apply to Luz, see Davies and Allison, *Matthew*, 165–67; Hagner, *Matthew 1–13*, 8.

lists without checking them against the Old Testament. Here I opt for a harder but (in my view) more compelling argument: Matthew has used both the Old Testament and nonbiblical sources for his genealogy, but his differences with the Old Testament fall within the acceptable range of flexibility for Jewish genealogies and do not constitute evidence for legendary intent.

Matthew seems to draw most of his genealogy from the Old Testament. The key Old Testament sources are 1 Chronicles 1–3 and Ruth 4 (see table 1). Matthew relies on the Greek version of Chronicles for the generations from Abraham to Zerubbabel.[11] Chronicles even provides Matthew with two of the four women whom he mentions: Tamar (1 Chr 2:4; Matt 1:3) and Solomon's mother (1 Chr 3:5), whom Matthew calls "the wife of Uriah" (Matt 1:6).[12] Matthew also seems to depend on Ruth, for while Chronicles says nothing about Ruth being Obed's mother, Ruth 4 makes this clear. The people of Bethlehem even connect Ruth to Tamar when they say to Boaz, "Through the children that the LORD will give you by this young woman, may your house be like that of Perez, whom Tamar bore to Judah" (Ruth 4:12).[13] Matthew therefore not only has sources for his genealogy; he relies on them significantly.

Matthew does, however, differ from Chronicles and Ruth at three key points: (1) the names used, (2) the addition of Rahab, and (3) the omission of some generations. Since each of these points might cause one to question Matthew's historiographic intent, we will investigate them in detail.

---

[11] Matthew's dependence on the Septuagint can be seen both in how he spells certain names and the fact that he presents Salathiel as the father of Zerubbabel (Matt 1:12). Whereas the Masoretic Text portrays Shealtiel (= Salathiel) as the uncle of Zerubbabel, the Septuagint is clear that Salathiel is Zerubbabel's father (1 Chr 3:17, 19; cf. Ezra 3:2, 8; Hag 1:1).

[12] Scripture quotations are from the NRSV unless otherwise noted. First Chronicles 3:5 LXX names Solomon's mother as Bersabee (Βηρσαβεε), the same name it uses for Uriah's wife in 2 Samuel (2 Kgdms) 11:3. First Chronicles 3:5 MT names Solomon's mother as Bathshua (בת־שׁוּעַ).

[13] Steven M. Bryan, "The Missing Generation: The Completion of Matthew's Genealogy," *BBR* 29.3 (2019): 300.

Table 1: Old Testament sources for Matthew's genealogy

	Matthew 1:2–16 (NRSV)	Old Testament sources (LXX)		Matthew 1:2–16 (NRSV)
From Abraham to David	Abraham	1 Chr 1:27	From David to the Exile	Solomon
	Isaac	1 Chr 1:28, 34		Rehoboam
	Jacob	1 Chr 1:34		Abijah
	Judah and his brothers	1 Chr 2:1–2; Ruth 4:12		Asaph
	Perez and Zerah	1 Chr 2:4; Ruth 4:12		Jehoshaphat
	Hezron	1 Chr 2:5; Ruth 4:18		Joram
	Aram	1 Chr 2:9; Ruth 4:19		Uzziah
	Aminadab	1 Chr 2:10; Ruth 4:19		Jotham
	Nahshon	1 Chr 2:10; Ruth 4:20		Ahaz
	Salmon	1 Chr 2:11; Ruth 4:20		Hezekiah
	Boaz	1 Chr 2:11; Ruth 4:21		Manasseh
	Obed	1 Chr 2:12; Ruth 4:13, 17, 21		Amos
	Jesse	1 Chr 2:12; Ruth 4:22		Josiah
	David	1 Chr 2:15; Ruth 4:22		Jechoniah and his brothers

Old Testament sources (LXX)		Matthew 1:2–16 (NRSV)	Old Testament sources (LXX)
1 Chr 3:5	From the Exile to the Messiah	Salathiel	1 Chr 3:17
1 Chr 3:10		Zerubbabel	1 Chr 3:19
1 Chr 3:10		Abiud	—
1 Chr 3:10		Eliakim	—
1 Chr 3:10		Azor	—
1 Chr 3:11		Zadok	—
1 Chr 3:12		Achim	—
1 Chr 3:12		Eliud	—
1 Chr 3:13		Eleazar	—
1 Chr 3:13		Matthan	—
1 Chr 3:13		Jacob	—
1 Chr 3:14		Joseph	—
1 Chr 3:14		Jesus	—
1 Chr 3:16 (cf. 2 Chr 36:10)			

Names

Matthew differs from one or both of his Old Testament sources regarding the names of eleven men in the genealogy (see table 2).[14] One of these differences can be explained easily: Uzziah (Ὀζίας) is another Old Testament name for Azariah (Ἀζαρία).[15] Scholars do not regard most of the remaining ten differences as significant, but two have drawn significant attention:

Chronicles		Matthew
Asa (Ἀσά)	→	Asaph (Ἀσάφ)
Amon (Ἀμών)	→	Amos (Ἀμώς)[16]

Some scholars propose that Matthew has changed these names deliberately to allude to the psalmist Asaph and the prophet Amos,[17] to achieve a gematrical scheme,[18] or both.[19] Others suggest

---

[14] Matthew also differs with the LXX regarding Rahab's name—see further below.

[15] See 2 Kgs 15:1, 13, 30, 34; Carson, *Matthew*, 67; Brown, *Birth of the Messiah*, 60. Scholars sometimes suggest that Matthew (or a hypothetical nonbiblical source) has confused the Greek names for Ahaziah and Uzziah—e.g., Brown, *Birth of the Messiah*, 82. But this is unlikely, for 1 Chr 3:12 LXX has Azariah (Ἀζαρία), which does not closely resemble the Greek names for Ahaziah. It is far more likely that Matthew has used Ahaziah's alternate name Uzziah and has intentionally omitted the three kings before him (Davies and Allison, *Matthew*, 1:176).

[16] Some manuscripts of Matthew have Asa (Ἀσά) and Amon (Ἀμών). However, it seems more likely that scribes would have changed Asaph to Asa and Amos to Amon than vice versa. See further Bruce M. Metzger, *A Textual Commentary on the Greek New Testament*, 2nd ed. (Deutsche Bibelgesellschaft, 1994), 1–2.

[17] Julius Schniewind, *Das Evangelium nach Matthäus*, 11th ed., NTD 2 (Vandenhoeck & Ruprecht, 1964), 10; Robert H. Gundry, *Matthew: A Commentary on His Literary and Theological Art* (Eerdmans, 1982), 15–16; Craig S. Keener, *A Commentary on the Gospel of Matthew* (Eerdmans, 1999), 76–77; John Nolland, *The Gospel of Matthew: A Commentary on the Greek Text*, NIGTC (Eerdmans, 2005), 79, 81; R. T. France, *The Gospel of Matthew*, NICNT (Eerdmans, 2007), 27. Proponents of this view sometimes note that Matthew quotes part of a psalm of Asaph (Ps 78:2) in Matt 13:35. Gundry and Nolland acknowledge that a deliberate change is less likely in the case of Amos since Ἀμώς appears in some manuscripts of 1 Chr 3:14 LXX.

[18] Steven M. Bryan, "Onomastics and Numerical Composition in the Genealogy of Matthew," *BBR* 30.4 (2020): 533–35.

[19] Bryan, "Onomastics," 535.

that Matthew (or a nonbiblical source) has confused these Davidic kings with the psalmist and the prophet.[20]

Table 2: Differences in names between Matthew's genealogy and its sources*

Matthew 1:2-16 (NRSV)	Matthew 1:2-16 (NA[28])	1 Chronicles 1:24-3:19 (LXX)	Ruth 4:12-22 (LXX)
Judah (Matt 1:2-3)	Ἰούδας	Ἰούδα (1 Chr 2:1-2)	Ἰούδας (Ruth 4:12)
Hezron (Matt 1:3)	Ἑσρώμ	Ἀρσών (1 Chr 2:5), but later Ἐσερών (1 Chr 2:9)	Ἑσρών (Ruth 4:18-19)
Aram (Matt 1:4)	Ἀράμ	Ἀράμ (1 Chr 2:9)	Ἀρράν (Ruth 4:19)
Boaz (Matt 1:5)	Βόες	Βόος (1 Chr 2:11)	Βόος (Ruth 4:21)
Obed (Matt 1:5)	Ἰωβήδ	Ὠβήδ (1 Chr 2:12)	Ὠβήδ (Ruth 4:13, 17, 21)
Solomon (Matt 1:6-7)	Σολομῶν	Σαλωμῶν (1 Chr 3:5)	—
Asaph (Matt 1:8)	Ἀσάφ	Ἀσά (1 Chr 3:10)	—
Uzziah (Matt 1:8-9)	Ὀζίας	Ἀζαρία (1 Chr 3:12)	—
Jotham (Matt 1:9)	Ἰωαθάμ	Ἰωαθάν (1 Chr 3:12)	—
Amos (Matt 1:10)	Ἀμώς	Ἀμών (1 Chr 3:14)	—
Josiah (Matt 1:10-11)	Ἰωσίας	Ἰωσία (1 Chr 3:14)	—

*All names are in the nominative case. The Göttingen edition of 1 Chronicles has not yet been published, so the text for 1 Chronicles is from Alfred Rahlfs and Robert Hanhart, eds., *Septuaginta: Editio altera* (Deutsche Bibelgesellschaft, 2006). Rahlfs and Hanhart do not include breathing marks and accents for the names, so I have added them. The text for Ruth is from Udo Quast, ed., *Ruth*, vol. 4.3 of *Septuaginta: Vetus Testamentum Graecum* (Vandenhoeck & Ruprecht, 2006).

---

[20] Brown, *Birth of the Messiah*, 60-61; Davies and Allison, *Matthew*, 1:175, 177; Hagner, *Matthew 1-13*, 11; Luz, *Matthew 1-7*, 80.

Before evaluating these options, let us clarify what is at stake: If Matthew (or his source) has made an error, this would impact the historiographic truth of his account, but it would not constitute evidence for legendary intent. On the other hand, if Matthew has changed the names on purpose, we must ask why he has done so. There are several possibilities:

(1) Matthew identifies Asa with the psalmist Asaph or, improbably, Amon with the prophet Amos.[21]
(2) Matthew intends to refer to Asa and Amon but has slightly altered one or both names for literary or theological reasons.
(3) Matthew does not intend to refer to Asa and Amon but to the Levite Asaph and the prophet Amos, respectively.

Options (1) and (2) are fully compatible with historiographic intent. On both counts, Matthew intends to refer to the Davidic kings Asa and Amon; he simply calls them by names that are slightly different but well within the normal range of flexibility (see table 2). Option (3) would pose a problem for Matthew's historiographic intent, but it is highly unlikely. The reason is simple: to insert two non-Davidic figures into the genealogy would undermine Jesus's status as son of David, which Matthew affirms and even goes out of his way to emphasize (Matt 1:1, 6, 17, 20).[22] So neither an unintentional error nor the deliberate changes Matthew might have made provide any grounds for legendary intent.

---

[21] Richard Bauckham, "Tamar's Ancestry and Rahab's Marriage: Two Problems in the Matthean Genealogy," *NovT* 37.4 (1995): 321n23. Bauckham suggests that Matthew's use of Asaph may be "an example of a frequent practice in Jewish exegesis of identifying two biblical persons with similar names." He goes on to provide other examples of this phenomenon (326–27).

[22] Cf. Matt 9:27; 12:23; 15:22; 20:30–31; 21:9, 15; 22:42–46.

Table 3: Amon's names in Kings and Chronicles**

Passage	Name	Witnesses†
2 Kgs 21:18–19, 23–25	Amon (Ἀμών) or Ammon (Ἀμμών)	O, L
	Amos (Ἀμώς)	B, A
1 Chr 3:14	Amon (Ἀμών)	L
	Amnon (Ἀμνών)	B*
	Amos (Ἀμώς)	A, B^C
2 Chr 33:20–25	Amon (Ἀμών)	L
	Amos (Ἀμώς)	B, A

** The data is based on the textual apparatus of Rahlfs and Hanhart, *Septuaginta: Editio altera*.

† A = Codex Alexandrinus; B = Codex Vaticanus; L = Lucian; O = Origen; * = original reading; ^C = corrector.

Moreover, the flexibility of Semitic names in Greek suggests that Matthew has not made an error and may not have made an intentional change in both cases. Asa (Ἀσά) is the best attested reading in 1 Chronicles 3:10 LXX, but one Septuagint manuscript reads Asab (Ἀσάβ),[23] and Josephus consistently refers to Asa as Asanos (Ἄσανος).[24] The names ascribed to Amon are even more diverse. Amon receives several names in the Septuagint manuscripts of 1 Chronicles 3:14 (Matthew's source) and two other passages (2 Kgs 21:18–19, 23–25; 2 Chr 33:20–25). Table 3 presents these names with the major textual witnesses that support them. Here we find that both Codex Vaticanus (B) and Codex Alexandrinus (A) read Ἀμώς in multiple passages. One might argue that they do so under the influence of Matthew.[25] However, the original reading of Vaticanus does not have Ἀμώς in 1 Chronicles 3:14 (Matthew's source), so Matthean influence seems unlikely here.

---

[23] Metzger, *Textual Commentary*, 1n1. Metzger cites manuscript 60, which dates to the tenth century AD.

[24] Josephus, *Ant.* 8.286, 287, 290, 292, 294, 295, 298, 303, 304, 306, 307, 312, 314.

[25] E.g., France, *Matthew*, 27.

Nor does Alexandrinus seem to depend on Matthew, for it differs from Matthew regarding several other names.[26] Steven Bryan has observed that Matthew tends to prefer readings preserved in Alexandrinus,[27] so if Alexandrinus is independent of Matthew, it is quite possible that Matthew found Ἀμώς in his text of Chronicles. Jeremiah 1:2 and 25:3 LXX refer to Amon as Ἀμώς as well.[28] A glance at the Septuagint textual apparatus for 1 Chronicles 1–3 and Ruth 4 also reveals significant fluidity in how Semitic names were spelled in Greek.[29] The upshot of all this is that Matthew is operating well within ancient orthographic conventions in referring to Asa as Asaph and Amon as Amos, and it is quite plausible that he found the name Amos in his text of 1 Chronicles 3:14.

Rahab

Matthew names Rahab, who does not appear in Chronicles or Ruth, as the mother of Boaz: "Salmon [was] the father of Boaz by Rahab" (Matt 1:5). Matthew, however, spells Rahab's name Ῥαχάβ, whereas the LXX and early Christian literature generally use Ῥαάβ.[30] The difference in spelling has led some interpreters to suggest that the Rahab in view is not the biblical Rahab.[31] How-

---

[26] E.g., Βοόζ (1 Chr 2:11–12 LXX A) / Βόες (Matt 1:5); Σαλωμών (1 Chr 3:5 LXX) / Σολομών (Matt 1:6–7); Ἀσά (1 Chr 3:10 LXX A) / Ἀσάφ (Matt 1:7–8); Ἰωναθάν (1 Chr 3:12 LXX A) / Ἰωαθάμ (Matt 1:9). I owe the final example and the broader point to Bryan, "Onomastics," 523n23.

[27] Bryan, "Onomastics," 523n23.

[28] For text and apparatus, see Joseph Ziegler, ed., *Ieremias, Baruch, Threni, Epistula Ieremiae*, 3rd ed., vol. 15 of *Septuaginta: Vetus Testamentum Graecum* (Vandenhoeck & Ruprecht, 2006), 149, 274. Josephus, *Ant.* 10.46, manuscript M (fourteenth century AD) also refers to Amon as Amosos (Ἀμώσος).

[29] For a limited apparatus for both passages see Rahlfs and Hanhart, *Septuaginta: Editio altera*. For a full apparatus for Ruth 4 see Quast, *Ruth*.

[30] Jerome D. Quinn, "Is ΡΑΧΑΒ in Mt 1:5 Rahab of Jericho?" *Bib* 63.2 (1981): 226; Bauckham, "Tamar's Ancestry," 320. The spelling Ῥαχάβη appears in some manuscripts of Josephus, *Ant.* 5.8–30 (Quinn, "ΡΑΧΑΒ," 226; Bauckham, "Tamar's Ancestry," 320).

[31] Origen, *Scholia in Matthaeum* 1.5; Quinn, "ΡΑΧΑΒ."

ever, all the other figures in Matthew 2:1–13a are biblical ones, and Matthew differs from the Septuagint spelling at numerous points, so it seems most likely that Matthew intends the biblical Rahab.[32] However, Rahab does not appear as the wife of Salmon or the mother of Boaz elsewhere in the Old Testament or in Jewish literature. Furthermore, interpreters often note that the biblical Rahab would have lived around two centuries before either Salmon or Boaz.[33] Davies and Allison accordingly comment, "Maybe we have here the product of Matthean fancy."[34] Such an interpretation, if correct, would cast significant doubt on Matthew's historiographic intent. However, there are good reasons to doubt it.

Let us begin with the chronological issue: Nahshon, the father of Salmon (1 Chr 2:11; Ruth 4:11; Matt 1:4), belongs to the period of the Exodus and the wilderness wanderings (Exod 6:23; Num 1:7; 2:3; 7:12–17; 10:14). Salmon, then, would be part of the generation that entered the promised land and a contemporary of Rahab.[35] So there is no chronological gap between Rahab and Salmon, and if there is a gap between Salmon and Boaz, Matthew did not create it but found it in his sources (1 Chr 2:11; Ruth 4:20–21). Indeed, if Matthew detected a chronological gap (i.e., omitted generations) in the genealogies of Chronicles and Ruth, he may have felt more at liberty to omit generations of his own (see below).

The question of sources, however, remains: Where did Matthew get his information about Rahab? It is possible that he found

---

[32] Brown, *Birth of the Messiah*; Raymond E. Brown, "*Rachab* in Matt 1:5 Probably Is Rahab of Jericho," *Bib* 63.1 (1982): 79–80; Bauckham, "Tamar's Ancestry," 321; Jason B. Hood, *The Messiah, His Brothers, and the Nations (Matthew 1.1–17)*, LNTS 441 (T&T Clark, 2011), 106; Erik Waaler, *The Use of the Old Testament in Matthew 1–4*, WUNT 2/595 (Mohr Siebeck, 2023), 136.

[33] Before Salmon: Davies and Allison, *Matthew*, 1:173; Keener, *Matthew*, 79n19. Before Boaz: Brown, *Birth of the Messiah*, 60; Jane Schaberg, *The Illegitimacy of Jesus: A Feminist Theological Interpretation of the Infancy Narratives* (Harper & Row, 1987), 25.

[34] Davies and Allison, *Matthew*, 1:173.

[35] Brown, "*Rachab*"; Bauckham, "Tamar's Ancestry," 322; Nolland, *Matthew*, 78.

it in Chronicles. Richard Bauckham has proposed that Matthew found the basis for Rahab's marriage to Salmon in 1 Chronicles 2:54–55, which refers "both to Salma (שלמא, as in 2:11, 51) and to Rechab (רכב, which could be transliterated Ῥαχαβ, as in Matt. 1:5)."[36] Bauckham notes that the Targum to Ruth 4:20 identifies the Salma of 1 Chronicles 2:11 (LXX Salmon) with the Salma of 2:51, 54, and he shows how a Jewish exegete such as Matthew might have derived the idea that Rahab married Salma from 1 Chronicles 2:54–55.[37] Bauckham's reconstruction is necessarily tentative since we do not know precisely what Hebrew text Matthew would have had in front of him or how he would have interpreted it. Yet it is plausible, especially given how extensively Matthew draws on Chronicles elsewhere in his genealogy.[38] But suppose Bauckham is wrong: it is unlikely that Matthew simply imagined Rahab into Jesus's genealogy. Part 1 has shown that ancient biographers used sources for their birth material, and Matthew's use of Chronicles and Ruth in the genealogy suggests that he is no exception to this rule. As Joel Kennedy notes, "Arguing that Matthew fabricates ancestors when he has been shown to closely utilize sources otherwise is problematic and difficult to maintain exegetically."[39] Therefore, if Matthew did not draw his information about Rahab from 1 Chronicles 2:54–55 (as Bauckham argues), the most logical conclusion is that he found it in a nonbiblical source.[40]

---

[36] Bauckham, "Tamar's Ancestry," 325.

[37] Bauckham, "Tamar's Ancestry," 325–29.

[38] In support of Bauckham, see Joel Kennedy, *The Recapitulation of Israel: Use of Israel's History in Matthew 1:1–4:11*, WUNT 2/57 (Mohr Siebeck, 2008), 91.

[39] Kennedy, *Recapitulation*, 91.

[40] Rabbinic literature portrays Rahab as the wife of Joshua (b. Meg. 14b–15a; Eccl. Rab. 8:10 §1) and even discusses Rahab's children (b. Meg. 14b–15a; Sifre Num. 78; Num. Rab. 8.9). While these specific traditions do not support Matthew's claim about Rahab, the fact that they exist suggests that Matthew may have had access to other nonbiblical traditions about Rahab. Strack and Billerbeck rightly comment on Matt 1:5, "Existing traditions indicate that Rahab was not counted among the ancestresses of the Davidic house. Since Matt 1:5 nevertheless indicates

Omissions

Matthew omits several generations that Chronicles includes: three generations between Joram and Uzziah (Ahaziah, Joash, and Amaziah), one between Josiah and Jechoniah (Jehoiakim),[41] and perhaps others after Zerubbabel, the last biblical figure in the genealogy.[42] Matthew's omissions have led some interpreters to charge him with making either an intentional or an unintentional error. Robert Miller, for example, asks, "Did Matthew rig the numbers by deliberately deleting four generations? Or did he omit them accidentally . . . ?"[43]

The problem with such an either-or, however, is that it ignores an important third option—namely, that Matthew omitted these generations intentionally but was operating within Jewish genealogical conventions in doing so. The Old

---

this . . . another older tradition must have existed" (*Commentary on the New Testament*, 1:25).

[41] Matthew says, "Josiah [was] the father of Jechoniah and his brothers" (Matt 1:11). Yet 1 Chr 3:16 describes Jechoniah as having only one brother, Zedekiah. One solution is to interpret "brothers" figuratively as referring to Jechoniah's fellow Jews (Gundry, *Matthew*, 17; Hood, *Messiah, His Brothers, and the Nations*, 76–86). However, Bryan rightly notes that "this reading does not explain how Jeconiah's brothers can be regarded as descendants of Josiah, which is what the genealogy seems to require" ("Missing Generation," 304). A more compelling explanation is that Matthew, based on 2 Chr 36:10 where Jechoniah's uncle Zedekiah is referred to as his "brother" (cf. 2 Kgs 24:7; Jer 37:1), uses "brothers" to refer to Jechoniah's father and two uncles, who all reigned over Judah and went into exile (Bryan, "Missing Generation," 304–7). Bryan notes that such genealogical compression is not without precedent (307), citing Ezra 8:18–19; 1 Chr 15:5–10. See also James T. Sparks, *The Chronicler's Genealogies: Towards an Understanding of 1 Chronicles 1–9*, Academia Biblica (SBL, 2008), 105–7; Robert R. Wilson, *Genealogy and History in the Biblical World* (Yale UP, 1977), 48–54.

[42] Matthew does not include any of the descendants of Zerubbabel listed in Chronicles (1 Chr 3:19–24). And whereas Luke has nineteen generations between Zerubbabel and Jesus, Matthew has only ten. It therefore seems likely that Matthew has omitted one or more generations listed in Chronicles. See further Bryan, "Missing Generation," 309–10.

[43] Robert J. Miller, *Born Divine: The Births of Jesus and Other Sons of God* (Polebridge, 2003), 81–82.

Testament and Jewish literature regularly omit generations when recounting genealogical information. The book of Joshua, for example, describes Achan as "son of Carmi son of Zabdi son of Zerah" (7:1) and then a few verses later as "Achan son of Zerah" (7:24). Similarly, whereas Genesis 11:10–26 lists eight generations between Shem and Abraham, the Apocalypse of Abraham gives only four.[44] Other genealogies give an unusually small number of generations for the time elapsed, suggesting that generations have been omitted. For example, we noted above that the time between Salmon and Boaz may suggest that Chronicles and Ruth have omitted generations, and it is possible that they omit other generations as well.[45] Such examples could be easily multiplied.[46] It seems that the goal of Jewish genealogies was not necessarily to list every generation but to trace a legitimate line of descent. The rabbinic saying "Grandchildren are reckoned as children" captures the

---

[44] Apocalypse of Abraham title. The missing generations are Shelah, Eber, Peleg, and Reu (Gen 11:12–18).

[45] For a concise account of the chronological gaps in the genealogy of Ruth 4:18–22 see Robert L. Hubbard Jr., *The Book of Ruth*, NICOT (Eerdmans, 1988), 284. Hubbard suggests that the gaps most likely occur between Hezron and Amminadab and between Nahshon and Boaz. On chronological gaps in 1 Chr 2:1–17, see Roddy Braun, *1 Chronicles*, WBC 14 (Word, 1986), 34.

[46] For omissions made clear by comparison see 1 Chr 6:7–9 (cf. Ezra 7:3); Ezra 5:1 (cf. Zech 1:1). For omissions implied by the time elapsed see Exod 6:16–20 / 1 Chr 7:22–27 (very different numbers of generations between Moses/Levi and Joshua/Ephraim); 1 Chr 6:33–43 (twenty-one ancestors for Heman and fourteen for Asaph over the same period); Josephus, *Life* 3–5. On Josephus see Jeremias, *Jerusalem in the Time of Jesus*, 214n212. For the view that this passage from Josephus contains a scribal or authorial error rather than an omission, see Emil Schürer, *The History of the Jewish People in the Age of Jesus Christ (175 B.C.–A.D. 135)*, ed. Géza Vermes and Fergus Millar, 3 vols. (T&T Clark, 1973–87), 1:46n3. I owe these references and those above to Wilson, *Genealogy and History*, 197n127; Brown, *Birth of the Messiah*, 75n36; Davies and Allison, *Matthew*, 1:176–77. Wilson also shows that the omission of generations ("telescoping") occurs in oral genealogies and in ancient Mesopotamian and Egyptian genealogies (*Genealogy and History*, 33–36, 65–69, 115–18, 126).

spirit well.[47] To say "*X* was the father of *Y*" in such a context would mean that *X* was the ancestor of *Y*, not necessarily that he had personally sired (or adopted) him.

Matthew's omissions, then, pose no difficulty for the idea that he has composed the genealogy with historiographic intent. Yet—some might say—the omissions themselves are only the tip of the iceberg. The effect of the omissions is to create the three series of fourteen generations that Matthew refers to at the end of the genealogy (Matt 1:17). Furthermore, one generation appears to be missing from the final group. Do such factors not suggest that Matthew intends the genealogy to be something other than historical? Let us consider the 3×14 structure first: Matthew may have omitted generations for a variety of reasons including but not limited to the realization of his 3×14 structure.[48] Such motives, however, are compatible with historiographic intent if exercised within the appropriate boundaries. And as we have seen

---

[47] See t. Yevam. 8.4; b. Yevam. 62b, 70a; b. Qidd. 4a. The translation here is from b. Yevam. 62b in Hersh Goldwurm, Yisroel Simcha Schorr, and Chaim Malinowitz, eds., *Talmud Bavli: The Schottenstein Edition*, Artscroll (Mesorah, 1990–2005). In b. Yevam. 62b, the principle is deduced from 1 Chr 2:21, Judg 5:14, and Ps 60:7 (MT 60:9). The rabbinic texts cited do not apply the saying to omitted generations in genealogies, but it seems open to such an application. A note on b. Yevam. 70a in the Schottenstein edition, for example, paraphrases the principle as follows: "one's legal relationship with his grandchildren is similar to his legal relationship with his children" (see n. 15). Numerous scholars have also seen the saying as relevant—e.g., Strack and Billerbeck, *Commentary on the New Testament*, 1:34; Brown, *Birth of the Messiah*, 75n36; Laurentin, *Truth of Christmas*, 351; Davies and Allison, *Matthew*, 1:177.

[48] Some interpreters have argued, for example, that Matthew omits Ahaziah, Joash, and Amaziah because of God's curse on the house of Ahab (1 Kgs 21:21–24, 29; cf. Exod 20:5). See Thomas C. Oden, ed., *Incomplete Commentary on Matthew (Opus Imperfectum)*, trans. James A. Kellerman, 2 vols., Ancient Christian Texts (IVP Academic, 2010), 1:16; G. Kuhn, "Die Geschlechtsregister Jesu bei Lukas und Matthäus, nach ihrer Herkunft untersucht," *ZNW* 22.2 (1923): 221n1; Jacques Masson, *Jesus, fils de David, dans les généalogies de saint Matthieu et de saint Luc* (Téqui, 1982), 116–24; Davies and Allison, *Matthew*, 1:176; John Nolland, "Jechoniah and His Brothers (Matthew 1:11)," *BBR* 7 (1997): 172; Nolland, *Matthew*, 80. I owe these references to Susan Rieske. For an alternative view, see Bryan, "Missing Generation," 308.

above, Matthew's omissions are consistent with Jewish genealogical conventions. Matthew may intend his genealogy to be more than a mere list of Jesus's ancestors, but that does not make it less than historical. What about the missing generation? Numerous scholars have argued that it is not missing or that Matthew made a mistake (a problem for the truth of his account, but not its historiographic intent).[49] But suppose the worst: Matthew mentions fourteen generations, knows there are only thirteen listed, and has a solution in mind that he expects the reader to discern using the resources of his Gospel. What of it? Scholars have offered a variety of solutions to the missing generation, but these generally do not involve anything ahistorical (e.g., inserting Judas Maccabeus as one of Jesus's ancestors).[50] Therefore, neither the 3×14 schema nor the missing generation provide grounds for doubting Matthew's historiographic intent.

Summary

The genealogy, then, turns out to provide strong support for Matthew's historiographic intent. Matthew draws most of his genealogy from Chronicles and Ruth, and his differences with these sources fall within the acceptable range of flexibility for Jewish genealogies. The nonbiblical source(s) that Matthew relies on are unfortunately lost to us, but the use of sources in the birth material of ancient biographies and Matthew's own use of Chronicles and Ruth suggests that he had additional sources and employed them responsibly. Neither the differences in names, nor the presence of Rahab, nor the omitted generations provide any evidence for legendary intent. The close dependence on sources that we observe in the genealogy poses a significant problem for the claim that Matthew intends his birth material to be ahistorical.

---

[49] For a survey, see Bryan, "Missing Generation," 296–98.
[50] E.g., Krister Stendahl, "Matthew," in *Peake's Commentary on the Bible*, ed. Matthew Black (Thomas Nelson, 1962), 771; Herman C. Waetjen, "The Genealogy as the Key to the Gospel According to Matthew," *JBL* 95.2 (1976): 209–15; Bryan, "Missing Generation"; Bryan, "Onomastics"; Susan M. Rieske, *"This Generation" and the Elect in the Book of Matthew: A Tale of Two Families*, LNTS 677 (T&T Clark, 2026), 179–91.

Birth Narrative

It is well known that Matthew quotes and alludes to the Old Testament repeatedly in his birth narrative. Interpreters often leverage Matthew's use of the Old Testament (or Jewish exegetical traditions) to argue that he intends the birth narrative to be something less than historical. In a monograph on Matthew's formula quotations, for example, George Soares Prabhu asserts that "the story of the massacre of the infants of Bethlehem (2,16–18) seems to derive wholly from the OT and rabbinic traditions of the birth of Moses."[51] He goes on to say regarding Matthew's birth narrative as a whole,

> One might, in fact, query the usefulness or even the legitimacy of asking such historical questions of narratives which, quite obviously, are not intended as history; and whose historicity is largely irrelevant to the point they intend to make.[52]

Our study above, however, has shown that it is less than obvious that Matthew intends the birth narrative to be ahistorical. If (1) ancient biographers composed their birth material with historiographic intent and (2) Matthew uses sources for the genealogy in his biography of Jesus, we have good reason to think that Matthew intends his birth narrative to be historical. But there is more: Matthew's use of the Old Testament—the very datum that supposedly indicates his legendary intent—actually provides evidence for historiographic intent.[53]

---

[51] Soares Prabhu, *Formula Quotations*, 299.
[52] Soares Prabhu, *Formula Quotations*, 299.
[53] Interpreters sometimes describe the Gospel birth narratives (especially that of Matthew) as "midrash." Some simply mean by this that the evangelists are using Jewish exegetical techniques; others use the term to describe the genre of the birth narratives, with the implication that they are meant to be ahistorical. The latter use is, in my view, incorrect, but here I focus on the more fundamental question: whether Matthew's use of the Old Testament in his birth narrative indicates an ahistorical intent. For a summary of the discussion on the birth narratives and midrash, see Brown, *Birth of the Messiah*, 557–63, 577–79, 598–600.

Quotations

Matthew quotes the Old Testament five times in his birth narrative, in each case introducing the quotation with a fulfillment formula (1:22-23; 2:5-6, 15, 17-18, 23).[54] The key question is whether Matthew fabricated the story based on the quotations or added the quotations to existing narrative traditions about Jesus.[55] The latter view is more likely for at least three reasons.

First, the quotations depend on the story. The fabrication hypothesis assumes that Matthew started with the Old Testament texts and created a story to fit them. But why *these* texts?[56] As R. T. France notes,

> Most of them are not texts which would naturally suggest themselves to someone looking for messianic proof texts. . . . The only plausible reason for Matthew's choosing such an improbable set of texts is that the traditions he was relating already contained specific features which called them to mind, viz. a "virgin" conception, a return from Egypt, the loss of children in Bethlehem, and Jesus' home in the obscure village of Nazareth, for each of which Matthew then seeks a scriptural precedent.[57]

Matthew has also adapted the wording of some quotations to fit the narrative context.[58] He has altered Micah 5:2 substantially, and "something so dreadful has apparently happened to whatever text lies behind [Matthew] 2.23 that no one can now be sure what

---

[54] For discussion of Matthew's formula quotations, see Soares Prabhu, *Formula Quotations*, 18-41. Soares Prabhu identifies eleven formula quotations; the ones outside the birth narrative are Matt 4:14-16; 8:17; 12:17-21; 13:35; 21:4-5; 27:9-10.

[55] Cf. Brown, *Birth of the Messiah*, 99.

[56] R. T. France, "The Formula-Quotations of Matthew 2 and the Problem of Communication," *NTS* 27 (1981): 236; idem, "Scripture, Tradition and History in the Infancy Narratives of Matthew," in *Gospel Perspectives*, ed. R. T. France and David Wenham (JSOT, 1981), 251.

[57] R. T. France, "The Birth of Jesus," in *Handbook for the Study of the Historical Jesus*, ed. Tom Holmén and Stanley E. Porter (Leiden: Brill, 2011), 2369. Cf. M. J. Down, "The Matthaean Birth Narratives: Matthew 1:18-2:23," *ExpTim* 90.2 (1978): 52; Keener, *Matthew*, 82.

[58] France, "Formula-Quotations," 236; idem, "Scripture, Tradition and History," 251-52; idem, "Birth of Jesus," 2370.

it was."[59] Such changes would be unnecessary if Matthew had created the story to fit the quotations. Therefore, both the texts Matthew quotes and the form in which he quotes them suggest that the story gave rise to the quotations, not the quotations to the story.

Second, the story does not depend on the quotations. If one omits the quotations and their introductory formulas, a coherent narrative remains.[60] The narrative also goes beyond the quotations in significant ways. Brown observes that "it is difficult to imagine how the narrative ever could have been made up by reflection" on the citations since they "deal with aspects that are only minor in the story line."[61] These observations do not square with the hypothesis that Matthew created the story to fit the quotations, but they make good sense if he added the quotations to existing traditions.

Third, the concept of fulfillment implies actual events. France rightly asks, "What would be the point of proclaiming 'then was fulfilled . . . ,' if nothing in fact happened 'then,' nor at all outside the author's own mind? . . . At least for the person who makes the claim, the 'fulfilling' events must be factual, otherwise the argument is meaningless."[62] Matthew's use of formula quotations elsewhere bears this out, for he generally adds these quotations to stories that he has received from Mark.[63] By claiming that the

---

[59] France, "Formula-Quotations," 236.

[60] Brown, *Birth of the Messiah*, 100; Down, "Birth Narratives," 52; Davies and Allison, *Matthew*, 1:191. Brown treats Matt 2:5b–6 (quoting Mic 5:2) as an exception. However, the quotation is not strictly necessary for the story; it only serves as the substantiation for chief priests and scribes' declaration that the Messiah was to be born "in Bethlehem of Judea" (Matt 2:5a).

[61] Brown, *Birth of the Messiah*, 100. Brown makes this statement about the citations in Matt 2:13–23 but goes on to say the same about the other citations.

[62] France, "Scripture, Tradition and History," 252.

[63] See Matt 4:12–16 (cf. Mark 1:14); Matt 8:16–17 (cf. Mark 1:32–34); Matt 13:34–35 (Mark 4:33–34); Matt 21:1–6 (cf. Mark 11:1–4). I owe the basic insight to Brown, who notes that "we have other instances of Matthew's appending formula citations to stories that already came to him"

events of his narrative fulfill the Old Testament quotations, then, Matthew implies that he believes the events really occurred.

The idea that Matthew invented the narrative based on the quotations becomes even less probable when we study the individual quotations. Space does not permit us to examine all Matthew's quotations in detail, but we will consider one that has provoked significant interest—Isaiah 7:14, which Matthew connects to the virginal conception (Matt 1:22–23). Beyond the general points noted above, two further factors suggest that Matthew did not fabricate the virginal conception based on Isaiah 7:14. First, Isaiah 7:14 does not require a virginal conception, and so far as we know early Judaism did not understand it to predict one.[64] Second, the virginal conception complicates Jesus's Davidic lineage by requiring Joseph to adopt him into the Davidic line.[65] Early Judaism did have a concept and practice of adoption, so the virginal conception does not present an insurmountable obstacle

---

(*Birth of the Messiah*, 100). Brown cites Matt 4:12–16 and Matt 27:9–10 (cf. Acts 1:18–19) as examples (see 100n7 for the latter).

[64] Strack and Billerbeck, *Commentary on the New Testament*, 1:55–56; J. Gresham Machen, *The Virgin Birth of Christ*, 2nd ed. (Harper & Row, 1932), 293–97; John McHugh, *The Mother of Jesus in the New Testament* (Doubleday, 1975), 282–83; Brown, *Birth of the Messiah*, 149; Vermes, *Jesus the Jew*, 215; Gundry, *Matthew*, 25; Laurentin, *Truth of Christmas*, 411; Davies and Allison, *Matthew*, 1:214; Greg Rhodea, "Did Matthew Conceive a Virgin? Isaiah 7:14 and the Birth of Jesus," *JETS* 56.1 (2013): 64–70. Some interpreters claim that the use of παρθένος in Isa 7:14 LXX would have led Matthew to fabricate the virginal conception—e.g., J. K. Elliott, *Questioning Christian Origins* (SCM, 1982), 10; Bart D. Ehrman, *Jesus, Interrupted: Revealing the Hidden Contradictions in the Bible (and Why We Don't Know About Them)* (HarperOne, 2009), 74. Against this view, see Rhodea, "Did Matthew Conceive a Virgin?" 67–68.

[65] Machen, *Virgin Birth*, 285; McHugh, *Mother of Jesus*, 276–77, 283, 320–21; Laurentin, *Truth of Christmas*, 344–45, 416; France, "Birth of Jesus," 2371n27; Rhodea, "Did Matthew Conceive a Virgin?" 72–76. McHugh goes too far when he says that the virginal conception "would entail denying that [Jesus] was truly 'of the seed of David'" (*Mother of Jesus*, 320–21), for lineal "seed" language is used in a nonbiological sense in the Old Testament and early Judaism (e.g., Gen 38:8–9; Deut 25:5–6 LXX; Jub. 41.4–5; Testament of Zebulun 3.4; Philo, *Unchangeable* 16; *Posterity* 180).

to Jesus being a legitimate son of David.⁶⁶ Nonetheless, it is hard to imagine Matthew fabricating a virginal conception that would complicate Jesus's Davidic lineage based on an Old Testament text that did not require a virginal conception. As France says, "One does not invent inconvenient facts in order to defend them."⁶⁷ The most likely explanation for why Matthew included the virginal conception is that it was part of the tradition he received.

In sum, the Old Testament quotations in Matthew's birth narrative provide no evidence that Matthew has fabricated material. On the contrary, they indicate that he drew on existing traditions (i.e., sources) and regards his story as historical. Matthew 1:18–2:23 appears to be "tradition scripturalized" rather than "prophecy historicized."⁶⁸

Indirect References

Scholars have also questioned Matthew's historiographic intent based on indirect references to the Old Testament (or Jewish exegetical traditions) in the birth narrative. We will first survey the major references that have been proposed and then consider their significance.

Interpreters have noted numerous connections between Matthew's birth narrative and traditions about Moses. The angel's command to Joseph to return to Israel "for those who were seeking the child's life are dead" (τεθνήκασιν γὰρ οἱ ζητοῦντες τὴν ψυχὴν τοῦ παιδίου; Matt 2:20) clearly alludes to Exodus 4:19 LXX, where God commands Moses to return to Egypt "for all those who were seeking your life are dead" (τεθνήκασιν γὰρ πάντες οἱ

---

⁶⁶ Caleb T. Friedeman, "Jesus' Davidic Lineage and the Case for Jewish Adoption," *NTS* 66 (2020): 249–67.

⁶⁷ France, "Birth of Jesus," 2371. Cf. Carson, *Matthew*, 72.

⁶⁸ I owe the expressions to Mark S. Goodacre, "Prophecy Historicized or Tradition Scripturalized? Reflections on the Origins of the Passion Narrative," in *The New Testament and the Church: Essays in Honour of John Muddiman*, ed. John Barton and Peter Groves, LNTS 532 (T&T Clark, 2016), 37–51. Yet whereas Goodacre seems to find some prophecy historicized in the passion narratives (51n46), the evidence presented here suggests that Matthew's birth narrative is thoroughly tradition scripturalized.

ζητοῦντές σου τὴν ψυχήν).⁶⁹ Scholars have proposed other parallels to biblical and extrabiblical traditions about Moses as well. The biblical parallels are as follows:⁷⁰

- Moses and Jesus both flee to another country from a king who is seeking to kill them (Exod 2:15; Matt 2:13–14).⁷¹
- Pharaoh and Herod both order the slaughter of children (Exod 1:22; Matt 2:16).
- Pharaoh and Herod both die (Exod 2:23; Matt 2:19).
- Moses and Joseph both take their families back to their countries of origin when God commands them to do so (Exod 4:19–20; Matt 2:19–21).

The extrabiblical parallels depend significantly on how far one is willing to reach chronologically and conceptually. The following, however, date to the first century AD or earlier and are often noted.⁷²

- Amram (Moses's father) and Joseph both receive a dream from God that reveals what to do regarding the birth of the child.⁷³
- It is said that the child will save God's people.⁷⁴
- Pharaoh and Herod are both warned about the birth of a Hebrew baby who poses a threat to their reign.⁷⁵
- The warning comes from one or more scribes.⁷⁶

---

⁶⁹ The translation of Exod 4:19 LXX is my own.
⁷⁰ The list below is adapted from Brown, *Birth of the Messiah*, 113.
⁷¹ There may also be an allusion here—compare Matt 2:13–14 (ζητεῖν ... τοῦ ἀπολέσαι ... ἀνεχώρησεν) with Exod 2:15 (ἐζήτει ἀνελεῖν ... ἀνεχώρησεν).
⁷² E.g., Brown, *Birth of the Messiah*, 114–15; Davies and Allison, *Matthew*, 1:192–93; Dale C. Allison Jr., *The New Moses: A Matthean Typology* (Fortress, 1993), 144–45; Hagner, *Matthew 1–13*, 34.
⁷³ Josephus, *Ant.* 2.212–216; Matt 1:18–21.
⁷⁴ LAB 9.10 (cf. Mekh. R. Ish. Shir. 10.58–61; b. Sotah 12b–13a; b. Meg. 14a); Matt 1:21.
⁷⁵ Josephus, *Ant.* 2.205–209; Tg. Ps.-J. Exod 1:15; Matt 2:2–12, 16–17.
⁷⁶ Josephus, *Ant.* 2.205, 234 (one of the sacred scribes); Matt 2:4–6 (multiple scribes).

Scholars have also proposed indirect references beyond the ones to Moses. It is not possible to discuss all these here, but we may note three that have garnered significant support. First, interpreters have suggested a variety of connections between Matthew's magi (Matt 2:1–2) and Balaam (Num 22–24).[77] Balaam comes from the east (Num 23:7; cf. Matt 2:1), prophesies about a star that symbolizes a messianic figure (Num 24:7), and is called a magus by Philo (*Moses* 1.276). Brown goes so far as to say that the story of Balaam in Numbers 22–24 provided the "immediate inspiration" for Matthew 2:1–2.[78] The second and third allusions that scholars have proposed are also connected to the magi. Matthew says, "On entering the house, they saw the child with Mary his mother; and they knelt down and paid him homage [προσεκύνησαν αὐτῷ]. Then, opening their treasure-chests, they offered [προσήνεγκαν] him gifts of gold [χρυσόν], frankincense [λίβανον], and myrrh" (Matt 2:11). Some have proposed that Matthew here alludes to Psalm 71:10–11 LXX (MT 72:10–11), where kings bring gifts to God's king and pay homage (προσκυνέω) to him, and to Isaiah 60:6 LXX, where gentiles bring gold (χρυσός) and frankincense (λίβανος) to Jerusalem.[79]

One might question the validity of some of the references above, but let us suppose that Matthew intended all of them. What do they tell us about his historiographic intent (or lack thereof)? They certainly indicate that Matthew wants to show how Jesus fulfills the Old Testament. But do they demonstrate that Matthew intends his story to be less historical than the rest of his Gospel? This seems unlikely for at least three reasons. First, as noted above, Matthew's repeated claim that the events of his narrative fulfill the Old Testament implies that he believes they really happened. Second, the differences between Matthew's birth narrative and the texts and traditions noted above suggest

---

[77] Gundry, *Use of the Old Testament*, 128–29; Brown, *Birth of the Messiah*, 117, 193–94; Gundry, *Matthew*, 27; Davies and Allison, *Matthew*, 1:234–35.

[78] Brown, *Birth of the Messiah*, 117.

[79] Gundry, *Use of the Old Testament*, 129–30; Brown, *Birth of the Messiah*, 187–88; Gundry, *Matthew*, 32; Davies and Allison, *Matthew*, 1:250.

a historiographic rather than a legendary intent. For every similarity noted above, there are multiple differences that imply that Matthew is conforming the texts and traditions in question to an existing story. Yes, Moses and Jesus both flee the country from an evil king, but whereas Moses flees from Egypt as an adult, Jesus flees to Egypt as an infant. Why, unless Matthew had a story before him in which Jesus and his family did just this? Yes, Pharaoh and Herod both order the slaughter of children, but whereas Pharaoh issues this command concerning male newborns before Moses's birth, Herod issues it concerning male children two years old and under after Jesus's birth.[80] Why, unless Matthew had traditions that indicated as much? And so on. It is telling that even Luz, who sees little historical value in Matthew's birth narrative, comments, "The Moses traditions have enriched our story. At the same time, however, our story [Matt 2:13–23] shows itself to be so independent of them . . . that it in no way can be understood as simply an imitation of the Moses Haggadah."[81] The same may be said for the allusions to Numbers, Psalms, and Isaiah. Matthew has certainly told his story in a way that reveals how Jesus fulfills the Old Testament, but a close examination of his indirect references suggests that he has done so with historiographic intent. Finally, Matthew alludes to the Old Testament throughout his Gospel, so the presence of Old Testament allusions alone cannot indicate that Matthew's birth narrative is less historical than the rest of the First Gospel.

Summary

Matthew's use of the Old Testament (and perhaps Jewish exegetical traditions) in the birth narrative therefore supports, rather than undermines, his historiographic intent. Matthew certainly intends to show how Jesus has fulfilled the Old Testament, but he seems to do so with historiographic intent, conforming his Old

---

[80] The plural τοὺς παῖδας (Matt 2:16) could refer to children in general (so NRSV), but Matt 2:1–6 suggests that male children are in view here.

[81] Luz, *Matthew 1–7*, 104. Cf. Hagner, *Matthew 1–13*, 35.

Testament quotations and allusions to his traditions about Jesus rather than fabricating a story to fit the Old Testament references.

Use of Mark

We may also gain insight by comparing Matthew's use of sources in the birth narrative to his use of Mark elsewhere.[82] Three brief points will suffice.

First, Matthew's use of Mark shows that for him a lack of source-citation does not necessarily imply a lack of sources. While Matthew uses Mark throughout his Gospel, he never cites Mark as a source. Indeed, to my knowledge, Matthew never explicitly cites any source in his Gospel. The fact that Matthew does not *cite* sources in the birth narrative does not mean that he does not *have* sources. On the contrary, not citing sources seems to be Matthew's normal practice.

Second, Matthew's use of Mark provides a standard by which to measure his use of sources in the birth narrative. For example, if Matthew were to use sources in the birth narrative with far greater flexibility than he uses Mark elsewhere, this would suggest that he intends the birth narrative to be less historical. We can unfortunately perform such a comparison only on the genealogy, the only part of Matthew's birth narrative for which we have literary sources. However, the changes Matthew has made to his sources for the genealogy do not seem to go beyond the sorts of changes he makes to Mark elsewhere. Matthew, for example, reorders, compresses, simplifies, expands, and paraphrases elements in Mark.[83] The changes we have observed in the genealogy fall well within this range of flexibility.

Third, interpreters tend to assume that where Matthew goes substantially beyond Mark, he does so based on another source, whether that be Q, another literary source, or an oral source. I

---

[82] With most scholars today, I hold that Mark is the earliest of the Synoptic Gospels and that Matthew used Mark as a source.

[83] Davies and Allison, *Matthew*, 1:73–74; Michael R. Licona, *Why Are There Differences in the Gospels? What We Can Learn from Ancient Biography* (Oxford UP, 2017), 112–202.

suggest that it is only fair to grant Matthew the same benefit of the doubt for the birth narrative.

Summary

A close reading therefore shows that while Matthew does not cite sources for his birth narrative, he does have sources and uses them responsibly by ancient standards. Matthew draws extensively on biblical sources for his genealogy, and his differences with these sources fall within the acceptable range of flexibility for Jewish genealogies. He has shaped his Old Testament references to fit an existing story, rather than creating a story to fit his references. And his use of Mark elsewhere further supports the idea that he has sources for the birth narrative and has used them according to similar standards. The use of sources that we observe in Matthew 1–2 not only fails to support a legendary intent; it provides strong evidence for historiographic intent.

TRANSPARENCY, EVALUATION, AND DISTANCING

Unlike our biographers in part 1, Matthew does not employ *transparency*, *evaluation*, or *distancing* in his birth narrative. Why? Perhaps because he was not aware of these historiographic features. Yet this seems unlikely, given how frequently they occur in ancient historiography and how commonsense they are. (One does not need to have read extensively in Thucydides or Polybius, for example, to evaluate a historical claim.) The idea that Matthew was ignorant of these features becomes even less likely when we recognize that he probably employs two of them elsewhere. Matthew recounts that after Jesus's resurrection, the chief priests and elders bribe the soldiers who guarded Jesus's tomb to say that Jesus's disciples came at night and stole his body while they were asleep (Matt 28:11–13). Matthew then comments, "So they took the money and did as they were directed. And this story is still told among the Jews to this day" (28:15). Here we seem to have both *transparency* and *evaluation*: Matthew is noting an alternative account for the empty tomb and passing a decidedly negative judgment on it. Matthew alludes to the motive for his evaluation when he notes that the soldiers' tale "is still told among the Jews to this day."[84]

The absence of *transparency*, *evaluation*, and *distancing* in the birth narrative therefore seems to be a conscious absence: Matthew is likely aware of these historiographic features but does not employ them. What should we make of this? Let us take the features one at a time. *Transparency* would have allowed Matthew to acknowledge any alternative accounts of Jesus's origins. However, *transparency* was not obligatory, so a lack of it does not necessarily indicate a lack of alternative accounts. All we can reasonably conclude is that if Matthew knew of other accounts of Jesus's origins, he did not find them important enough to mention. *Evaluation* would have given Matthew a way to pass judgment on the reliability of the traditions he relates. The fact that he does not utilize evaluation suggests that he regards the information he recounts as reliable. *Distancing* would have allowed Matthew to separate his authorial reputation from certain historical claims. The lack of *distancing* in Matthew 1–2 is quite striking, given that Matthew recounts multiple supernatural events—not least a virginal conception. If Matthew had doubted the truth of any of the miracles he narrates, he could easily have distanced himself from them. Overall, then, the absence of *transparency*, *evaluation*, and *distancing* (particularly the latter two) in Matthew 1–2 suggests that Matthew is very confident in the truth of his account, supernatural events notwithstanding.

SUPERNATURAL ELEMENTS

Matthew recounts multiple supernatural events in his birth narrative:

- The virginal conception
- The star that guides the magi to Jesus
- Three dreams in which an angel appears to Joseph
- A dream that warns the magi not to return to Herod

---

[84] Justin Martyr indicates that this story was still being told in his day (*Dialogue with Trypho* 108).

Scholars sometimes assume that these weigh against the historiographic intent of the story. However, part 1 has shown that some ancient biographers regarded supernatural events as a legitimate part of history and included them throughout their biographies. Matthew seems to affirm the legitimacy of supernatural events as well, for he recounts many of them beyond the birth narrative. These include:

- Jesus's baptism, where the Spirit of God appears and God speaks (3:16–17)
- Jesus's temptation (4:1–11)
- Healings (e.g., 4:23–24; 8:5–13, 14–17)
- Exorcisms (e.g., 4:24; 8:16, 28–34)
- Nature miracles (8:23–27; 14:22–33)
- Feedings of the five thousand and four thousand (14:13–21; 15:32–39)
- Jesus's transfiguration (17:1–8)
- Jesus's resurrection (28:1–10, 16–20)

One might, of course, protest that the miracles in the birth narrative are more numerous or significant than those in the rest of the Gospel. However, this does not seem to be the case. With respect to frequency, the Gospel of Matthew contains many two-chapter sections that have at least as many miracles as Matthew 1–2 (e.g., Matt 3–4, 8–9, 14–15). With respect to significance, the virginal conception is no more miraculous than Jesus's resurrection.[85] The miracles in the birth narrative therefore provide no evidence that Matthew intends this material to be ahistorical.

TIME ELAPSED

The time elapsed between Jesus's birth and Matthew's writing provides important insights regarding Matthew's ability to actualize his historiographic intent. Jesus was probably born around 5 BC (before Herod the Great's death in 4 BC).[86] Schol-

---

[85] France, *Matthew*, 44.
[86] John P. Meier, *A Marginal Jew: Rethinking the Historical Jesus*, 5 vols., ABRL (Doubleday, 1991–2016), 1:229, 375–76 (7–4 BC); N. T. Wright, *The New Testament and the People of God*, Christian Origins

ars have proposed a variety of dates for the Gospel of Matthew. Jonathan Bernier divides these into "lower," "middle," and "higher" chronologies, with the middle being the majority view.[87] Lower chronologies date Matthew to AD 45–59, middle chronologies to AD 70–75, and higher chronologies to AD 130.[88] Let us take the middle (majority) view as our starting point: From this perspective, Matthew would be writing 74–79 years after Jesus's birth.[89] Part 1 has shown us that this is nothing short of exceptional. Cornelius Nepos, Philo, Plutarch, and Suetonius are generally writing hundreds of years after the births of their subjects. Of the biographies analyzed in part 1, only five stand so close to the subject's birth:

- Nepos, *Atticus* (76 years)
- Plutarch, *Otho* (69 years)
- Suetonius, *Domitian* (69 years)
- Suetonius, *Persius* (72 years)
- Suetonius, *Lucan* (67 years)[90]

Plutarch's *Otho*, however, does not have birth material. So of the ninety-five biographies analyzed in part 1, only four are as close to the events they report about the subject's birth and childhood as Matthew is. Therefore, even on a middle chronology, Matthew is breathing rarefied air when it comes to his proximity to the events he reports. And if a lower chronology is correct, then Matthew's proximity to the birth of his subject is not only elite; it is unsurpassed by any biography analyzed here.[91] If Matthew wrote at any time in AD 45–59, he would be closer to Jesus's birth than

---

and the Question of God 1 (Fortress, 1992), 147 (4 BC); E. P. Sanders, *The Historical Figure of Jesus* (Penguin, 1993), 10–11 (ca. 4 BC).

[87] Jonathan Bernier, *Rethinking the Dates of the New Testament: The Evidence for Early Composition* (Baker, 2022), 3.

[88] Bernier, *Rethinking the Dates*, 3, 84, 277.

[89] Recall that there is no year zero between 1 BC and AD 1.

[90] Suetonius has three other lives that are close: *Nero* (83 years), *Titus* (81 years), and *Pliny* (82 years).

[91] For a recent defense of a lower chronology for Matthew, see Bernier, *Rethinking the Dates*, 35–84.

Nepos, Philo, Plutarch, and Suetonius are to the births of any of their subjects. Two related points arise from this basic insight.

First, Matthew would have enjoyed exceptional access to sources about Jesus's birth. He may have had access to eyewitnesses such as Jesus's mother Mary, who apparently was a member of the early church (Acts 1:14). But even if he did not, he almost certainly would have had access to individuals close to her such as Jesus's brother James. The low time elapsed also makes it improbable that Matthew's sources (oral or literary) had been corrupted by legendary accretions, as some scholars have assumed.[92] The time elapsed between Jesus's birth and Matthew's writing therefore suggests that Matthew had ample access to reliable sources about Jesus's birth.

Second, the low time elapsed may explain Matthew's confidence about the miracles he reports. We observed in part 1 that ancient biographers often employ *transparency*, *evaluation*, or *distancing* when recounting miracles (and sometimes omens). Matthew, however, reports a virginal conception, a guiding star, and multiple divinely given dreams without using any of these historiographic devices. I suggest that Matthew's proximity to the events and his consequent access to reliable sources may explain why he is so confident about the miracles that he reports.

In sum, the time elapsed suggests that Matthew had exceptional resources with which to carry out his historiographic intent. Few ancient biographers would have enjoyed Matthew's proximity to the events he reports and the sources that would have been available to him. A truly historical approach to Matthew 1–2 must therefore recognize that Matthew not only intends his birth narrative to be historical but also is elite among ancient biographers in his access to sources.

CONCLUSION

Matthew—like Nepos, Philo, Plutarch, and Suetonius—has composed his birth narrative with historiographic intent. While Matthew does not cite sources for his birth narrative, he does have

---

[92] E.g., Soares Prabhu, *Formula Quotations*, 299.

sources and appears to use them responsibly by ancient standards. The lack of *transparency, evaluation,* or *distancing* (especially the latter two) suggests that Matthew is quite confident in the reliability of his account. Matthew does recount multiple miracles in the birth narrative, but his attitude toward miracles elsewhere shows that the presence of miracles provides no evidence for ahistorical intent. Finally, the time elapsed reveals that Matthew enjoys an elite status among ancient biographers when it comes to his proximity to his subject's birth and the sources that would have been available to him. Matthew therefore both intends his birth narrative to be historical and is well-positioned to actualize his historiographic intent.

7
LUKE

The historiographic intent of Luke's birth material is even clearer than that of Matthew. As we will see below, Luke identifies his Gospel as a work of ancient historiography (Luke 1:1–4) and employs historiographic features repeatedly with reference to his birth material. Before examining the evidence for Luke's historiographic intent, however, we first need to define the boundaries of his birth material. Luke 1:5–2:52 constitutes the birth narrative proper, but Luke also includes a genealogy of Jesus amid adult material (3:23–38). Two factors suggest that we should regard the genealogy as birth material despite its position later in the Gospel. First, ancient biographies often provide an account of the subject's lineage alongside the birth narrative.[1] Second, ancient biographies include material regarding the subject's origins amid adult material.[2] It therefore seems best to treat both Luke 1:5–2:52 and 3:23–38 as birth material.

---

[1] Part 1 provides numerous examples. See further David E. Aune, *The New Testament in Its Literary Environment*, Library of Early Christianity 8 (Westminster, 1987), 32; Richard A. Burridge, *What Are the Gospels? A Comparison with Graeco-Roman Biography*, 2nd ed. (Eerdmans, 2004), 141; Gerard Mussies, "Parallels to Matthew's Version of the Pedigree of Jesus," *NovT* 28.1 (1986): 33.

[2] E.g., Suetonius, *Jul.* 56.7; *Aug.* 94.1–9; *Nero* 52; *Tib.* 14.2; 57.1.

Here I focus on the historiographic intent of Luke's birth material and intentionally leave aside truth-oriented questions about how Luke's account relates to that of Matthew or to other historical sources. Such questions are, of course, important, but it only makes sense to ask them once we have determined whether Luke has composed his account with historiographic intent.

SOURCES

Preface (Luke 1:1–4)

Luke begins his Gospel with a preface that discusses the precedent, sources, and purpose for his work.

> Since many have undertaken to compose a narrative about the things that have been fulfilled among us, just as those who from the beginning were eyewitnesses and servants of the word handed them down to us, it seemed good to me also, as one who has a thoroughly informed familiarity with all these things from the beginning, to write to you in order, most excellent Theophilus, so that you may know the certainty of the things about which you have been taught. (Luke 1:1–4)[3]

Scholars today generally agree that Luke's preface identifies his Gospel as a work of ancient historiography.[4] Clare Rothschild

---

[3] My translation. I owe the phrase "as one who has a thoroughly informed familiarity with" to David P. Moessner, *Luke the Historian of Israel's Legacy, Theologian of Israel's "Christ": A New Reading of the "Gospel Acts" of Luke*, BZNW 182 (de Gruyter, 2016), 68–107. On this interpretation of παρηκολουθηκότι ... ἀκριβῶς, see further below.

[4] Daryl D. Schmidt, "Rhetorical Influences and Genre: Luke's Preface and the Rhetoric of Hellenistic Historiography," in *Jesus and the Heritage of Israel: Luke's Narrative Claim upon Israel's Legacy*, ed. David P. Moessner, Luke the Interpreter of Israel 1 (Trinity Press International, 1999), 27–60; David E. Aune, "Luke 1.1–4: Historical or Scientific *Prooimion*?" in *Paul, Luke and the Graeco-Roman World: Essays in Honour of Alexander J. M. Wedderburn*, ed. Alf Christophersen et al., JSNTSup 217 (Sheffield Academic, 2002), 138–48; Todd C. Penner, *In Praise of Christian Origins: Stephen and the Hellenists in Lukan Apologetic Historiography*, Emory Studies in Early Christianity 10 (T&T Clark, 2004), 219–22; Clare K. Rothschild, *Luke-Acts and the Rhetoric of History*, WUNT 2/175 (Mohr Siebeck, 2004), 93–94; Nathalie Siffer-Wiederhold, "Le projet littéraire de Luc d'après le prologue de l'évangile (Lc 1,1–4)," *RevScRel*

notes six claims that attained the status of convention in the prologues to ancient historiographic works:

- The claim to truth (ἀλήθεια and/or τὸ σαφές)
- The claim to "accuracy" (ἀκρίβεια)
- The claim to research (ἱστορία) or at least, a "narrative" (διήγησις) and often a narrative that begins in or from the "beginning" (e.g., ἀπ' ἀρχῆς)
- The claim to avoid style
- The claim to "order" the sources (e.g., καθεξῆς)
- The claim to rely on autopsy (αὐτοψία)[5]

As Rothschild notes, "Not every historian includes every claim, and the terminology is flexible."[6] It is therefore significant that Luke employs all these claims in his preface except the claim to

---

79.1 (2005): 39–54; Sean A. Adams, "Luke's Preface and Its Relationship to Greek Historiography: A Response to Loveday Alexander," *JGRChJ* 3 (2006): 177–91; Armin D. Baum, "Lk 1,1–4 zwischen antiker Historiografie und Fachprosa: Zum literaturgeschichtlichen Kontext des lukanischen Prologs," *ZNW* 101 (2010): 33–54; J. L. Moles, "Luke's Preface: The Greek Decree, Classical Historiography and Christian Redefinitions," *NTS* 57 (2011): 461–82; Michael Wolter, *The Gospel According to Luke*, trans. Wayne Coppins and Christoph Heilig, 2 vols., Baylor-Mohr Siebeck Studies in Early Christianity (Baylor UP, 2016–17), 1:43; Richard Bauckham, *Jesus and the Eyewitnesses: The Gospels as Eyewitness Testimony*, 2nd ed. (Eerdmans, 2017), 216–24; Craig S. Keener, *Christobiography: Memory, History, and the Reliability of the Gospels* (Eerdmans, 2019), 221–39; John J. Peters, "Luke's Source Claims in the Context of Ancient Historiography," *JSHJ* 18 (2020): 36–45; idem, *Luke Among the Ancient Historians: Ancient Historiography and the Attempt to Remedy the Inadequate "Many"* (Pickwick, 2022), 13–15. The main challenge to the historiographic character of Luke's preface has come from Loveday Alexander, *The Preface to Luke's Gospel: Literary Convention and Social Context in Luke 1.1–4 and Acts 1.1*, SNTSMS 78 (Cambridge UP, 1993). Most scholars, however, have remained convinced that Luke 1:1–4 is a historiographic preface (see above), and Alexander has since affirmed that Luke intends to write history of some sort (*Acts in Its Ancient Literary Context: A Classicist Looks at the Acts of the Apostles*, Early Christianity in Context [T&T Clark, 2005], 19).

[5] Quoted with minor adaptations from Rothschild, *Luke-Acts*, 67–69. Rothschild cites primary sources for each claim.

[6] Rothschild, *Luke-Acts*, 69.

avoid style.[7] Through the use of such conventions, "Luke consciously aligns his work with the tradition of ancient historiography."[8] And if Luke knows ancient historiography well enough to give his Gospel a historiographic preface, it seems likely that he is also aware of the historiographic expectations for his work—including the expectation that his birth narrative be based on sources.[9]

Luke discusses his sources both implicitly and explicitly in the preface. First, he says that "many" have undertaken to compile similar accounts (Luke 1:1). Francis Watson rightly notes, "Given that Mark is Luke's primary source, he must belong among the 'many' who attempted to compose an account, and whose work provides the occasion for Luke's."[10] Interpreters who subscribe to the two-source theory or Farrer hypothesis might also include Q or the Gospel of Matthew, respectively, among these accounts. Second, Luke says that he and the "many" have received their traditions from "those who from the beginning were eyewitnesses and servants of the word" (1:2). The phrase likely refers to a single group with a twofold role: "They saw, and then they reported."[11] Luke claims to have a thoroughly informed familiarity (παρηκολουθηκότι ... ἀκριβῶς) with everything the

---

[7] Peters, "Luke's Source Claims," 43.

[8] Penner, *In Praise of Christian Origins*, 220.

[9] On Luke's knowledge of Greco-Roman literature, see C. Kavin Rowe, *World Upside Down: Reading Acts in the Graeco-Roman Age* (Oxford UP, 2009); Steve Reece, *The Formal Education of the Author of Luke-Acts*, LNTS 669 (T&T Clark, 2022).

[10] Francis Watson, *Gospel Writing: A Canonical Perspective* (Eerdmans, 2013), 124.

[11] Darrell L. Bock, *Luke*, 2 vols., BECNT (Baker Academic, 1994/1996), 1:58. Bock comments, "The single article οἱ ... and the trailing participle γενόμενοι ... argue for this view, though the plural makes it less than certain, since the Granville-Sharp rule does not apply in plural constructions" (1:58). Cf. Joseph A. Fitzmyer, *The Gospel According to Luke (I–IX)*, AB 28 (Doubleday, 1981), 294; Alexander, *Preface to Luke's Gospel*, 119; Bauckham, *Jesus and the Eyewitnesses*, 122. James Edwards perceptively notes, "Eyewitnesses of the Christ-event alone would not qualify one for this particular company, for Antipas, Pilate, members of the Sanhedrin, and countless individuals saw Jesus of Nazareth but did not respond in faith and become 'servants of the word'" (James R.

eyewitnesses have handed on, and this qualifies him to add his account to those of the "many."[12]

Luke therefore presents his Gospel—including the birth narrative—as based on the testimony of the eyewitnesses. One might, of course, protest that the preface does not apply to the birth narrative. But on what grounds? As I. I. du Plessis notes, "The fact that the prologue is directly followed by the birth stories makes it hard to believe that Luke did not consider this part of the narrative also as presenting an eyewitness report."[13] Luke also says nothing in the preface to suggest that it does not apply to the birth narrative. The legendary-intent advocate might argue that Luke and his ideal reader would instinctively bracket out the birth narrative because they knew that birth narratives in ancient biographies were not meant to be historical. However, such an argument is no longer tenable in light of part 1. Indeed, part 1 has highlighted several places where ancient biographers provide blanket source discussions at the beginning of the biography that apply to the birth material.[14] I suggest that if we found Luke's preface at the beginning of any other ancient biography, we would

---

Edwards, *The Gospel According to Luke*, Pillar New Testament Commentary [Eerdmans, 2015], 25).

[12] David Moessner argues compellingly that παρηκολουθηκότι means "to follow with the mind" or to have an "informed familiarity" rather than "to investigate." See David P. Moessner, "'Eyewitnesses,' 'Informed Contemporaries,' and 'Unknowing Inquirers': Josephus' Criteria for Authentic Historiography and the Meaning of ΠΑΡΑΚΟΛΟΥΘΕΩ," *NovT* 38.2 (1996): 105–22; idem, "The Appeal and Power of Poetics (Luke 1:1–4): Luke's Superior Credentials (παρηκολουθηκότι), Narrative Sequence (καθεξῆς), and Firmness of Understanding (ἡ ἀσφάλεια) for the Reader," in *Jesus and the Heritage of Israel: Luke's Narrative Claim upon Israel's Legacy*, Luke the Interpreter of Israel 1 (Trinity Press International, 1999), 84–123; idem, *Luke*, 68–107. Cf. Alexander, *Preface to Luke's Gospel*, 128–30; Bauckham, *Jesus and the Eyewitnesses*, 123; Wolter, *Luke*, 1:49–50; Keener, *Christobiography*, 226–27. Yet if παρηκολουθηκότι does not mean "to investigate," it does imply investigation; as Bock notes, "Luke is not an eyewitness, so his ability 'to follow' the events carefully can result only from investigation" (*Luke*, 1:60).

[13] I. I. Du Plessis, "Once More: The Purpose of Luke's Prologue (Lk 1:1–4)," *NovT* 16.4 (1974): 266.

[14] E.g., Nepos, *Ag.* 1.1; Philo, *Moses* 1.4; Plutarch, *Thes.* 1.1–3; *Lyc.* 1.1.

naturally conclude that its claims apply to the whole life, including the birth narrative.

Luke, then, claims that his birth narrative depends on the testimony of the eyewitnesses. It is important to distinguish between two ways of understanding this claim. First, Luke might be saying that he received the traditions from one or more eyewitnesses of Jesus's birth and childhood.[15] Mary the mother of Jesus would be the most plausible candidate, since Luke places her among the disciples in Acts 1:14. Second, Luke might be saying that he received the traditions from the apostles and others who were eyewitnesses of Jesus's ministry (cf. Acts 1:21–22). These would not, of course, have been eyewitnesses of Jesus's birth and childhood, but according to Luke they had access to Mary (Acts 1:14) and to Jesus himself, whose testimony would be especially relevant to the events of Luke 2:41–52. The idea that Luke received the birth narrative traditions from one or more eyewitnesses therefore does not require Mary to be one of those eyewitnesses. The key point for our purposes is that, on either view, Luke employs *sources* with respect to his birth narrative and indicates his historiographic intent.

In sum, Luke opens his Gospel with a historiographic prologue that presents its contents—including the birth material—as based on the testimony of the "eyewitnesses and servants of the word." From the start, then, Luke indicates that he intends the birth narrative to be historical. And as we will see below, the birth narrative and genealogy corroborate Luke's historiographic intent.

Birth Narrative (Luke 1:5–2:52)

Luke confirms that he intends the birth narrative to be historical by (1) including a number of agreements with Matthew that

---

[15] Scholars who take this view include Du Plessis, "Once More," 266; René Laurentin, *The Truth of Christmas Beyond the Myths: The Gospels of the Infancy of Christ*, trans. Michael J. Wrenn and associates, Studies in Scripture (St. Bede's, 1986), 427; Bock, *Luke*, 1:61; Karl A. Kuhn, "Beginning the Witness: The αὐτόπται καὶ ὑπηρέται of Luke's Infancy Narrative," *NTS* 49.2 (2003): 237–55.

suggest he has drawn on a source and (2) explicitly acknowledging a source within the birth narrative. We will examine each of these points in detail below.

Agreements with Matthew

Raymond Brown notes eleven points of agreement between the birth narratives of Matthew and Luke:

1. The parents to be are Mary and Joseph who are legally engaged or married, but have not yet come to live together or have sexual relations (Matt 1:18; Luke 1:27, 34).
2. Joseph is of Davidic descent (Matt 1:16, 20; Luke 1:27, 32; 2:4).
3. There is an angelic announcement of the forthcoming birth of the child (Matt 1:20–23; Luke 1:30–35).
4. The conception of the child by Mary is not through intercourse with her husband (Matt 1:20, 23, 25; Luke 1:34).
5. The conception is through the Holy Spirit (Matt 1:18, 20; Luke 1:35).
6. There is a directive from the angel that the child is to be named Jesus (Matt 1:21; Luke 1:31).
7. An angel states that Jesus is to be Savior (Matt 1:21; Luke 2:11).
8. The birth of the child takes place after the parents have come to live together (Matt 1:24–25; Luke 2:5–6).
9. The birth takes place at Bethlehem (Matt 2:1; Luke 2:4–6).
10. The birth is chronologically related to the reign (days) of Herod the Great (Matt 2:1; Luke 1:5).
11. The child is reared at Nazareth (Matt 2:23; Luke 2:39).[16]

It is highly unlikely that Matthew and Luke arrived at all these by chance, by applying messianic prophecies to Jesus, or by reading

---

[16] Raymond E. Brown, *The Birth of the Messiah: A Commentary on the Infancy Narratives in the Gospels of Matthew and Luke*, rev. ed., ABRL (Doubleday, 1993), 34–35.

Jesus's adult character back into his origins. We are left with two possibilities: (1) Matthew and Luke rely on a common source; (2) either Matthew or Luke depends on the other. With respect to (2), it seems more likely that Luke relies on Matthew than vice-versa, not least because Luke acknowledges the existence of other narratives about Jesus (Luke 1:1).[17] Fortunately, we need not choose between (1) and (2) at present; the salient point is that Luke has used a source for significant elements of his birth narrative. Note also that the virginal conception—the most significant miracle in Luke 1–2—is one of the elements Luke draws from this source. We will consider Luke's use of supernatural elements below, but suffice it to say that his dependence on sources for the virginal conception should caution us against assuming that supernatural elements necessarily indicate legendary intent. The agreements between Matthew and Luke therefore confirm that Luke has drawn on a source for the birth narrative.

Preservation Sayings (Luke 2:19, 51)

Luke includes in his birth narrative two enigmatic sayings about Mary preserving words in her heart:

> And Mary was preserving all these words and pondering them in her heart [πάντα συνετήρει τὰ ῥήματα ταῦτα συμβάλλουσα ἐν τῇ καρδίᾳ αὐτῆς]. (2:19)

> And his mother was preserving all the words in her heart [διετήρει πάντα τὰ ῥήματα ἐν τῇ καρδίᾳ αὐτῆς]. (2:51)[18]

Interpreters have understood these sayings in at least five ways:[19]

---

[17] A. M. Farrer, "On Dispensing with Q," in *Studies in the Gospels: Essays in Memory of R. H. Lightfoot*, ed. D. E. Nineham (Blackwell, 1955), 56. On Luke's use of Matthew, see further M. D. Goulder, *Luke: A New Paradigm*, 2 vols., JSNTSup 20 (JSOT, 1989); Mark S. Goodacre, *The Case Against Q: Studies in Markan Priority and Synoptic Problem* (Trinity Press International, 2002), esp. 49–66; Watson, *Gospel Writing*, 117–55.

[18] My translations.

[19] Caleb T. Friedeman, *The Revelation of the Messiah: The Christological Mystery of Luke 1-2 and Its Unveiling in Luke-Acts*, SNTSMS 181 (Cambridge UP, 2023), 138–42. I emphasize there that "with a few

- Source: Luke 2:19, 51 indicate that Mary preserves memories of the events that have occurred and designate Mary as the source of Luke's birth narrative.[20]
- Comprehension: Luke 2:19, 51 show that Mary fully understands the significance of what she has witnessed.[21]
- Puzzle: Luke 2:19, 51 indicate Mary's incomprehension and her attempt to understand what she has seen.[22]

---

exceptions, these types [of interpretations] are not mutually exclusive but represent distinct emphases in explicating Mary's actions in 2:19, 51" (138).

[20] F. Godet, *The Gospel of St. Luke*, trans. E. W. Shalders and M. D. Cusin, 4th ed., 2 vols. (T&T Clark, 1889), 1:135, 150; W. M. Ramsay, *Was Christ Born at Bethlehem? A Study on the Credibility of St. Luke*, 3rd ed. (Hodder & Stoughton, 1905), 74–75; Adolf Harnack, *The Date of the Acts and of the Synoptic Gospels*, trans. J. R. Wilkinson, Crown Theological Library 33 (Williams & Norgate, 1911), 154–56; Marie-Joseph Lagrange, *Évangile selon Saint Luc*, 3rd ed., Études bibliques (Victor Lecoffre, 1927), 79, 98; J. Gresham Machen, *The Virgin Birth of Christ*, 2nd ed. (Harper & Row, 1932), 200–202; Norval Geldenhuys, *Commentary on the Gospel of Luke*, NICNT (Eerdmans, 1951), 114, 129; René Laurentin, *Structure et théologie de Luc I–II* (Gabalda, 1957), 97; Geoffrey Graystone, *Virgin of All Virgins: The Interpretation of Luke 1:34* (Pontifical Biblical Institute, 1968), 52–54; Heikki Räisänen, *Die Mutter Jesu im Neuen Testament*, Annales Academiae Scientiarum Fennicae 2/158 (Suomalainen Tiedeakatemia, 1969), 124; John McHugh, *The Mother of Jesus in the New Testament* (Doubleday, 1975), 147; Rainer Riesner, *Jesus als Lehrer: Eine Untersuchung zum Ursprung der Evangelien-Überlieferung*, WUNT 2/7 (Mohr, 1981), 210–12; André Feuillet, *Jesus and His Mother: The Role of the Virgin Mary in Salvation History and the Place of Woman in the Church*, trans. Leonard Maluf, Studies in Scripture (St. Bede's, 1984), 67–68; Samuel Byrskog, *Story as History—History as Story: The Gospel Tradition in the Context of Ancient Oral History* (Brill Academic, 2002), 89–90; R. T. France, *Luke*, Teach the Text Commentary Series (Baker, 2013), 35, 46.

[21] Willem C. van Unnik, "Die rechte Bedeutung des Wortes treffen: Lukas 2,19," in *Verbum: Essays on Some Aspects of the Religious Function of Words. Dedicated to Dr. H. W. Obbink, Professor in the History of Religions and Egyptology, University of Utrecht, on November 14th, 1964*, ed. Theodorus Petrus van Baaren, Studia theologica Rheno-Traiectina 6 (Kemink, 1964), 129–47.

[22] Brown, *Birth of the Messiah*, 430–31, 494; John Nolland, *Luke 1–9:20*, WBC 35A (Word, 1989), 110, 128, 134.

- Piety: Luke 2:19, 51 express Mary's exemplary faith, virtue, or devotion.[23]
- Prolepsis: Luke 2:19, 51 point to a future fulfillment of the things Mary has witnessed.[24]

I have argued at length elsewhere that the source interpretation is essentially correct but needs to be integrated into a more holistic model that incorporates the strengths of the other views.[25] Here I will summarize the key points and show how they support and nuance the source interpretation.

First, Luke 2:19, 51 are allusions to Daniel 7:28 LXX. The book of Daniel has survived in two Greek versions (Old Greek and Theodotion); I include both versions of Daniel 7:28 below:

> I, Daniel, was very much seized with astonishment, and my condition spread within me, and I preserved the word in my heart [τὸ ῥῆμα ἐν καρδίᾳ μου ἐτήρησα]. (Dan 7:28 OG)

> I, Daniel, my thoughts were greatly troubling me, and my appearance was changed, and I preserved the word in my heart [τὸ ῥῆμα ἐν τῇ καρδίᾳ μου διετήρησα]. (Dan 7:28 TH)[26]

Daniel 7:28 OG and TH provide closer verbal parallels to Luke 2:19, 51 than any other text does. Luke also encourages the association with Daniel by alluding to Daniel 9–10 repeatedly in Luke 1. The most obvious link to Daniel is the appearance of Gabriel, whose biblical appearances are limited to Daniel 8:16

---

[23] Alfred Loisy, *L'Évangile selon Luc* (Minerva, 1924), 118; Fitzmyer, *Luke (I–IX)*, 398.

[24] Gottfried Erdmann, *Die Vorgeschichten des Lukas- und Matthäus-Evangeliums und Vergils vierte Ekloge*, Forschungen zur Religion und Literatur des Alten und Neuen Testaments 2/30 (Vandenhoeck & Ruprecht, 1932), 20; Frans Neirynck, "Maria bewaarde al de woorden in haar hart. Lk. 2, 19. 51 in hun context verklaard," *Collationes Brugenses et Gandavenses* 5 (1959): 457, 461–66; Heinz Schürmann, *Das Lukasevangelium, erster Teil: Kommentar zu Kap. 1, 1–9, 50*, HThKNT 3 (Herder, 1969), 117. For an English translation of Neirynck, "Maria," see Caleb T. Friedeman and Jeremy D. Otten, "A Reception History and English Translation of Frans Neirynck, *Maria bewaarde al de woorden in haar hart*," *ETL* 97.4 (2021): 647–76.

[25] Friedeman, *Revelation of the Messiah*, 137–78, cf. 99–110, 112–15.

[26] My translations.

and 9:21 and Luke 1:19, 26. However, Luke includes a number of more subtle allusions as well.[27] Luke uses these allusions to portray Zechariah and Mary as Daniel-figures in relation to Gabriel, so a further connection between Mary and Daniel in Luke 2:19, 51 coheres thematically with Luke's earlier use of Daniel. The fact that Luke alludes to Daniel 7:28 in Luke 2:19, 51 is significant, for it suggests that we can only understand these verses in close dialogue with Daniel 7:28.

Second, in Daniel 7 preservation in the heart serves as an intermediate stage between receiving divine revelation and communicating it in writing:

revelation → preservation → communication

Daniel receives revelation in the form of a vision (7:2–27), preserves it in his heart (7:28), and eventually writes it down (7:1). That the preservation is "in the heart" likely indicates "both that the revelation was kept secret prior to the written record (thus enhancing the value of the account) and that it was preserved securely during this period (thus elevating its trustworthiness)."[28] Preservation in the heart became a stock motif in revelatory literature from the second century BC to the second century AD (especially apocalypses and testaments), some of which were demonstrably influenced by Daniel.[29] All these works portray divine revelation as the object of preservation, and most of them use preservation in the heart as an intermediate stage between revelation and written communication (as Dan 7 does).

Third, Luke would have "interpreted Daniel 7:28 as a legitimate appeal to Daniel as the origin of Daniel 7."[30] Unlike many

---

[27] Friedeman, *Revelation of the Messiah*, 92–98.
[28] Friedeman, *Revelation of the Messiah*, 149–50.
[29] Daniel 4:28 OG; Genesis Apocryphon (1QapGen) VI, 12; Aramaic Levi 7; Testament of Reuben 1.4; Testament of Simeon 2.1; Testament of Levi 6.2; 8.19; Apocalypse of Moses (= Greek Life of Adam and Eve) 3.2–3; 4 Ezra 14.7–9; 2 Baruch 50.1; Testament of Abraham A 3.4, 12; Testament of Abraham B 3.4; Targum Pseudo-Jonathan Gen 37:11. The ones most clearly influenced by Daniel are Genesis Apocryphon VI, 12 and 4 Ezra 14.7–9.
[30] Friedeman, *Revelation of the Messiah*, 167–68.

modern scholars, early Jews and Christians uniformly attributed the book of Daniel to the sixth-century prophet Daniel.[31] Other than the Neoplatonist philosopher Porphyry (late third century AD), we are unaware of anyone who challenged the Danielic authorship of the book prior to the seventeenth century.[32] As an early Christian, Luke would naturally have understood Daniel 7:28 to emphasize the secrecy and security with which Daniel preserved the vision of Daniel 7 prior to recording it (7:1).

Finally, Luke uses preservation in the heart in continuity with Daniel 7, but with some important adjustments. Luke, like Daniel, employs it in a revelatory context: each of the seven scenes in Luke's birth narrative focuses on the speech of one or more characters whom Luke portrays as speaking on God's behalf.[33] Also like Daniel, Luke places the preservation in the heart after an instance of divine revelation, which he refers to as a "word" (ῥῆμα; Luke 2:15, 17, 50). But where Daniel preserves a single "word" (ῥῆμα, Dan 7:28), Luke has Mary preserve "all these words" (πάντα . . . τὰ ῥήματα ταῦτα; Luke 2:19) and "all the words" (πάντα τὰ ῥήματα; 2:51). Since Luke describes the inspired speech in the individual scenes as a "word" (2:15, 17, 50), the phrase "all the words" most likely refers to all the instances of inspired speech in the preceding narrative (and, by implication, the related events). Luke also replaces Daniel's aorist verb (OG: ἐτήρησα; TH: διετήρησα; Dan 7:28) with imperfects (συνετήρει, Luke 2:19; διετήρει, 2:51) and emphasizes Mary's incomprehension by noting her pondering and lack of understanding (2:19, 50). The latter suggests that Mary is preserving the words not only for future communication but also for future

---

[31] Jewish sources: Josephus, *Ant.* 10.267–80; 11.337; 4Q174 1 II, 1–5; 11Q13 II, 18; b. Ber. 31a. Christian sources: Jerome, *Explanatio in Danielem* proem 8–11; Hippolytus, *Commentarium in Danielem* 1.1.

[32] P. M. Casey, "Porphyry and the Origin of the Book of Daniel," *JTS* 27.1 (1976): 15–33; John J. Collins, *Daniel: A Commentary on the Book of Daniel*, Hermeneia (Fortress, 1993), 25.

[33] Friedeman, *Revelation of the Messiah*, 26–51. The seven scenes with their speakers are: Luke 1:5–25 (Gabriel); 1:26–38 (Gabriel); 1:39–56 (Elizabeth and Mary); 1:57–80 (Zechariah); 2:1–21 (angel of the Lord, heavenly host); 2:22–40 (Simeon and Anna); 2:41–52 (Jesus).

comprehension; the former encourages the reader to pay attention to Mary as the narrative unfolds. The preservation sayings therefore "indicate that Mary alone preserves all of the instances of divine revelation in the preceding narrative in secret for later communication (a result of which is Luke 1–2) and interpretation."[34] Luke intends the reader to understand from 2:19, 51 that Mary "has communicated the revelation so that it is no longer in the heart alone, but also on the page."[35]

The preservation sayings are therefore more than source indicators, but not less. Luke uses these sayings to designate Mary as the source of Luke 1–2, in the same way that Daniel 7:28 designates Daniel as the source of Daniel 7. One might object that the preservation sayings do not seem like a normal way for an ancient biographer to indicate his source. Such an objection, however, fails for three reasons: (1) Ancient biographers do not seem to have followed a set formula in citing their sources. The instances of *sources* discussed in part 1, for example, exhibit a significant diversity of phrasing, and these only constitute a small fraction of the relevant data. (2) Our only extant Jewish biography is Philo's *Life of Moses*, so we know little about how biographers steeped in the Old Testament (such as Luke) cited their sources. (3) Luke is under no obligation to cite sources in the same way that other biographers did. Indeed, I would argue that the preservation sayings are precisely the sort of source markers we would expect based on who Luke is and the traditions he is working with. Imagine: You are an early Christian whose mind is soaked in Israel's Scriptures, and you are writing a biography of Jesus. The traditions you have received about his birth and childhood come from his mother Mary and contain many instances of divine revelation in the form of inspired speech. You also know that Mary did not initially comprehend everything she heard but came to understand it after the resurrection. How do you convey all this succinctly without distracting from the flow of your narrative? One could hardly do better than to allude to Daniel 7:28 with precisely the modifications we observe in Luke 2:19, 51.

---

[34] Friedeman, *Revelation of the Messiah*, 176.
[35] Friedeman, *Revelation of the Messiah*, 174.

We may therefore conclude that Luke employs *sources* in Luke 2:19, 51. Indeed, he indicates his sources more clearly in the birth narrative than anywhere else in his Gospel beyond the preface. Of course, Luke may intend to portray other characters besides Mary as sources.[36] But nowhere else does he acknowledge a source as explicitly as he does in Luke 2:19, 51.

Summary

The birth narrative therefore confirms what Luke has already indicated in the preface: Luke is relying on sources. Luke's agreements with Matthew indicate that he has drawn on a source for key elements of the birth narrative, and in the preservation sayings Luke designates Mary as a source. Based on *sources* alone, then, we would have to say that if Luke intends any part of his Gospel to be historical, it is the birth narrative.

Genealogy (Luke 3:23–38)

Our first clue to the historiographic intent of Luke's genealogy is its placement. Luke locates the genealogy amid adult material (between the baptism and temptation) and frames it as a statement about the adult Jesus, saying, "Jesus, when he began his ministry, was about thirty years of age, being the son (as was supposed) of Joseph, the son of Heli . . ." (3:23).[37] The lack of clarity about where Luke transitions from adult material to birth material makes it unlikely that he expects the reader to interpret the genealogy as less historical than the adult material that surrounds it. Hence Luke—like our biographers in part 1—does not seem to regard birth material as a special case with respect to historiographic intent.

Luke, like Matthew, does not cite sources for his genealogy. Scholars, however, generally agree that he used sources. The two basic views are: (1) Luke drew on the Old Testament and supplemented it with other sources;[38] (2) Luke used an

---

[36] Bauckham, *Jesus and the Eyewitnesses*, 129–32.
[37] On the theological significance of this placement, see Friedeman, *Revelation of the Messiah*, 62–63.
[38] Bock, *Luke*, 1:349.

existing nonbiblical genealogy and perhaps edited it.[39] Richard Bauckham, for example, argues that the Lukan genealogy came from the family circle of Jesus's brother Jude and that Luke only added two phrases—ὡς ἐνομίζετο ("as was thought"; Luke 3:23) and τοῦ θεοῦ ("the son of God"; 3:38)—and perhaps reversed the order of the names.[40] Such a view would constitute strong evidence for Luke's historiographic intent, for Luke would have made minor edits to a source he had good reason to trust. It also allows one to attribute any differences between the Lukan genealogy and the Old Testament to Luke's nonbiblical source. However, I am not convinced that Luke, who knows the Old Testament quite well,[41] would have used a nonbiblical genealogy without checking it against the Old Testament. Here—as with Matthew above—I therefore opt for the more difficult case that Luke has drawn on both the Old Testament and nonbiblical sources for his genealogy, but that his differences with the Old Testament do not constitute evidence for legendary intent.

Luke appears to draw much of his genealogy from the Old Testament, particularly the Greek version of Genesis 4–5, 10–11, and 1 Chronicles 1–3 (see table 4).[42]

---

[39] Brown, *Birth of the Messiah*, 93–94; Fitzmyer, *Luke (I–IX)*, 491, 497–98; Nolland, *Luke 1–9:20*, 173; Gerhard Schneider, *Das Evangelium nach Lukas Kapitel 1–10*, 3rd ed., Ökumenischer Taschenbuch-Kommentar 3/1 (Mohn, 1992), 94; François Bovon, *Luke 1: A Commentary on the Gospel of Luke 1:1–9:50*, trans. Christine M. Thomas, Hermeneia (Fortress, 2002), 134.

[40] Richard Bauckham, *Jude and the Relatives of Jesus in the Early Church* (T&T Clark, 1990), 315–73, esp. 364, 368–69.

[41] On Luke's use of the Old Testament, see, e.g., Darrell L. Bock, *Proclamation from Prophecy and Pattern: Lucan Old Testament Christology*, JSNTSup 12 (JSOT, 1987); David W. Pao and Eckhard J. Schnabel, "Luke," in *Commentary on the New Testament Use of the Old Testament*, ed. G. K. Beale and D. A. Carson (Baker Academic, 2007), 251–414; Richard B. Hays, *Echoes of Scripture in the Gospels* (Baylor UP, 2016), 191–280.

[42] Luke may also depend on Ruth 4, but the only place where he is closer to Ruth than to Chronicles is Ἑσρώμ (Luke 3:33)—cf. Ἑσρών (Ruth 4:18–19); Ἀρσών (1 Chr 2:5); Ἐσερών (1 Chr 2:9).

Table 4: Old Testament sources for Luke's genealogy

Luke 3:23–38 (NRSV)	Old Testament sources (LXX)
Jesus, Joseph, Heli, Matthat, Levi, Melchi, Jannai, Joseph, Mattathias, Amos, Nahum, Esli, Naggai, Maath, Mattathias, Semein, Josech, Joda, Joanan, Rhesa	—
Zerubbabel	1 Chr 3:19
Salathiel*	1 Chr 3:17
Neri, Melchi, Addi, Cosam, Elmadam, Er, Joshua, Eliezer, Jorim, Matthat, Levi, Simeon, Judah, Joseph, Jonam, Eliakim, Melea, Menna, Mattatha	—
Nathan	1 Chr 3:5 (cf. 2 Sam 5:14; 1 Chr 14:4)
David	1 Chr 2:15 (cf. Ruth 4:22)
Jesse	1 Chr 2:12 (cf. Ruth 4:22)
Obed	1 Chr 2:12 (cf. Ruth 4:13, 17, 21)
Boaz	1 Chr 2:11 (cf. Ruth 4:21)
Sala	1 Chr 2:11 (cf. Ruth 4:20)
Nahshon	1 Chr 2:10 (cf. Ruth 4:20)
Aminadab	1 Chr 2:10 (cf. Ruth 4:19)
Admin, Arni†	—
Hezron	1 Chr 2:5; Ruth 4:18
Perez	1 Chr 2:4; Ruth 4:12
Judah	1 Chr 2:1–2; Ruth 4:12
Jacob	1 Chr 1:34
Isaac	1 Chr 1:28, 34
Abraham	Gen 11:26–27; 1 Chr 1:27
Terah	Gen 11:24; 1 Chr 1:26
Nahor	Gen 11:22; 1 Chr 1:26
Serug	Gen 11:20; 1 Chr 1:26
Reu	Gen 11:18; 1 Chr 1:25

Luke 3:23-38 (NRSV)	Old Testament sources (LXX)
Peleg	Gen 11:16; 1 Chr 1:25
Eber	Gen 10:24; 11:14; 1 Chr 1:25
Shelah	Gen 10:24; 11:13; 1 Chr 1:24
Cainan	Gen 10:24; 11:12
Arphaxad	Gen 10:22; 11:10; 1 Chr 1:17
Shem	Gen 5:32; 1 Chr 1:4
Noah	Gen 5:28-29; 1 Chr 1:4
Lamech	Gen 5:25; 1 Chr 1:3
Methuselah	Gen 5:21; 1 Chr 1:3
Enoch	Gen 5:18; 1 Chr 1:3
Jared	Gen 5:15; 1 Chr 1:2
Mahalaleel	Gen 5:12; 1 Chr 1:2
Cainan	Gen 5:9; 1 Chr 1:2
Enos	Gen 4:26; 5:6; 1 Chr 1:1
Seth	Gen 4:25-26; 1 Chr 1:1
Adam	Gen 2:7; 1 Chr 1:1

* Here I use the Greek spelling, as in Matt 1:12 NRSV.

† See discussion in the body of the text. If Aram is the correct reading, then the source is 1 Chr 2:10 (cf. Ruth 4:19).

Luke may have used the simple list of Chronicles rather than gathering the names from the more diffuse and complex genealogies of Genesis.[43] However, he seems to rely on Genesis 10:24 or 11:12 LXX for Cainan (Luke 3:36), who does not appear in Chronicles (except in codex A of 1 Chr 1:18).[44]

---

[43] William S. Kurz, "Luke 3:23-38 and Greco-Roman and Biblical Genealogies," in *Luke-Acts: New Perspectives from the Society of Biblical Literature Seminar*, ed. Charles H. Talbert (Crossroad, 1984), 176.

[44] I. Howard Marshall, *The Gospel of Luke: A Commentary on the Greek Text*, NIGTC (Eerdmans, 1978), 165; Kurz, "Luke 3:23-38," 176; Gert J. Steyn, "The Occurrence of 'Kainam' in Luke's Genealogy: Evidence of Septuagint Influence?" *ETL* 65.4 (1989): 409-11. Richard Bauckham argues that the author of the Lukan genealogy (not Luke himself) relies on Jub 8.1-5 or a similar tradition rather than the LXX ("More on Kainam the Son of Arpachshad in Luke's Genealogy," *ETL* 67.1 [1991]:

Luke does, however, diverge from Chronicles at several points: (1) the postexilic generations from Jesus to Zerubbabel, (2) the preexilic generations from Salathiel to Nathan, and possibly (3) the names Admin and Arni in Luke 3:33. Each of these involves otherwise unknown figures. On the face of it, this does not bode well for the legendary intent hypothesis. Luke exhibits historiographic intent by following Chronicles closely elsewhere in the genealogy, so when he deviates from Chronicles and lists otherwise unknown figures, the most reasonable conclusion is that he is using another source. Indeed, some scholars regard Luke's genealogy as more reliable than Chronicles at these points! Bauckham claims that Luke's genealogy "is historically more credible than the Chronicler's" in tracing Zerubbabel's descent through the non-royal line of Nathan.[45] Joachim Jeremias similarly concludes that Luke's differences with Chronicles in the postexilic section "suggest a favourable judgment on the value of the Lucan genealogy."[46] The burden of proof therefore rests on those who regard Luke's genealogy as legendary in intent. For the sake of thoroughness, however, I provide a more detailed discussion of Luke's differences with Chronicles below.

From Jesus to Zerubbabel (Luke 3:23–27)

None of the nineteen names that Luke gives between Jesus and Zerubbabel appear in 1 Chronicles 3:19–24. We should not be particularly surprised by this, since Chronicles names eight children

---

95–102). Bauckham, however, acknowledges that one cannot completely rule out dependence on the LXX (102). Andrew E. Steinmann has questioned the authenticity of Cainan ("Challenging the Authenticity of Cainan, Son of Arpachshad," *JETS* 60.4 [2017]: 697–711). For a response to Steinmann, see Henry B. Smith Jr. and Kris J. Udd, "On the Authenticity of Kainan, Son of Arpachshad," *Detroit Baptist Seminary Journal* 24 (2019): 119–54.

[45] Bauckham, *Jude and the Relatives of Jesus*, 339. Bauckham does regard Levi, Simeon, Judah, and Joseph (Luke 3:29–30) as fabricated, though not by Luke (343). See further below.

[46] Joachim Jeremias, *Jerusalem in the Time of Jesus: An Investigation into Economic and Social Conditions During the New Testament Period*, trans. F. H. Cave and C. H. Cave (Fortress, 1969), 296.

of Zerubbabel but lists descendants for only one of them (Hananiah). What is striking is that Rhesa, whom Luke names as the son of Zerubbabel, does not appear among Zerubbabel's descendants in Chronicles.[47] There are several potential explanations for this. For example: (1) Luke follows the line of Hananiah but omits the generations that Chronicles gives. (2) Luke follows the line of one of Zerubbabel's other children but omits one or more generations directly after Zerubbabel. (3) Rhesa is an alternate name for one of Zerubbabel's sons named in Chronicles. (4) Rhesa is a son of Zerubbabel not mentioned by Chronicles—perhaps because he was an adopted or levirate son.[48] We do not have enough information to decide between these options, but each is plausible. Luke might have omitted the generations noted in (1) and (2) to achieve the seventy-seven generations of his genealogy. Our study of Matthew's genealogy has also shown that such omissions

---

[47] Some interpreters argue that Rhesa was not originally a name at all but an Aramaic word for "chief" or "prince" (ריש or רישא) that was a title for Zerubbabel ("Zerubbabel, the prince") and was copied into Greek as Ῥησά. See Arthur Hervey, *The Genealogies of Our Lord and Saviour Jesus Christ* (Macmillan, 1853), 111–14; Alfred Plummer, *A Critical and Exegetical Commentary on the Gospel According to St. Luke*, 5th ed., ICC (T&T Clark, 1922), 104; Jeremias, *Jerusalem in the Time of Jesus*, 296; Bauckham, *Jude and the Relatives of Jesus*, 328. This theory seems to require a simple list of names in the reverse order of Luke's genealogy ("Zerubbabel the prince, Joanan," etc.), and the main benefit is that it might allow one to identify Zerubbabel's son Hananiah (1 Chr 3:19, 21) with Johanan (Luke 3:27) in this pre-Lukan list (though not in Luke's understanding). The theory is compatible with my thesis, for it emphasizes Luke's dependence on his sources, but in my view it is too speculative to be probable.

[48] Nancy S. Dawson, Eugene H. Merrill, and Andreas J. Köstenberger, *All the Genealogies of the Bible: Visual Charts and Exegetical Commentary* (Zondervan Academic, 2023), 193. The authors also suggest that Rhesa may have been the son-in-law of Zerubbabel (the husband of his daughter Shelomith) and carried on Zerubbabel's line in this capacity. The son-in-law suggestion is possible, but it seems that it would still require Zerubbabel to adopt Rhesa. Such a situation would be most likely if Zerubbabel's sons other than Hananiah failed to produce male offspring. A similar situation occurs in Ezra 2:61; see Caleb T. Friedeman, "Jesus' Davidic Lineage and the Case for Jewish Adoption," *NTS* 66 (2020): 258.

were conventional in Jewish genealogies, so (1) and (2) would pose no problem for Luke's historiographic intent. And in favor of (3) and (4), Chronicles seems to use alternate names and leave known sons unmentioned elsewhere.[49]

Whichever of these explanations one prefers, they are all more likely than the idea that Luke has fabricated the postexilic portion of his genealogy. Why would Luke diverge from the well-known line of Zerubbabel in Chronicles and give a different line of otherwise unknown figures? The most compelling answer is that Luke depends on a source other than Chronicles. The generations closest to Jesus are also the ones most likely to be remembered in the first century AD, so it would be unnecessary (and unwise) for Luke to fabricate names here. The genealogy from Joseph to Zerubbabel therefore does not seem to exhibit legendary intent.

From Salathiel to Nathan (3:27–31)

Luke traces Salathiel's lineage through the non-royal line of Nathan rather than the royal line of Solomon, as in Chronicles. This, however, in no way supports legendary intent. It is again difficult to conceive of why Luke would depart from the royal line of Chronicles unless he had a source that gave him other information about Jesus's lineage.[50] Two proposals, however, are worth mentioning. First, one might argue that Luke follows Nathan's line because he wants to distance Jesus from the sins of Solomon and his progeny. Yet this is not a compelling reason to fabricate a whole lineal line, particularly when the rest of the genealogy

---

[49] With respect to omitted names, Gen 46:21 lists ten sons of Benjamin, Num 26:38 five, 1 Chr 7:6 three, and 1 Chr 8:1–2 five. These four lists differ significantly as to the names as well. For a helpful table see Roddy Braun, *1 Chronicles*, WBC 14 (Word, 1986), 108. Braun suggests that three of the names in 1 Chr 8:1–5 are variants of names in Gen 46 and Num 26 (125).

[50] Zechariah 12:12 portrays the house of Nathan as a prominent Davidic family (Bauckham, *Jude and the Relatives of Jesus*, 341–43). However, this alone does not explain why Luke would trace the lineage of Jesus through Nathan rather than Solomon.

contains many sinful ancestors—not least the original sinner Adam. Second, Johnson argues that Luke depends on a tradition that identified Nathan the son of David with Nathan the prophet and follows Nathan's line because he wants to give Jesus a prophetic pedigree.[51] However, there is no evidence that such a tradition existed in the first century AD, and in any case "prophets are not legitimized by descent."[52] The best explanation, then, is that Luke is following a source other than Chronicles.

The specific point where Luke diverges from Chronicles has to do with the father of Salathiel. Whereas 1 Chronicles 3:17 LXX portrays Salathiel as the son of Jeconiah, Luke describes him as the son of Neri (Luke 3:27). It is possible to reconcile Luke and Chronicles through an adoption or levirate marriage, and the destruction of Jerusalem and the Babylonian exile may have created a situation where one of these was necessary to perpetuate the Davidic line.[53] We need not solve this puzzle, however, to see how unlikely it is that Luke would deviate from Chronicles to fabricate the otherwise unknown Neri as father of Salathiel. Once again, the most reasonable explanation is that Luke is drawing on a source besides Chronicles.

The final potential objection to Luke's historiographic intent in this section of the genealogy comes from a row of four patriarchal names: Levi, Simeon, Judah, and Joseph (3:29–30). Interpreters often contend that:

1. The custom of using the names of the patriarchs as personal names did not develop in Israel until after the exile.
2. The four patriarchal names in Luke 3:29–30 are therefore an anachronism.

---

[51] Marshall D. Johnson, *The Purpose of the Biblical Genealogies with Special Reference to the Setting of the Genealogies of Jesus*, SNTSMS 8 (Cambridge UP, 1969), 240–52.
[52] Mussies, "Parallels," 43. Cf. Bauckham, *Jude and the Relatives of Jesus*, 353.
[53] Dawson, Merrill, and Köstenberger, *All the Genealogies*, 191–92.

3. The anachronism undermines the credibility of (a) these names[54] or (b) the whole monarchic section of the genealogy.[55]

Let us take these points one at a time: (1) The case against the pre-exilic use of patriarchal names is an argument from silence. Furthermore, there is some evidence that the names of the patriarchs were used as personal names before the exile.[56] It would be better, then, to say that we have limited evidence for the preexilic use of patriarchal names and that Luke 3:29–30 may accrue to this body of evidence. (2) Even if the names were an anachronism, it is not clear that they would be the sort of anachronism that supports (3). Would Luke, for example, be applying patriarchal names to figures with similar names, to figures with dissimilar names, or to totally fabricated figures? These are very different claims with correspondingly different implications. (3) The conclusion is a claim about truth, not intent. To demonstrate that the anachronism entails legendary intent, one would need to show that Luke did not find these names in his source but fabricated them himself. And this would be no easy task, since scholars generally agree that Luke has drawn this section of the genealogy from a nonbiblical source. The patriarchal names of Luke 3:29–30 therefore do not seem to constitute evidence for legendary intent.

Admin and Arni (Luke 3:33)

Luke 3:33 contains a thorny text-critical problem that may amount to a difference between Luke and Chronicles. Here NA[28] and UBS[5] read τοῦ Ἀμιναδὰβ τοῦ Ἀδμὶν τοῦ Ἀρνὶ τοῦ Ἑσρώμ

---

[54] Brown, *Birth of the Messiah*, 92; Marshall, *Luke*, 160; Bauckham, *Jude and the Relatives of Jesus*, 343.

[55] Jeremias, *Jerusalem in the Time of Jesus*, 296; Johnson, *Purpose of the Biblical Genealogies*, 229–30; Fitzmyer, *Luke (I–IX)*, 496.

[56] Bauckham notes the prophet Gad (1 Sam 22:5; 2 Sam 24:11–14), king Manasseh (2 Kgs 21:1–18), and the "more dubious examples" of 1 Chr 7:10, 25:2, and 26:5 (*Jude and the Relatives of Jesus*, 343n89). The examples from Chronicles are presumably more dubious because they may reflect the Chronicler's own time; cf. Marshall, *Luke*, 160. But if this is so, then why are there not more of them?

("Amminadab, son of Admin, son of Arni, son of Hezron").[57] Chronicles, however, places Aram between Amminadab and Hezron and knows nothing of Admin or Arni (1 Chr 2:10; cf. Ruth 4:19). How can we explain this?

First, it is possible that τοῦ Ἀμιναδὰβ τοῦ Ἀράμ τοῦ Ἑσρώμ is the better reading. Bruce Metzger describes the NA-UBS reading as "the least unsatisfactory form of the text,"[58] which does not exactly inspire confidence. Metzger also comments,

> Although the reading τοῦ Ἀμιναδὰβ τοῦ Ἀράμ is supported by an impressive range of witnesses (A D 33 565 1079 many versions), with a reading that involves three names (such as that adopted by the Committee) Luke's entire genealogy falls into an artistically planned pattern, even more elaborate than Matthew's (cf. Mat 1.17); thus, from Adam to Abraham, 3 x 7 generations; from Isaac to David, 2 x 7 generations; from Nathan to Salathiel (pre-exilic), 3 x 7 generations; from Zerubbabel (post-exilic) to Jesus, 3 x 7 generations, making a total of 11 x 7, or 77 generations from Adam to Jesus.[59]

However, as Homer Heater notes, "Impressive evidence should not be ignored in favor of a supposed schematic plan of the genealogy."[60] Heater also observes that if one reads Aram as the only name between Amminadab and Hezron and counts God, Luke's genealogy still follows the same pattern as Matthew's and yields seventy-seven names.[61] Indeed, the NIV and CSB adopt precisely this reading.[62] Such factors should at least caution us against accepting the NA-UBS reading uncritically.

Second, if the NA-UBS reading is correct, Luke's practice elsewhere makes it unlikely that he has fabricated Admin and Arni.

---

[57] *The Greek New Testament, Produced at Tyndale House, Cambridge*, ed. Dirk Jongkind (Crossway, 2017) reads τοῦ Ἀμιναδὰβ τοῦ Ἀδμεὶν τοῦ Ἀρνεὶ τοῦ Ἑσρώμ.

[58] Bruce M. Metzger, *A Textual Commentary on the Greek New Testament*, 2nd ed. (Deutsche Bibelgesellschaft, 1994), 113.

[59] Metzger, *Textual Commentary*, 113n1.

[60] Homer Heater Jr., "A Textual Note on Luke 3:33," *JSNT* 28 (1986): 29.

[61] Heater, "Textual Note," 29.

[62] The NIV and CSB both translate Ἀράμ as "Ram."

The analysis above indicates that Luke has drawn his entire genealogy either from the Old Testament or a nonbiblical source. It makes little sense that he would deviate from that practice (1) by omitting Aram and adding two otherwise unknown figures or (2) by renaming Aram as Arni and adding one otherwise unknown figure. One might argue that Luke did (1) or (2) to reach seventy-seven generations. Yet as Heater has reminded us, the genealogy can contain seventy-seven generations without Admin and Arni. And even if Luke counted only the human names, the simplest way to reach seventy-seven would have been to retain Aram and add another figure. It therefore seems unlikely that the seventy-seven generations would have motivated Luke to do something he does nowhere else and fabricate names. If Admin and Arni are original, then the most compelling explanation is that Luke has drawn these names from a nonbiblical source.

Summary (Genealogy)

Luke's genealogy, like his birth narrative, is source-based. Luke has drawn significant elements of his genealogy from the Old Testament. While he does differ from the Old Testament at points, all these involve otherwise unknown figures who are far better explained by a nonbiblical source than by invention.

Summary (Sources)

Luke indicates the historiographic intent of his birth narrative and genealogy through his use of sources. He begins his Gospel with a historiographic preface that presents his work—including the birth narrative—as based on the testimony of the "eyewitnesses and servants of the word" (Luke 1:1–4). Luke confirms that this claim applies to the birth narrative by designating Mary a source within it (2:19, 51). His agreements with Matthew also indicate that he has drawn on a source for key elements of his birth narrative. In the genealogy, Luke relies on the Old Testament and other sources, and his differences from the Old Testament provide no evidence for legendary intent. Luke, it seems, intends his birth material to be historical.

TRANSPARENCY, EVALUATION, AND DISTANCING

Luke does not employ *transparency* in his birth material. He does, however, use *evaluation* or *distancing* in the genealogy when he says that Jesus "was the son (as was thought [ὡς ἐνομίζετο]) of Joseph" (Luke 3:23). Luke uses νομίζω nine times in Luke-Acts, usually to describe an incorrect assumption.[63] Either *evaluation* or *distancing* therefore seems possible. The scales tip toward *evaluation*, though, when we consider that the purpose of the comment is to qualify Jesus's relationship to Joseph in light of the virginal conception: Jesus was not Joseph's biological son because he was conceived by the Holy Spirit (Luke 1:34–35).[64] So while in the abstract ὡς ἐνομίζετο might indicate *distancing* or *evaluation*, in the context of Luke's narrative it indicates a negative judgment on the biological paternity of Joseph. Whether one opts for *distancing* or *evaluation*, though, the salient point is that Luke employs yet another historiographic feature in his birth material. The fact that this historiographic feature appears in the genealogy is yet another strike against the idea that Luke has spun the genealogy (or any part of it) out of thin air.

When we consider Luke's use of *sources* and *evaluation* in the birth material together, an interesting picture emerges: Beyond the general notice of sources in the preface, Luke employs *sources* twice (Luke 2:19, 51) and *evaluation* once (3:23) in the birth material. To my knowledge, nowhere else in the body of the Gospel does Luke utilize historiographic features so explicitly. Therefore, based on the use of historiographic features, the birth material has a better claim to historiographic intent than any other section of the Gospel.

---

[63] Joel B. Green, *The Gospel of Luke*, NICNT (Eerdmans, 1997), 189. The nine occurrences are Luke 2:44; 3:23; Acts 7:25; 8:20; 14:19; 16:13, 27; 17:29; 21:29. The one case where the assumption might be correct is Acts 16:13. Wolter also notes that the term is used for "uncertain or false attribution of paternity" in a number of nonbiblical sources (*Luke*, 1:178–79).

[64] Machen, *Virgin Birth*, 125–26; Marshall, *Luke*, 162; Bauckham, *Jude and the Relatives of Jesus*, 369; Bock, *Luke*, 1:352; Mark L. Strauss, *The Davidic Messiah in Luke-Acts: The Promise and Its Fulfillment in Lukan Christology*, JSNTSup 110 (Sheffield Academic, 1995), 126–29.

SUPERNATURAL ELEMENTS

Luke narrates numerous miracles in his birth narrative. These include:

- Three angelic appearances
- Zechariah being struck mute by Gabriel (and later healed)
- The miraculous conception of John
- The virginal conception of Jesus
- Multiple instances of God inspiring humans to speak

Such events, however, do not constitute evidence that Luke intends the birth material to be less historical than the rest of the Gospel. To determine what these tell us about Luke's intent, we must examine the rest of Luke-Acts to see how Luke views miracles. As it turns out, Luke affirms divine action in the world quite robustly. Here is a sampling of miracles he narrates in the Gospel:

- Jesus's baptism, where the Spirit of God appears and God speaks (3:21–22)
- Jesus's temptation (4:1–13)
- Healings (e.g., 4:38–39, 40; 5:12–13, 17–26; 6:18–19)
- Exorcisms (e.g., 4:33–36, 41; 6:18)
- Nature miracles (8:22–25)
- Feeding of the five thousand (9:10–17)
- Jesus's transfiguration (9:28–36)
- Jesus's resurrection (24:1–49)
- Jesus's ascension (24:50–53)

Acts provides many more examples. One might object that the miracles in the birth narrative are more numerous or significant than those in the rest of the Gospel and in Acts. Such an objection, however, does not square with the evidence. The rest of Luke and Acts contain many two-chapter sections that have at least as many miracles as Luke 1–2 (e.g., Luke 4–5, 7–8; Acts 1–2). And as noted in our study of Matthew, the virginal conception is no more significant than Jesus's resurrection. The miracles in the birth narrative therefore do not constitute evidence for legendary intent.

TIME ELAPSED

The time elapsed between Jesus's birth and Luke's writing suggests that Luke is well-positioned to actualize his historiographic intent. The proposed dates for the Gospel of Luke vary significantly. Lower chronologies date Luke to AD 59–60, middle chronologies to AD 80–95, and higher chronologies to AD 110.[65] Following our earlier discussion of Matthew, let us assume 5 BC as Jesus's date of birth and take the middle (majority) view as our starting point: Luke would then be writing 84–99 years after Jesus's birth—a decade later than Matthew but still exceptionally close by the standards of ancient biography. Of the biographies analyzed in part 1, nine have a comparable time elapsed:

- Nepos, *Atticus* (76 years)
- Plutarch, *Otho* (69 years)
- Suetonius, *Nero* (83 years)
- Suetonius, *Otho* (88 years)
- Suetonius, *Titus* (81 years)
- Suetonius, *Domitian* (69 years)
- Suetonius, *Persius* (72 years)
- Suetonius, *Lucan* (67 years)
- Suetonius, *Pliny* (82 years).[66]

Two of these, however, do not have birth material (Plutarch, *Otho*; Suetonius, *Pliny*). Thus, only seven of the ninety-five biographies analyzed in part 1 stand as close to their subject's birth and childhood as Luke does. And this is based on a middle chronology. With a lower chronology, Luke—like Matthew—would be closer to the birth of Jesus than Nepos, Philo, Plutarch, and Suetonius are to the births of any of their subjects. The previous chapter discussed the implications of this for Matthew, but I summarize them below for Luke.

First, Luke would have had exceptional access to sources about Jesus's birth. Luke 1:1–4, of course, indicates as much, but

---

[65] Jonathan Bernier, *Rethinking the Dates of the New Testament: The Evidence for Early Composition* (Baker, 2022), 3, 84, 277.

[66] The smallest times elapsed after these are Plutarch, *Galba* (103 years); Suetonius, *Vitellius* (105 years); Suetonius, *Caligula* (108 years).

what the time elapsed tells us (that the preface does not) is how rare it was for an ancient biographer to be so close to sources about his subject's birth. Whether Luke received his traditions from Mary or from the apostles and other eyewitnesses of Jesus's ministry, he enjoyed excellent access to sources by the standards of ancient biography.

Second, the low time elapsed may explain why Luke seems so confident about the miracles he reports. Whereas ancient biographers often employ *transparency*, *evaluation*, or *distancing* when reporting miracles, Luke reports numerous miracles without using any of these historiographic devices. Luke's proximity to the events and his consequent access to reliable sources may explain his apparent confidence about the miracles he reports.

To sum up: The time elapsed suggests that Luke—like Matthew—had exceptional resources with which to accomplish his historiographic intent. Few ancient biographers wrote so close to the events they report and had access to the sorts of sources that Luke did. Luke therefore not only intends his birth material to be historical but also is in an excellent position to actualize his historiographic intent.

CONCLUSION

The birth narrative and genealogy of Luke are textbook examples of historiographic intent. Luke opens his Gospel with a historiographic preface in which he presents his work—including the birth material—as based on the testimony of the "eyewitnesses and servants of the word" (Luke 1:1–4). He confirms that the birth narrative is source-based by (1) including numerous points that agree with Matthew and can only have come from a source and (2) designating Mary as a source (2:19, 51). The genealogy, too, seems to be based on sources, for much of it follows the Old Testament, and all the points where Luke differs from the Old Testament involve otherwise unknown figures who are far better explained by a nonbiblical source than by fabrication. Luke also employs *evaluation* in the genealogy (3:23), further confirming his historiographic intent. While Luke recounts many miracles in the birth narrative, he also includes many in the rest of the Gospel and in Acts, so these cannot indicate that the birth narrative is less historical. Finally, the time elapsed suggests that Luke is elite among ancient biographers in his proximity to his subject's birth and the sources available to him. Luke therefore both intends for his birth material to be historical and is well-positioned to enact his historiographic intent.

CONCLUSION

The present book has challenged the skepticism of intent that is responsible for the unique distrust of the Gospel birth narratives in modern historical scholarship. I have argued that ancient biographers—including Matthew and Luke—intended their birth material to be historical rather than legendary, and so we cannot casually dismiss it from historical inquiry. In this concluding chapter, I would like to reflect on where we have come from, where we have arrived, and where we might go from here.

FROM AMBIGUITY TO CLARITY

One of the reasons scholars have been able to dismiss the Gospel birth narratives from historical inquiry so easily is ambiguity—both about the questions under discussion and how to answer them. Throughout this book, I have tried to provide greater clarity on both fronts. I distinguished at the outset between two sorts of historiographic skepticism: skepticism of intent and skepticism of truth. These imply that the question of history really involves two questions: "Is this meant to be true?" and "Is this actually true?" I have primarily focused on the question of intent in this study but have also arrived at some insights relevant to the question of truth. I submit that if we wish to make genuine progress toward understanding the historical value of the Gospel birth narratives in the future, the first step is to distinguish much more explicitly between the issues of intent and truth.

The second step is to be clear about how we are answering the historical question(s) we choose to pursue. One of the challenges I have encountered in writing this book is that scholars who assert that the Gospel birth narratives are meant to be legendary rarely explain and defend what counts as legendary intent. Here I have tried to be clear about my own method by identifying four historiographic features (*sources, transparency, evaluation,* and *distancing*) that have served as the basis of my analysis. I am reasonably confident in these features because of how consistently they occur across ancient historiography (see appendixes A–F). I offer them, however, not as a final word but as a starting point for a more robust discussion about how to discern whether an ancient source is meant to be historical.

FROM LEGENDARY TO HISTORICAL

The notion that the Gospel birth narratives are meant to be legendary is a myth. I do not mean that it is not intended to be true—its proponents are sincere—but that it is not true. I recognize that this can be hard for many of us to accept because we have been told it is true by people who seem like they should know. But that is precisely the point: we have been told. We have not tested this theory for ourselves, and in all likelihood the people who told us have not tested it either. The legendary intent hypothesis is a chimera, a creature conceived in a scholarly echo chamber that survives only on its own reverberations and careless readings of ancient sources. It is not based on close readings of ancient biographies or the Gospels.

I speak from personal experience. The seeds for the present book were planted in 2013 when I began to read scholarly literature on the Gospel birth narratives and repeatedly encountered the claim that ancient birth narratives—including the Gospel birth narratives—were not meant to be historical. I examined the ancient biographies that were cited, and what I found did not square with the story I had been told. The ancient biographers in question cited sources, noted differences among their sources, evaluated the historical reliability of claims, and distanced themselves from claims—all in birth material and often in the same passages that supposedly proved their legendary intent. When I returned to the Gospel birth narratives, I found not only that they gave no evidence of legendary intent but also that Luke indicated the historiographic intent of his birth narrative and genealogy using the same historiographic features that appear in ancient biographies.

The present book has attempted to put the key insights from the primary literature before the reader and to place them in dialogue with modern scholarship. Part 1 has shown that ancient biographers composed their birth material with historiographic intent. Part 2 has demonstrated that Matthew and Luke, too, exhibit historiographic intent in their birth material. The Gospel birth narratives, then, are intended to be historical. I recognize that such a conclusion contradicts the oft-repeated maxim that ancient birth narratives are meant to be legendary, but I would invite readers to evaluate my case based not on what they have heard from others but on the primary sources themselves.

Where do we go from here? My proposal is simple: we should approach the Gospel birth narratives the same way we approach any other part of the Gospels (or ancient biographies in general) with respect to their intent. The Gospel birth narratives are not a special case with respect to historiography. They are historical sources that deserve to be studied as such—and it is to this matter that we now turn.

FROM CLOSED CASE TO OPEN HORIZON

The Gospel birth narratives have long been regarded as a closed case in historical Jesus scholarship.[1] And if the Gospel birth narratives are meant to be legendary, this makes good sense. The foregoing study, however, has shown that the Gospel birth narratives are meant to be historical. Now that the question of intent has been answered, the question of truth remains—which is to say that it is time for the real historical work to begin. To

---

[1] See the introduction for examples.

pursue the question of truth would require a monograph of its own, but here I would like to offer three suggestions about how the inquiry should proceed.

First, the inquiry should respect the genre of the Gospel birth narratives and the literary conventions they employ. The Gospel birth narratives appear in ancient biographies, and so we should expect them to operate by the literary and historiographic conventions of ancient biography.[2] We must also be sensitive to other ancient literary conventions, such as the Jewish genealogical conventions that Matthew seems to employ (and Luke may as well). While the modern historian may desire greater accuracy than ancient sources provide, it is unfair to accuse ancient authors of errors when they are simply operating by the historiographic standards of their day.

Second, the inquirers should be transparent about their metaphysical commitments. Our investigation has shown that ancient biographers—including Matthew and Luke—regarded supernatural events as a legitimate aspect of history. Interpreters who subscribe to methodological naturalism will, of course, dismiss the miracle claims of the Gospel birth narratives as improbable a priori. Others who are open to miracle claims may find in the Gospel birth narratives sufficient reason for belief. Yet wherever we find ourselves on this spectrum, we need to articulate our metaphysical commitments rather than pretending that they do not exist.

Third, the inquiry should take seriously Matthew and Luke's proximity to the events they report. Our study has shown that

---

[2] On the literary and historiographic conventions of ancient biography see J. L. Moles, introduction to *The Life of Cicero*, by Plutarch, ed. and trans. J. L. Moles (Aris & Phillips, 1988), 36–39; Christopher Pelling, "Plutarch's Adaptation of His Source-Material," in *Plutarch and History: Eighteen Studies* (Classical Press of Wales, 2002); Craig S. Keener and Edward T. Wright, eds., *Biographies and Jesus: What Does It Mean for the Gospels to Be Biographies?* (Emeth, 2016); Michael R. Licona, *Why Are There Differences in the Gospels? What We Can Learn from Ancient Biography* (Oxford UP, 2017), esp. 19–21; Craig S. Keener, *Christobiography: Memory, History, and the Reliability of the Gospels* (Eerdmans, 2019), 303–27.

Matthew and Luke are breathing rarefied air when it comes to the time elapsed between the birth of their subject and their writing. Whereas Nepos, Philo, Plutarch, and Suetonius are writing on average over 360 years after their subjects' births, Matthew and Luke are probably writing less than 100 years and possibly less than 65 years after Jesus's birth. Such a time elapsed would have given Matthew and Luke exceptional access to sources by the standards of ancient biography. Luke even indicates that he has made good use of this access by citing the "eyewitnesses and servants of the word" (Luke 1:2) and Jesus's mother Mary (2:19, 51) as sources for his birth narrative. A truly historical approach must therefore recognize not only that the Gospel birth narratives are meant to be historical but also that they are more likely to contain reliable information than most ancient birth narratives.

CONCLUSION

Sometime in the mid to late first century AD, two followers of Jesus wrote biographies about him. They did not have to include an account of his origins, but they did, presumably for the same reason as other ancient biographers: they had sources with relevant information. Their sources told a remarkable story. Some of it was quite inconvenient—not least the part about Joseph the son of David not being Jesus's biological father. The two authors, however, told the story they received. They told it with literary and theological artistry, of course, but they did so within the range of flexibility that was normal for ancient biographies. And while they could have distanced themselves from the miracles they found in their sources, they did not, apparently because they thought the miracles really happened.

Scholars today generally dismiss these stories from historical inquiry. They do so primarily because—they have been told—ancient birth narratives were not meant to be historical in the first place. The present study, however, has shown that ancient biographers—including those two biographers of Jesus—composed their birth material with historiographic intent. Of course, the fact that something is intended to be true does not necessarily mean that it is true. But I submit that those who doubt the truth of the Gospel birth narratives should at least do their authors the courtesy of disagreeing with them.

The ultimate contribution of this book is therefore to open a horizon that was previously closed. Matthew and Luke—like other ancient biographers—composed their birth narratives with historiographic intent, and so we must engage them precisely as historical documents. The end of this journey, then, turns out to be the beginning of another. *Ad fontes.*

APPENDIX A
Historiographic Features in Ancient Historians

The table in this appendix presents historiographic features (*sources*, *transparency*, *evaluation*, and *distancing*) in the works of major ancient historians. An em-dash (—) indicates the absence of a particular feature.[1]

---

[1] I owe some of these references to H. D. Westlake, "ΛΕΓΕΤΑΙ in Thucydides," *Mnemosyne* 30 (1977): 345–62; Samuel Byrskog, *Story as History—History as Story: The Gospel Tradition in the Context of Ancient Oral History* (Brill Academic, 2002), 95–97, 124, 149–52, 178, 189.

	Sources	Transparency	Evaluation	Distancing
Herodotus, Histories	1.47, 49, 87, 95, 140, 170, 171, 214; 2.3, 10, 13, 19, 28, 29, 44, 50, 99–146 (passim), 147, 148, 150, 182; 3.55, 115–116, 117; 4.5, 14, 16, 24–25, 27, 76, 81, 150, 192, 196; 5.9, 59, 60, 63, 77; 6.47; 7.60, 224; 8.35, 87, 128, 133; 9.16, 84, 85	1.2, 5, 20, 51, 65, 70, 75, 95, 171, 172, 202; 2.2, 20, 44, 55, 103, 116, 134, 146, 181; 3.2, 3, 9, 32, 45, 47; 4.8, 11, 77, 95, 103, 154; 5.44–45, 85–87; 6.53–54, 75, 84, 137; 7.55, 150–152, 165, 214, 220, 230; 8.84, 94, 120; 9.74	1.1, 5, 20, 51, 70, 75, 172, 182, 214; 2.2, 5, 15, 21, 22, 23, 44, 45, 49, 56, 73, 120, 121, 131, 134, 146, 150; 3.2, 3, 9, 16; 4.5, 11, 25, 77, 96, 105, 155, 195; 5.10, 57, 86, 88; 6.84, 121–124; 7.137, 152, 153, 214, 220–221, 238; 8.8, 94, 119–120, 129; 9.71	1.1, 3, 4, 23, 24, 51, 87, 114, 182, 183, 191, 202; 2.28, 43, 54, 63, 73, 75, 86, 91, 123, 127, 130, 131, 156, 174, 175, 177; 3.1, 16, 18, 20, 24, 26, 30, 33, 34, 116; 4.5, 7, 8, 9, 10, 11, 14, 15, 27, 82, 90, 110, 176, 178, 179, 180, 184, 187, 191, 195; 5.7, 10, 32, 42, 49, 57, 86, 105, 113; 6.14, 44, 52, 54, 61, 69, 76, 105, 117; 7.12, 56, 150–152, 153, 189, 212, 226, 227, 232, 239; 8.8, 38, 39, 55, 65, 88, 129, 134, 138; 9.82, 84, 93, 95*

Appendix A | 207

	Sources	Transparency	Evaluation	Distancing
Thucydides, *Peloponnesian War*	1.9.2; 1.13.2–3; 1.22.2; 1.97.2; 1.132.5; 1.138.1, 6; 3.104.4–6; 6.2.4	1.22.3; 2.5.6; 6.54.1; 6.60.2; 8.87.2–3	1.10.3; 1.20; 1.21.1; 3.113.6; 5.68.2; 6.2.2, 4; 6.54.1; 6.55.1; 6.60.2, 5; 8.87.4–5	1.1.2; 1.22.1; 1.24.4; 1.118.3; 1.134.1; 2.18.5; 2.20.1; 2.47.3; 2.48.1; 2.57.1; 2.77.6; 2.93.4; 2.98.3; 2.102.5; 3.79.3; 3.88.3; 3.94.5; 3.96.1; 3.116.2; 4.24.4; 4.104.2; 5.74.2; 6.2.1; 6.2.2; 6.2.4; 7.44.1; 7.86.4; 8.50.3†
Xenophon, *Hellenica*	—	5.4.7; 6.4.37	5.4.13	2.3.56; 3.1.14; 3.2.27; 3.5.21; 4.2.17, 22; 4.4.10; 4.8.36; 5.3.2; 5.4.57; 6.2.6, 16; 6.4.8, 12, 29, 30, 37; 6.5.26, 29, 49; 7.1.30, 31, 32; 7.4.40

	Sources	Transparency	Evaluation	Distancing
Polybius, *Histories*	3.4.13; 3.8.1; 3.26.1; 3.33.18; 3.48.12; 4.2.1, 2; 4.33.2–3; 4.81.14; 5.33.1; 6.45.1; 9.25.2–4; 10.3.2; 10.28.3; 29.8.10	1.65.9; 2.56.1; 3.6.1; 4.78.3–4; 12.5.4; 12.9.1	1.14.1–3; 1.65.9; 2.16.15; 2.56.3–2.63.6; 3.6.3–6; 3.9.1–5; 3.20.1–5; 3.26.2–7; 3.28.1; 3.47.6–3.48.11; 3.91.7; 4.39.11; 4.42.7–8; 4.78.5; 5.9.7; 10.3.2; 10.28.3; 12 (passim)	1.62.7; 2.16.13; 3.22.3–4; 3.24.2; 4.39.6; 4.43.2; 4.59.5; 5.38.10; 12.5.9; 12.16.9; 12.25.4

* Herodotus: "I am obliged to record the things I am told, but I am certainly not required to believe them—this remark may be taken to apply to the whole of my account" (*Hist.* 7.152; cf. 2.123).

† On λέγεται ("it is said") phrases in Thucydides, see Westlake, "ΛΕΓΕΤΑΙ."

APPENDIX B

Historiographic Data for Cornelius Nepos,
De viris illustribus

The table in this appendix presents the following for Cornelius Nepos, *De viris illustribus* (listed in alphabetical order): (1) location of the birth material; (2) historiographic features (*sources, transparency, evaluation,* and *distancing*); (3) omens; (4) miracles; (5) time elapsed between the subject's birth and Nepos's writing. In the *sources* through miracles columns, features within birth material appear first, with features outside birth material following the double vertical bar (||). An em-dash (—) indicates the absence of a particular feature.

210 | Appendix B

	Birth material	Sources*	Transparency	Evaluation	Distancing	Omens	Miracles	Time elapsed (years)
Agesilaus	1.2	1.1 ‖ 1.1	—‖—	—‖—	—‖—	—‖—	—‖—	411
Alcibiades	1.1–2; 2.1	1.1 ‖ 1.1; 2.2	11.1–2 ‖ 11.1–2	11.1–2 ‖ 7.3; 11.1–2	2.1 ‖ 3.5	—‖—	—‖—	416
Aristides	1.1	—‖—	—‖—	—‖—	—‖—	—‖—	—‖—	486
Atticus	1.1–3; 2.1	—‖ 13.7; 16.3; 17.1–3; 18.1–6	—‖—	—‖—	—‖—	—‖—	—‖—	76
Cato	1.1a	3.5 ‖ 1.1b; 3.5	—‖—	—‖—	—‖—	—‖—	—‖—	200
Chabrais	—	—‖—	—‖—	—‖—	—‖—	—‖—	—‖—	386
Cimon	1.1; 2.1	—‖—	—‖—	—‖—	—‖—	—‖—	—‖—	476
Conon	—	—‖—	—‖ 5.4	—‖ 5.4	—‖—	—‖—	—‖—	411
Datames	1.1	—‖—	—‖—	—‖—	—‖—	—‖—	—‖—	377
Dion	1.1	—‖—	—‖—	—‖—	—‖—	—‖—	—‖—	374
Epaminondas	1.1; 2.1–3	—‖—	—‖—	—‖—	—‖—	—‖—	—‖—	376
Eumenes	1.2, 4	—‖—	—‖—	—‖—	—‖—	—‖—	—‖—	327

Hamilcar	1.1	—||—	—||—	—||—	—||—	—||—	—||—	257
Hannibal	1.1; 2.3–3.1	2.3–6 || 13.2–3	—||—	—||— 8.2; 13.1	—||—	—||—	—||—	219
Iphicrates	—	—||— 3.2	—||—	—||—	—||—	—||—	—||—	384
Lysander	—	—||— 3.5	—||—	—||—	—||— 3.5	—||—	—||—	426
Miltiades	1.1	—||—	—||—	—||—	—||—	—||— 1.2–4	—||—	521
Pausanias	—	—||—	—||—	—||—	—||— 5.3	—||— 5.5	—||—	476
Pelopidas	—	—||—	—||—	—||—	—||—	—||—	—||—	376
Phocion	—	—||—	—||—	—||—	—||—	—||—	—||—	367
Themistocles	1.1–2	—||—	—||— 9.1; 10.4	—||— 9.1; 10.4	—||— 10.1	—||— 2.6–7	—||—	490
Thrasybulus	1.1	—||—	—||—	—||—	—||—	—||—	—||—	416
Timoleon	1.1	—||—	—||—	—||—	—||—	—||—	—||—	377
Timotheus	1.1	—||—	—||—	—||—	—||—	—||—	—||—	377

* On Nepos's use of sources, see James R. Bradley, *The Sources of Cornelius Nepos: Selected Lives*, Harvard Dissertations in Classics (Garland, 1991); Francis Titchener, "Cornelius Nepos and the Biographical Tradition," *Greece & Rome* 50.1 (2003): 88–90; Chris Alfred, "Source Valuation in Greek and Roman Biography: From Xenophon to Suetonius," in *Biographies and Jesus: What Does It Mean for the Gospels to Be Biographies?* ed. Craig S. Keener and Edward T. Wright (Emeth, 2016), 82–84; Timothy J. Christian, "Cornelius Nepos's *Themistocles*: A Targeted Comparison with the Histories of Herodotus and Thucydides with Implications for the Historical Reliability of the Gospels," in Keener and Wright, *Biographies and Jesus*; Fasil Woldemariam, "A Targeted Comparison of Plutarch's, Xenophon's, and Nepos's Biographies of Agesilaus, with Implications for the Historical Reliability of the Synoptics," in Keener and Wright, *Biographies and Jesus*; John Alexander Lobur, *Cornelius Nepos: A Study in the Evidence and Influence* (University of Michigan Press, 2021), 70–88.

APPENDIX C
Historiographic Data for Philo, *On the Life of Moses*

The table in this appendix presents the following for Philo, *On the Life of Moses* (listed in alphabetical order): (1) location of the birth material; (2) historiographic features (*sources, transparency, evaluation,* and *distancing*); (3) omens; (4) miracles; (5) time elapsed between the subject's birth and Philo's writing. In the *sources* through miracles columns, features within birth material appear first, with features outside birth material following the double vertical bar (||). An em-dash (—) indicates the absence of a particular feature.

	Birth material	Sources*	Transparency	Evaluation	Distancing	Omens	Miracles	Time elapsed (years)
On the Life of Moses	1.5–24	1.4, 9, 13 ‖ 1.4, 124, 126, 135, 158, 165, 234, 304; 2.38, 84, 132	–‖ 1.1	–‖–	–‖–	–‖–	1.12, 17, 19 ‖ 1.57, 65–84, 91–95, 96–145, 165–166, 176–179, 184–186, 198–209, 210–211, 277–291; 2.69, 280–288, 291	1,240

* I owe some of these references to Esteban Hidalgo, "A Redaction-Critical Study on Philo's *On the Life of Moses*, Book One," in *Biographies and Jesus: What Does It Mean for the Gospels to Be Biographies?* ed. Craig S. Keener and Edward T. Wright (Emeth, 2016), 278–80. One might classify some of these references as *distancing*; I have listed them as *sources* because Philo seems to trust his sources (*Moses* 1.4) and so would have less need for *distancing*.

APPENDIX D
Historiographic Data for Plutarch, *Lives*

The table in this appendix presents the following for Plutarch, *Lives* (listed in alphabetical order): (1) location of the birth material; (2) historiographic features (*sources, transparency, evaluation,* and *distancing*); (3) omens; (4) miracles; (5) time elapsed between the subject's birth and Plutarch's writing. In the *sources* through miracles columns, features within birth material appear first, with features outside birth material following the double vertical bar (||). An em-dash (—) indicates the absence of a particular feature.

216 | Appendix D

	Birth material	Sources*	Transparency	Evaluation†	Distancing	Omens	Miracles	Time elapsed (years)
Aemilius Paulus	2.1–3	2.1 || 10.4; 19.2	–|| 16.1; 21.3; 37.2	–|| 25.2	–|| 9.4; 21.3; 24.3; 25.1, 2	–|| 24.1	–|| 24.1; 25.1, 2	329
Agesilaus	1.1–2.1	–||	–||	–||	1.2	–||	–||	545
Agis	3.2	–||	–|| 9.2; 15.2	–|| 15.2	–|| 18.4	–||	–||	362
Alcibiades	1.1–6.4	1.2, 4; 3.1; 6.2 || 13.2; 16.2; 20.4; 33.1	–|| 39.2	1.2; 3.1 || 32.2	–|| 1.1; 13.2	–|| 39.2	–||	550
Alexander	2.1–3.5; 4.4–8.4	3.2; 4.2; 8.2 || 16.7; 17.3; 24.8; 26.1; 30.7; 31.2; 47.2; 54.1; 55.3; 60.1, 6; 70.1	2.5–6; 3.2 || 18.2; 20.5; 33.6; 38.4; 46.1; 55.3, 4; 60.3; 61.1	2.1 || 46.2; 75.3; 77.3	2.1, 4 || 10.4; 18.2; 24.5; 53.3; 54.1; 60.3; 64.1; 77.1	3.3–5 || 14.5; 25.1, 3–4; 50.2–3; 52.1; 57.3; 73.2, 3	–||	456
Antonius	1.1–2.1	–|| 2.2; 6.1; 9.3; 28.7; 59.4; 68.4; 82.2	–|| 86.1–2, 5	–|| 2.2; 6.1–2; 86.2	–|| 4.1; 9.4; 17.3; 27.2; 42.3; 44.2; 52.1	–|| 16.3–4; 60.2	–||	183
Aratus	2.1–3	–|| 3.2, 4; 13.2; 54.1	–|| 32.2–3; 33.2; 38.7–8	–|| 3.2; 33.3; 38.8	–|| 3.4; 13.3; 17.2; 22.1	–||	–|| 22.1	371
Aristides	1.1a	–||	–|| 1.1b; 5.7; 26.1; 27.2	–|| 5.7; 19.5; 26.2–3; 27.3	–||	–|| 19.1	–||	620

Appendix D | 217

Artaxerxes	1.1–2.1	–‖ 4.1; 9.1, 4; 13.3; 18.1; 19.3; 22.1	1.2 ‖ 4.1; 6.6; 10.1–11.6; 13.3; 19.4; 23.2, 4; 29.6	1.2 ‖ 4.1; 6.6; 13.3–4; 18.5	1.2 ‖ 7.2	–‖–	–‖–	504
Brutus	1.1–5	–‖ 2.4–5; 13.2; 23.1, 4; 26.4; 27.2; 28.2; 29.6; 40.1; 41.4; 42.4; 45.1; 51.1; 53.4	1.4 ‖ 24.5; 48.1; 52.5; 53.5	1.5 ‖ 53.5	–‖ 4.3; 5.1, 2; 9.2; 17.1; 27.4; 29.5; 36.1; 39.2; 48.1; 53.2	–‖ 12.6; 36.1–4; 37.4; 39.2; 41.4; 48.1, 2	–‖–	185
Caesar	—	–‖ 47.2; 63.2	–‖ 48.2; 54.1; 66.6	–‖ 8.3; 54.1	–‖ 28.5; 32.6; 46.2; 49.4; 63.3; 69.5	–‖ 19.4; 42.1; 43.2; 47.1; 63.1, 3; 68.2; 69.3	–‖ 66.1	200
Caius Gracchus	Tiberius Gracchus 1.1–5	–‖ 4.4	–‖ 13.3; 17.2, 3	–‖–	–‖ 11.1; 16.3, 5; 19.1	–‖ 11.1	–‖–	253
Caius Marius	3.1; 36.5–6a	–‖ 2.1; 17.3; 26.3	36.6a ‖ 11.8; 39.1	–‖ 11.7; 36.6b	–‖ 2.2; 3.2; 4.1; 5.1; 11.5; 17.4; 18.4; 25.1	36.5 ‖ 5.1; 17.1, 3; 26.3; 40.6	–‖–	257
Camillus	—	–‖–	–‖ 20.3; 33.6	–‖–	–‖ 5.4; 13.2	–‖–	–‖–	546

218 | Appendix D

	Birth material	Sources*	Transparency	Evaluation†	Distancing	Omens	Miracles	Time elapsed (years)
Cato Major	1.1–4	1.1, 3 ‖ 4.3; 17.4; 19.6; 20.5, 8; 24.6	–‖ 7.2; 17.4	–‖ 7.2; 12.4	–‖ 24.5, 6	–‖–	–‖–	334
Cato Minor	1.1–2.6	–‖ 25.1	–‖–	–‖ 11.4; 44.2	1.2, 5 ‖ 9.1; 11.4; 21.2; 23.3; 24.1; 25.5; 42.4; 44.1; 70.2; 72.2; 73.1	–‖–	–‖–	195
Cicero	1.1–2; 1.5–2.4	2.3 ‖ 24.3; 37.3; 45.2	1.1 ‖ 4.1	1.1; 2.2	1.1; 2.1 ‖ 1.3, 4; 4.4; 5.3; 6.3; 9.1; 17.1; 33.4; 36.3; 39.5; 40.2; 41.1; 44.2, 3, 5; 46.3; 48.2; 49.3	2.2 ‖ 20.1; 47.5	–‖–	206
Cimon	4.1–4	4.1, 4 ‖ 5.3; 9.1; 10.2, 4, 5; 14.4; 15.3; 16.3, 7, 8; 19.1, 4	–‖ 16.1; 19.1	–‖–	4.2 ‖ 14.2; 16.5; 18.6	–‖ 6.5; 18.3, 4	–‖–	610
Cleomenes	2.2	–‖ 9.2; 19.3	–‖ 5.3; 28.3	–‖–	2.2 ‖ 1.1; 27.2; 37.2	–‖ 7.2	–‖–	360
Coriolanus	1.1–2; 2.1	–‖–	–‖–	–‖–	–‖ 3.4; 37.3; 38.1	–‖–	–‖ 3.4	620

Crassus	1.1	—|| 5.4; 13.3	—|| 31.6	—|| 31.6	—|| 8.3; 13.1; 19.4; 23.1; 25.12; 31.7	—|| 8.3; 17.6; 18.5; 19.3-6	—||	215
Demetrius	2.1	2.1 || 13.1-2; 27.2	—|| 27.2	—||	—|| 19.4; 22.3; 34.2	—|| 29.1	—||	436
Demosthenes	4.1-5.5	4.1, 5; 5.4 || 9.4; 11.1, 3; 12.4; 15.2; 22.2; 27.5	4.3; 5.4 || 10.2; 15.2; 30.1	4.1	5.1 || 7.1	—|| 29.2	—||	484
Dion	4.1-5.3	4.2 || 6.2; 11.2; 14.4; 20.2; 24.5; 54.1	—|| 31.2; 35.3-5	—|| 20.2; 31.2; 36.1-2	5.3 || 7.4; 13.2, 3; 17.4; 20.2; 21.5; 24.3; 56.2	—|| 24.3-4; 29.3; 55.1-2	—||	508
Eumenes	1.1-2	1.1 || —	—||	1.2 || —	—|| 9.6	—|| 6.5	—||	461
Fabius	1.1-2	—||	1.1-2 || 21.4	—||	1.1-2 || 2.3	—||	—|| 2.3	380
Flamininus	—	—|| 16.3-4	—|| 18.4; 20.5	—||	—||	—||	—||	329
Galba	—	—||	—|| 14.4; 19.5; 27.2	—|| 25.3	—|| 3.1, 3; 4.2; 19.4, 5; 22.7; 25.1; 27.3	—|| 15.4; 23.2	—||	103
Lucullus	1.1-5	1.3 || 26.6; 28.7	—|| 43.1	—||	—|| 2.3, 6; 10.1; 11.6; 12.1; 23.3; 43.1	—|| 2.3; 12.1-2; 23.3-4; 24.6-7	—||	217

	Birth material	Sources*	Transparency	Evaluation†	Distancing	Omens	Miracles	Time elapsed (years)
Lycurgus	1.4–2.3	1.3 ‖ 1.3; 5.7; 23.1; 28.1; 31.3	1.1, 4 ‖ 1.1; 5.8; 8.3; 11.4; 23.1; 31.4	1.4 ‖ 4.5–6; 5.8; 14.1; 27.3; 28.6	1.1 ‖ 4.4–5; 14.4; 31.3	–‖–	–‖–	900
Lysander	2.1–3	2.3 ‖ 18.3	–‖–	–‖–	2.1 ‖ 12.1; 22.4; 26.1	–‖ 12.1	–‖ 26.1	550
Marcellus	1.1	1.1	–‖ 8.4; 19.5–6; 30.4	–‖ 8.5	–‖–	–‖ 4.1; 12.1; 28.2	–‖–	370
Nicias	2.1	2.1 ‖ 1.5–6; 4.2, 4, 5, 6; 8.2; 11.5–6; 17.4	–‖–	–‖–	–‖ 13.1; 15.3	–‖ 13.1	–‖–	570
Numa Pompilius	—	–‖ 21.4	–‖ 1.1–2; 9.8; 21.1	–‖ 13.4	–‖ 1.4; 4.1, 6; 6.4; 8.4, 6, 10; 9.1, 5; 10.1; 11.1; 13.1; 14.2; 15.2–3, 6	–‖ 6.4	–‖–	853
Otho	—	–‖ 3.2; 9.3; 14.1; 18.1	–‖ 6.5; 9.1, 3	–‖–	–‖–	–‖ 4.4	–‖–	69

Appendix D | 221

Pelopidas	3.1	—||—	—||—	—||—	—||—	—|| 20.4; 22.1–2; 31.2	—||—	510
Pericles	3.1–6.1	3.3–4 || 8.3–5; 9.1–2; 10.7; 13.5; 15.5–16.2; 23.1; 24.6; 26.3; 28.1, 5–6; 33.1; 38.2	4.1; 5.3 || 9.1; 10.4; 26.1; 31.1, 5	5.3 || 10.6–7; 26.1; 28.2–3; 31.1	3.2 || 6.2; 10.5; 13.8; 16.7; 24.2–3, 7; 26.4; 30.1	3.2	—||—	595
Philopoemen	1.1–4	—|| 2.3	—|| 16.4	—|| 2.1	—||—	—||—	—||—	353
Phocion	—	—|| 17.6; 19.1	—|| 27.5	—||—	—|| 10.3	—|| 28.2	—||—	501
Pompey	1.1–3	—|| 10.4	—||—	—|| 10.4	—|| 2.2; 10.4	—||—	—||—	206
Publicola	1.1	—||—	—|| 8.4; 16.5; 19.5	—||—	—|| 1.2	—||—	—||—	650
Pyrrhus	1.1–3.3	1.1 || 8.2	1.1–2; 2.5 || 17.4; 27.4	—||—	—|| 8.2, 3; 21.9	—|| 11.2; 30.2; 31.2	—||—	419

222 | Appendix D

	Birth material	Sources*	Transparency	Evaluation†	Distancing	Omens	Miracles	Time elapsed (years)
Romulus	2.1b–6.2	–‖ 8.7; 14.1; 16.7; 17.5; 29.7	1.1–2.1a; 2.1b–4.3; 6.1 ‖ 1.1–2.1a; 10.1; 13.2; 14.6; 15.2; 21.2, 6–7; 23.3; 27.5; 29.1, 3	2.3; 3.1; 6.1 ‖ 2.1a; 12.1; 13.3; 14.2, 7; 15.3; 16.8; 17.2, 5; 20.2; 21.2–3; 25.3; 28.6	2.3, 6; 4.2–3; 5.3, 4; 6.1–2 ‖ 1.4; 9.3, 5; 12.1, 2; 15.1; 20.5–6; 22.1; 28.1, 4, 6	–‖ 9.3, 5	–‖ 8.7	870
Sertorius	2	–‖–	–‖–	–‖–	–‖ 9.3–4	–‖–	–‖–	226
Solon	1.1–2	1.1–2 ‖ 6.3; 14.5–6; 15.2; 5; 16.2; 18.4; 19.3; 23.3; 25.1; 26.1, 4	1.1 ‖ 4.4; 5.1; 9.1; 10.1–2; 14.4; 15.4; 25.2; 27.1	–‖ 15.5; 19.4; 27.1; 32.4	1.2 ‖ 4.1; 6.1; 14.5; 18.5; 27.2	–‖–	–‖–	730
Sulla	1.1–3	–‖ 14.2, 6; 17.1; 37.1	–‖–	–‖–	1.1 ‖ 14.1; 29.6; 34.5	–‖ 7.2; 11.1; 17.1–2	–‖ 34.5	238
Themistocles	1.1–2.6	1.1 ‖ 4.3; 7.5–6; 8.2–3; 10.4; 13.3; 14.1; 17.1; 25.1; 27.5; 32.1	1.2; 2.3 ‖ 5.1; 25.3; 27.1, 5	1.3; 2.4, 6 ‖ 25.1, 3; 27.1	1.1; 2.1 ‖ 5.1; 15.1	–‖ 26.2–3	–‖–	624

Theseus	2.1; 3.1–6.1	3.2 ‖ 11.2; 14.3; 19.1; 23.3; 25.2, 5; 26.2–3; 35.2; 36.3	2.1; 4.1 ‖ 10.1–2; 15.2–16.2; 17.3–6; 19.1–7; 20.1–5; 26.1; 27.4; 29.1, 3; 30.4; 31.1; 32.4; 33.2; 34.2	–‖ 16.3; 26.1–2; 27.2, 5; 28.1–2; 29.4–5; 30.5; 31.1–4; 32.5; 34.2	1.3; 2.1; 3.2–3; 6.1 ‖ 1.3; 2.1; 12.3; 18.2; 21.2; 22.1, 3; 23.2, 3; 25.1; 30.1; 32.1; 34.1; 35.5; 36.1	3.3 ‖ 35.5	900
Tiberius Gracchus	1.1–5	–‖ 2.4; 4.3; 8.7	–‖ 4.3; 8.5; 21.2	–‖ 4.3; 21.2	1.2 ‖ 2.2; 7.3; 20.1	–‖ 17.1, 3	264
Timoleon	—	–‖—	–‖—	–‖—	–‖—	–‖—	511

* See further A. J. Gossage, "Plutarch," in *Latin Biography*, ed. T. A. Dorey, Studies in Latin Literature and Its Influence (Basic, 1967), 51–52; John Buckler, "Plutarch and Autopsy," *ANRW* 33.6:4788–830; Christopher Pelling, "Plutarch's Method of Work in the Roman Lives," in *Plutarch and History: Eighteen Studies* (Classical Press of Wales, 2002), 11–19; Christopher Pelling, "Plutarch's Adaptation of His Source-Material," in *Plutarch and History*, 91–115; Alfred, "Source Valuation," 86–93; Benson Goh, "Galba: A Comparison of Suetonius's and Plutarch's Biographies and Tacitus's Histories with Implications for the Historical Reliability of the Gospels," in *Biographies and Jesus: What Does It Mean for the Gospels to Be Biographies?* ed. Craig S. Keener and Edward T. Wright (Emeth, 2016); Fasil Woldemariam, "A Targeted Comparison of Plutarch's, Xenophon's, and Nepos's Biographies of Agesilaus, with Implications for the Historical Reliability of the Synoptics," in Keener and Wright, *Biographies and Jesus*.

† See further Brad L. Cook, "Plutarch's Use of λέγεται: Narrative Design and Source in Alexander," *Greek, Roman, and Byzantine Studies* 42 (2001): 335–42; Pelling, "Plutarch's Adaptation," 144–52; Alfred, "Source Valuation," 86–93.

APPENDIX E

Historiographic Data for Suetonius, *Lives of the Caesars*

The table below presents the following for Suetonius, *Lives of the Caesars* and *Lives of Illustrious Men* (listed in order of appearance in the LCL edition): (1) location of the birth material; (2) historiographic features (*sources, transparency, evaluation,* and *distancing*); (3) omens; (4) miracles; (5) time elapsed between the subject's birth and Suetonius's writing. In the *sources* through miracles columns, features within birth material appear first, with features outside birth material following the double vertical bar (||). An em-dash (—) indicates the absence of a particular feature.

The LCL edition does not provide reference numbers for *Horace, Tibullus, Persius, Lucan, Pliny the Elder,* and *Passienus Crispus,* so here I cite the paragraph and line in the corresponding Latin text of the LCL edition.

	Birth material	Sources	Transparency	Evaluation	Distancing	Omens	Miracles	Time elapsed (years)
Julius	56.7	56.7 ‖ 1.3; 9.2–3; 30.5; 49; 50.1; 51; 52.1, 3; 55.1–2, 3, 4–5; 56.1–2; 81	–‖ 30.2–3; 52.2; 78; 86	–‖ 30.4; 55.3; 87	–‖ 13.1; 30.3; 45.1; 47; 48; 49; 55.2; 88	–‖ 1.3; 7.2; 81.1–3; 88	–‖ 32	219
Augustus	1.1–8.1; 94.1–9	1; 2.3; 3.2; 5; 7.1; 94.3, 4, 5, 6 ‖ 10.4; 15	2.3; 3.1; 4.2; 6; 94.8 ‖ 27.4	3.1; 4.2 ‖ 27.4	94.4, 7 ‖ 23.2	94.1–9 ‖ 94.10–97.3	–‖ 6	182
Tiberius	1–6; 14.2; 57.1	2.1, 3; 6.3; 57.1 ‖ 21.3–6; 59; 61.1, 6; 62.2; 66; 67.1	5 ‖ 21.2; 52.3; 67.2; 73.2	5 ‖ 21.3; 62.3; 67.3–4	3.2 ‖ 51.1; 52.3; 54.2; 62.3; 69; 70.1	2.2; 14.2 ‖ 14.3–4; 19; 74	–‖ –	161
Gaius Caligula	1–8	–‖ 49.3	8.1–2 ‖ 19.3; 25.1; 58.2–3	8.2–5 ‖ 12.3; 19.3; 23.2	1.2; 2; 3.1; 4; 5 ‖ 8.5; 12.2; 20; 22.4	5 ‖ 57	–‖ 60	108
Claudius	1.1–2.1	1.4 ‖ 2.2; 3.2–4.6; 15.3; 21.2; 41.2–3	–‖ 27.1; 44.2–3	1.4, 6 ‖ 29.3	1.1, 4 ‖ 9.1; 15.3; 32; 37.2	–‖ 7; 13.2; 37; 46	–‖ –	129

Nero	1.1–7.1; 52 (cf. 20.1; 22.1)	2.2 ‖ 34.4; 52; 57.2	—‖—	6.4 ‖—	1.1,2; 6.1; 7.1 ‖ 12.2; 21.3; 23.2; 28.2; 29; 32.3; 37.2; 43.1	6.1–2 ‖ 19.1; 36.1; 40.1–3; 41.2; 46	—‖—	83
Galba	2.1–4.2	2; 4.1 ‖	3.1 ‖ 20.1	—‖ 20.1	3.2, 4 ‖ 18.3; 22	4.2 ‖ 1; 6.2; 9.2; 10.4; 18.1–19.1	—‖—	122
Otho	1.1–2.1	—‖ 10.1	—‖ 6.2	—‖—	2.1 ‖ 3.2; 7.2; 12.1	—‖ 4.1	—‖—	88
Vitellius	1.1–3.2	—‖—	1.1–2.1 ‖ 7.1	2.2 ‖ 7.1	3.2 ‖—	3.2 ‖ 9; 14.5; 18	—‖—	105
Vespasian	1.1–2.1; 5.2	1.2, 3 ‖	1.2, 4 ‖ 16.3	1.2, 4 ‖ 16.3	5.2 ‖ 4.3; 7.1; 21; 25	5.2 ‖ 4.5; 5.3–7; 7.1–3; 24	—‖—	111
Titus	1.1–3.1	—‖ 3.2	—‖ 10.2	—‖ 10.2	2 ‖ 9.2; 10.1	—‖ 10.1	—‖—	81
Domitian	1.1	1.1 ‖ 17.2; 18.2	—‖—	—‖—	1.1 ‖ 14.2; 23.2	—‖ 14.1; 15.2–3	—‖—	69
Terence	1	1 ‖ 1; 2; 3; 4; 5	1 ‖—	1 ‖—	—‖ 1; 3; 5	—‖—	—‖—	290

	Birth material	Sources	Transparency	Evaluation	Distancing	Omens	Miracles	Time elapsed (years)
Virgil	1–6a; 17	17 ‖ 18; 29; 30; 38; 43–46	1 ‖—	—‖ 10	4 ‖ 9; 22; 32; 34; 42	3; 5 ‖—	—‖—	175
Horace	1.1–5	1.1–2 ‖ 1.10–16; 2.1–7, 10–19, 28–31; 3; 4.6–8	1.2–5 ‖—	—‖ 4.8–10	—‖ 4.1	—‖—	—‖—	170
Tibullus	—	—‖ 1.1–4	—‖—	—‖—	—‖ 2.5–6	—‖—	—‖—	153
Persius	1.1–3.2	—‖ 9.1–3	—‖ 8.2–3	—‖—	—‖—	—‖—	—‖—	72
Lucan	3.1–2	—‖ 1.5–2.2; 5.13–15	—‖—	—‖—	—‖—	—‖—	—‖—	67
Pliny the Elder	—	—‖—	—‖ 1.11–13	—‖—	—‖—	—‖—	—‖—	82
Passienus Crispus	—	—‖—	—‖—	—‖—	—‖—	—‖—	—‖—	115

* On Suetonius's use of sources see Jacques Gascou, *Suétone historien*, Bibliothèque des écoles françaises d'Athènes et de Rome 255 (École française, 1984), 457–567; Alfred, "Source Valuation," 93–99; Benson Goh, "Galba: A Comparison of Suetonius's and Plutarch's Biographies and Tacitus's *Histories* with Implications for the Historical Reliability of the Gospels," in *Biographies and Jesus: What Does It Mean for the Gospels to Be Biographies?* ed. Craig S. Keener and Edward T. Wright (Emeth, 2016); Craig S. Keener, "Otho: A Targeted Comparison of Suetonius's Biography and Tacitus's History, with Implications for the Gospels' Historical Reliability," in Keener and Wright, *Biographies and Jesus*, 143–71.

APPENDIX F

Historiographic Data for Other Ancient Biographers

The table in this appendix presents the following for other ancient biographers (listed in chronological order): (1) location of the birth material; (2) historiographic features (*sources, transparency, evaluation,* and *distancing*); (3) omens; (4) miracles; (5) time elapsed between the subject's birth and the biographer's writing. In the *sources* through miracles columns, features within birth material are presented first, with features outside birth material following the double vertical bar (||). An em-dash (—) indicates the absence of a particular feature.[1]

---

[1] One work discussed by Miller and Lincoln that I do not include here is Philostratus, *Life of Apollonius of Tyana* (Robert J. Miller, *Born Divine: The Births of Jesus and Other Sons of God* [Polebridge, 2003], 147–49; Andrew T. Lincoln, *Born of a Virgin? Reconceiving Jesus in the Bible, Tradition, and Theology* [Eerdmans, 2013], 64–65, 121). The birth material of *Apollonius* does contain historiographic features. However, I do not include it here because there is significant doubt about whether it is an ancient biography. For a discussion of the issues, see Craig S. Keener, *Christobiography: Memory, History, and the Reliability of the Gospels* (Eerdmans, 2019), 46–48.

	Birth material	Sources	Transparency	Evaluation	Distancing	Omens	Miracles	Time elapsed (years)
Tacitus, *Agricola* (first century AD)	4	4 ‖ 22; 43*	–‖ 40	–‖ 38	–‖ 29	–‖–	–‖–	58
Lucian, *Demonax* (second century AD)†	3	1 ‖ 1	–‖–	–‖–	–‖–	–‖–	–‖–	105
Diogenes Laertius, *Lives of Eminent Philosophers* (third century AD)‡	3.1–5a (Plato)	3.1, 2, 3, 4–5a ‖ 3.5b, 6, 7, 8, 9–17, 21–22, 23, 24, 25, 26, 27–28, 29–30, 31–32, 34, 36, 37, 39, 40, 41–43a, 43b–45, 55, 80, 109	3.4 ‖ 3.6, 19, 20, 40, 48, 51	3.5 ‖ 47, 48	3.1, 2, 3, 5 ‖ 3.6, 18, 24, 30, 31, 33, 35, 36, 37, 38, 39, 46, 56–62	–‖–	–‖–	658
	10.1a, 14b (Epicurus)	10.1a, 14b ‖ 10.1b, 2, 12, 13, 14a, 15, 16–21, 22, 23, 24, 25, 26–28, 35–117, 119, 121–135, 136, 138, 139–154	–‖ 10.2, 3–12	–‖ 10.9	–‖ 10.2	–‖–	–‖–	570

Porphyry, Life of Pythagoras (third century AD)	1–2, 10–11a	—‖ 3, 4, 7, 9, 15, 32, 59, 61	1, 2, 10–11a ‖ 5, 55–56, 57	—‖ 56	2 ‖ 4, 14, 23–25, 27, 28, 44, 60	—‖—	—‖ 29, 30, 31, 33	829
Iamblichus, On the Pythagorean Life (fourth century AD)**	3–10	—‖ 93, 145, 157, 158, 189, 233	5 ‖ 126, 146, 241–42, 248, 251, 254	7 ‖ 62, 134, 137, 143, 148, 221, 248, 265	3, 4 ‖ 11, 25, 29, 33, 34, 58, 60, 61, 74, 82, 89, 91, 112, 114, 122, 126, 127, 130, 131, 132, 135, 139, 140, 143, 151, 158, 163, 170, 185, 197, 200, 237, 239, 245, 246, 247, 249, 263, 265	3–4, 5 ‖ 25, 221	8 ‖ 31–32, 62, 63, 70, 91, 134, 135–36, 143, 148	859

* Tacitus cites Livy and Fabius Rusticus as sources in *Agr.* 10, but not regarding Agricola's life.

† On *Demonax* as an ancient biography, see Mark Beck, "Lucian's *Life of Demonax*: The Socratic Paradigm, Individuality, and Personality," in *Writing Biography in Greece and Rome: Narrative Technique and Fictionalization*, ed. Koen De Temmerman and Kristoffel Demoen (Cambridge University Press, 2016), 80; Keener, *Christobiography*, 92.

‡ I focus on the lives of Plato and Epicurus because they are cited by Miller or Lincoln. See Miller, *Born Divine*, 145–47; Lincoln, *Born of a Virgin?* 62–65, 95.

** The numbers cited here are paragraph numbers rather than chapter numbers.

BIBLIOGRAPHY

Adams, Sean A. "Luke's Preface and Its Relationship to Greek Historiography: A Response to Loveday Alexander." *JGRChJ* 3 (2006): 177–91.

Adams, Sean A. "What Are *Bioi/Vitae*? Generic Self-Consciousness in Ancient Biography." In *The Oxford Handbook of Ancient Biography*. Edited by Koen De Temmerman. Oxford University Press, 2020.

Albrecht, Michael von. *A History of Roman Literature: From Livius Andronicus to Boethius: With Special Regard to Its Influence on World Literature*. Rev. ed. 2 vols. *Mnemosyne: Bibliotheca Classica Batavia* 165. Brill, 1997.

Alexander, Loveday. *Acts in Its Ancient Literary Context: A Classicist Looks at the Acts of the Apostles*. Early Christianity in Context. T&T Clark, 2005.

Alexander, Loveday. *The Preface to Luke's Gospel: Literary Convention and Social Context in Luke 1.1–4 and Acts 1.1*. SNTSMS 78. Cambridge University Press, 1993.

Alfred, Chris. "Source Valuation in Greek and Roman Biography: From Xenophon to Suetonius." In Keener and Wright, *Biographies and Jesus*.

Allison, Dale C., Jr. *The New Moses: A Matthean Typology*. Fortress, 1993.

Aune, David E. "Luke 1.1–4: Historical or Scientific *Prooimion*?" In *Paul, Luke and the Graeco-Roman World: Essays in Honour of Alexander J. M. Wedderburn*. Edited by Alf Christophersen,

Carsten Claussen, Jörg Frey, and Bruce Longenecker. JSNTSup 217. Sheffield Academic, 2002.

Aune, David E. *The New Testament in Its Literary Environment*. Library of Early Christianity 8. Westminster, 1987.

Aus, Roger David. *Matthew 1–2 and the Virginal Conception: In Light of Palestinian and Hellenistic Judaic Traditions on the Birth of Israel's First Redeemer, Moses*. Studies in Judaism. University Press of America, 2004.

Baldwin, Barry. *Suetonius*. Hakkert, 1983.

Bauckham, Richard. *Jesus and the Eyewitnesses: The Gospels as Eyewitness Testimony*. 2nd ed. Eerdmans, 2017.

Bauckham, Richard. *Jude and the Relatives of Jesus in the Early Church*. T&T Clark, 1990.

Bauckham, Richard. "More on Kainam the Son of Arpachshad in Luke's Genealogy." *ETL* 67.1 (1991): 95–102.

Bauckham, Richard. "Tamar's Ancestry and Rahab's Marriage: Two Problems in the Matthean Genealogy." *NovT* 37.4 (1995): 313–29.

Baum, Armin D. "Lk 1,1–4 zwischen antiker Historiografie und Fachprosa: Zum literaturgeschichtlichen Kontext des lukanischen Prologs." *ZNW* 101 (2010): 33–54.

Berger, Klaus. "Hellenistische Gattungen im Neuen Testament." *ANRW* 25.2. Part 2, Principat, 25.2. Edited by H. Temporini and W. Haase. de Gruyter, 1984.

Bernier, Jonathan. *Rethinking the Dates of the New Testament: The Evidence for Early Composition*. Baker, 2022.

Blomberg, Craig L. "Matthew." In *Commentary on the New Testament Use of the Old Testament*. Edited by G. K. Beale and D. A. Carson. Baker Academic, 2007.

Bock, Darrell L. *Luke*. 2 vols. BECNT. Baker Academic, 1994–96.

Bock, Darrell L. *Proclamation from Prophecy and Pattern: Lucan Old Testament Christology*. JSNTSup 12. JSOT, 1987.

Bond, Helen K. *The First Biography of Jesus: Genre and Meaning in Mark's Gospel*. Eerdmans, 2020.

Borg, Marcus J. *Jesus: Uncovering the Life, Teachings, and Relevance of a Religious Revolutionary*. HarperSanFrancisco, 2006.

Bovon, François. *Luke 1: A Commentary on the Gospel of Luke 1:1–9:50*. Translated by Christine M. Thomas. Hermeneia. Fortress, 2002.

Bradley, James R. *The Sources of Cornelius Nepos: Selected Lives*. Harvard Dissertations in Classics. Garland, 1991.

Bradley, Keith R. Introduction to *Lives of the Caesars*, by Suetonius. Volume 1, *Julius. Augustus. Tiberius. Gaius Caligula*. Translated by John C. Rolfe. Rev. ed. LCL 31. Harvard University Press, 1998.

Bradley, Keith R. "Suetonius." *OCD*, 1409–10.

Bradley, Keith R. *Suetonius' Life of Nero: An Historical Commentary*. Collection Latomus 157. Latomus, 1978.

Braithwaite, A. W. Notes to C. Suetoni Tranquili, *Divus Vespasianus*. Clarendon, 1927.

Braun, Roddy. *1 Chronicles*. WBC 14. Word, 1986.

Brown, Raymond E. *The Birth of the Messiah: A Commentary on the Infancy Narratives in the Gospels of Matthew and Luke*. Rev. ed. ABRL. Doubleday, 1993.

Brown, Raymond E. "*Rachab* in Matt 1:5 Probably Is Rahab of Jericho." *Bib* 63.1 (1982): 79–80.

Bryan, Steven M. "The Missing Generation: The Completion of Matthew's Genealogy." *BBR* 29.3 (2019): 294–316.

Bryan, Steven M. "Onomastics and Numerical Composition in the Genealogy of Matthew." *BBR* 30.4 (2020): 515–39.

Buckler, John. "Plutarch and Autopsy." *ANRW* 33.6. Part 2, *Principat*, 33.6. Edited by H. Temporini and W. Haase. de Gruyter, 1992.

Burridge, Richard A. *What Are the Gospels? A Comparison with Graeco-Roman Biography*. 2nd ed. Eerdmans, 2004.

Byrskog, Samuel. *Story as History—History as Story: The Gospel Tradition in the Context of Ancient Oral History*. Brill Academic, 2002.

Carson, D. A. *Matthew*. In vol. 8 of *The Expositor's Bible Commentary*. Zondervan, 1984.

Carter, John M. Commentary to *Divus Augustus*, by Suetonius. Edited by John M. Carter. Bristol Classical, 1982.

Casey, P. M. "Porphyry and the Origin of the Book of Daniel." *JTS* 27.1 (1976): 15–33.

Cassius Dio. *Roman History*. Translated by Earnest Cary and Herbert B. Foster. 9 vols. LCL. Harvard University Press, 1914–27.

Christian, Timothy J. "Cornelius Nepos's *Themistocles*: A Targeted Comparison with the Histories of Herodotus and Thucydides with Implications for the Historical Reliability of the Gospels." In Keener and Wright, *Biographies and Jesus*.

Cohen, Jonathan. *The Origins and Evolution of the Moses Nativity Story*. Studies in the History of Religions 58. Brill, 1993.

Collins, John J. *Daniel: A Commentary on the Book of Daniel*. Hermeneia. Fortress, 1993.

Colson, F. H. General introduction to *On Abraham. On Joseph. On Moses*, by Philo. LCL 289. Harvard University Press, 1935.

Cook, Brad L. "Plutarch's Use of λέγεται: Narrative Design and Source in Alexander." *Greek, Roman, and Byzantine Studies* 42 (2001): 329–60.

Crossan, John Dominic. *The Historical Jesus: The Life of a Mediterranean Jewish Peasant*. HarperSanFrancisco, 1991.

Crossan, John Dominic. "The Infancy and Youth of the Messiah." In *The Search for Jesus: Modern Scholarship Looks at the Gospels*. Edited by Hershel Shanks. Biblical Archaeology Society, 1994.

Damon, Cynthia. "Rhetoric and Historiography." In *A Companion to Roman Rhetoric*. Edited by William Dominik and Jon Hall. Blackwell Companions to the Ancient World. Blackwell, 2007.

Davies, W. D., and Dale C. Allison Jr. *The Gospel According to Saint Matthew*. 3 vols. ICC. T&T Clark, 1988–97.

Dawes, Gregory W. "Why Historicity Still Matters: Raymond Brown and the Infancy Narratives." *Pacifica* 19.2 (2006): 156–76.

Dawson, Nancy S., Eugene H. Merrill, and Andreas J. Köstenberger. *All the Genealogies of the Bible: Visual Charts and Exegetical Commentary*. Zondervan Academic, 2023.

De Temmerman, Koen. "Ancient Biography and Formalities of Fiction." In *Writing Biography in Greece and Rome: Narrative Technique and Fictionalization*. Edited by Koen De Temmerman and Kristoffel Demoen. Cambridge University Press, 2016.

Down, M. J. "The Matthaean Birth Narratives: Matthew 1:18–2:23." *ExpTim* 90.2 (1978): 51–52.

Du Plessis, I. I. "Once More: The Purpose of Luke's Prologue (Lk 1:1–4)." *NovT* 16.4 (1974): 259–71.

Dunn, James D. G. *Jesus Remembered*. Vol. 1 of Christianity in the Making. Eerdmans, 2003.

Edwards, James R. *The Gospel According to Luke*. Pillar New Testament Commentary. Eerdmans, 2015.

Ehrman, Bart D. *Jesus, Interrupted: Revealing the Hidden Contradictions in the Bible (and Why We Don't Know About Them)*. HarperOne, 2009.

Elliott, J. K. *Questioning Christian Origins*. SCM, 1982.

Erdmann, Gottfried. *Die Vorgeschichten des Lukas- und Matthäus-Evangeliums und Vergils vierte Ekloge*. Forschungen zur Religion und Literatur des Alten und Neuen Testaments 2/30. Vandenhoeck & Ruprecht, 1932.

Farrer, A. M. "On Dispensing with Q." In *Studies in the Gospels: Essays in Memory of R. H. Lightfoot*. Edited by D. E. Nineham. Blackwell, 1955.

Feldman, Louis H. "Philo's View of Moses' Birth and Upbringing." *CBQ* 64 (2002): 258–81.
Fenton, J. C. *Saint Matthew*. Westminster Pelican Commentaries. Westminster, 1963.
Feuillet, André. *Jesus and His Mother: The Role of the Virgin Mary in Salvation History and the Place of Woman in the Church*. Translated by Leonard Maluf. Studies in Scripture. St. Bede's, 1984.
Fitzmyer, Joseph A. *The Gospel According to Luke (I–IX)*. AB 28. Doubleday, 1981.
France, R. T. "The Birth of Jesus." In *Handbook for the Study of the Historical Jesus*. Edited by Tom Holmén and Stanley E. Porter. Brill, 2011.
France, R. T. "The Formula-Quotations of Matthew 2 and the Problem of Communication." *NTS* 27 (1981): 233–51.
France, R. T. *The Gospel of Matthew*. NICNT. Eerdmans, 2007.
France, R. T. *Luke*. Teach the Text Commentary Series. Baker, 2013.
France, R. T. "Scripture, Tradition and History in the Infancy Narratives of Matthew." In *Gospel Perspectives*. Edited by R. T. France and David Wenham. JSOT, 1981.
Freed, Edwin D. *The Stories of Jesus' Birth: A Critical Introduction*. Sheffield Academic, 2001.
Friedeman, Caleb T. "Jesus' Davidic Lineage and the Case for Jewish Adoption." *NTS* 66 (2020): 249–67.
Friedeman, Caleb T. *The Revelation of the Messiah: The Christological Mystery of Luke 1–2 and Its Unveiling in Luke-Acts*. SNTSMS 181. Cambridge University Press, 2023.
Friedeman, Caleb T., and Jeremy D. Otten. "A Reception History and English Translation of Frans Neirynck, *Maria bewaarde al de woorden in haar hart*." *ETL* 97.4 (2021): 647–76.
Friedlander, Gerald, ed. and trans. *Pirḳê de Rabbi Eliezer*. 4th ed. Sepher-Hermon, 1981.
Gascou, Jacques. *Suétone historien*. Bibliothèque des écoles françaises d'Athènes et de Rome 255. École française, 1984.
Geldenhuys, Norval. *Commentary on the Gospel of Luke*. NICNT. Eerdmans, 1951.
Ginzberg, Louis. *The Legends of the Jews*. 7 vols. Jewish Publication Society, 1909–38.
Godet, F. *The Gospel of St. Luke*. Translated by E. W. Shalders and M. D. Cusin. 4th ed. 2 vols. T&T Clark, 1889.
Goh, Benson. "Galba: A Comparison of Suetonius's and Plutarch's Biographies and Tacitus's Histories with Implications for the

Historical Reliability of the Gospels." In Keener and Wright, *Biographies and Jesus*.

Goldwurm, Hersh, Yisroel Simcha Schorr, and Chaim Malinowitz, eds. *Talmud Bavli: The Schottenstein Edition*. Artscroll. Mesorah, 1990–2005.

Goodacre, Mark S. *The Case Against Q: Studies in Markan Priority and Synoptic Problem*. Trinity Press International, 2002.

Goodacre, Mark S. "Prophecy Historicized or Tradition Scripturalized? Reflections on the Origins of the Passion Narrative." In *The New Testament and the Church: Essays in Honour of John Muddiman*. Edited by John Barton and Peter Groves. LNTS 532. T&T Clark, 2016.

Gossage, A. J. "Plutarch." In Latin Biography. Edited by T. A. Dorey. Studies in Latin Literature and Its Influence. Basic, 1967.

Goulder, M. D. *Luke: A New Paradigm*. 2 vols. JSNTSup 20. JSOT, 1989.

Graystone, Geoffrey. *Virgin of All Virgins: The Interpretation of Luke 1:34*. Pontifical Biblical Institute, 1968.

The Greek New Testament, Produced at Tyndale House, Cambridge. Edited by Dirk Jongkind. Crossway, 2017.

Green, Joel B. *The Gospel of Luke*. NICNT. Eerdmans, 1997.

Gundry, Robert H. *Matthew: A Commentary on His Literary and Theological Art*. Eerdmans, 1982.

Gundry, Robert H. *The Use of the Old Testament in St. Matthew's Gospel. With Special Reference to the Messianic Hope*. NovTSup 18. Brill, 1967.

Hadas, Moses, and Morton Smith. *Heroes and Gods: Spiritual Biographies in Antiquity*. Religious Perspectives 13. Harper & Row, 1965.

Hägg, Tomas. *The Art of Biography in Antiquity*. Cambridge University Press, 2012.

Hagner, Donald A. *Matthew 1–13*. WBC 33A. Word, 1993.

Hamilton, J. R. *Plutarch: Alexander. A Commentary*. Clarendon, 1969.

Harnack, Adolf. *The Date of the Acts and of the Synoptic Gospels*. Translated by J. R. Wilkinson. Crown Theological Library 33. Williams & Norgate, 1911.

Hays, Richard B. *Echoes of Scripture in the Gospels*. Baylor University Press, 2016.

Heater, Homer, Jr. "A Textual Note on Luke 3:33." *JSNT* 28 (1986): 25–29.

Henderson, John Jordan. "A Comparison of Josephus' *Life* and *Jewish War*: An Attempt at Establishing the Acceptable Outer Limits of Biographies' Historical Reliability." In Keener and Wright, *Biographies and Jesus*.

Hendrickx, Herman. *The Infancy Narratives*. Rev. ed. Studies in the Synoptic Gospels. Chapman, 1984.

Herodotus. *The Histories*. Translated by Robin Waterfield. Oxford University Press, 1998.

Hervey, Arthur. *The Genealogies of Our Lord and Saviour Jesus Christ*. Macmillan, 1853.

Hidalgo, Esteban. "A Redaction-Critical Study on Philo's *On the Life of Moses*, Book One." In Keener and Wright, *Biographies and Jesus*.

Hood, Jason B. *The Messiah, His Brothers, and the Nations (Matthew 1.1–17)*. LNTS 441. T&T Clark, 2011.

Hornblower, Simon, Antony Spawforth, and Esther Eidinow, eds. *The Oxford Classical Dictionary*. 4th ed. Oxford University Press, 2012.

Horsfall, Nicholas. "Life of Atticus." In *Cornelius Nepos: A Selection, Including the Lives of Cato and Atticus*. Clarendon Ancient History Series. Clarendon, 1989.

Horsfall, Nicholas. "Prose and Mime." In *Latin Literature*. Edited by E. J. Kenney and W. V. Clausen. Vol. 2 of *The Cambridge History of Classical Literature*. Cambridge University Press, 1982.

Hubbard, Robert L., Jr. *The Book of Ruth*. NICOT. Eerdmans, 1988.

Hurley, Donna W. *An Historical and Historiographical Commentary on Suetonius' Life of C. Caligula*. American Philological Association American Classical Studies 32. Scholars Press, 1993.

Jackson, John L. "A Commentary on Nepos' Life of Alcibiades." MA thesis, Rhodes University, 1982.

Jeremias, Joachim. *Jerusalem in the Time of Jesus: An Investigation into Economic and Social Conditions During the New Testament Period*. Translated by F. H. Cave and C. H. Cave. Fortress, 1969.

Johnson, Marshall D. *The Purpose of the Biblical Genealogies with Special Reference to the Setting of the Genealogies of Jesus*. SNTSMS 8. Cambridge University Press, 1969.

Jones, C. P. "Towards a Chronology of Plutarch's Works." *Journal of Roman Studies* 56 (1966): 61–74.

Kagan, Donald. *Pericles of Athens and the Birth of Democracy*. Free Press, 1991.

Keener, Craig S. *Acts: An Exegetical Commentary*. 4 vols. Baker Academic, 2012–15.

Keener, Craig S. *Christobiography: Memory, History, and the Reliability of the Gospels.* Eerdmans, 2019.
Keener, Craig S. *A Commentary on the Gospel of Matthew.* Eerdmans, 1999.
Keener, Craig S. *The Historical Jesus of the Gospels.* Eerdmans, 2009.
Keener, Craig S. *Miracles: The Credibility of the New Testament Accounts.* 2 vols. Baker Academic, 2011.
Keener, Craig S. "Otho: A Targeted Comparison of Suetonius's Biography and Tacitus's History, with Implications for the Gospels' Historical Reliability." In Keener and Wright, *Biographies and Jesus*.
Keener, Craig S., and Edward T. Wright, eds. *Biographies and Jesus: What Does It Mean for the Gospels to Be Biographies?* Emeth, 2016.
Kennedy, Joel. *The Recapitulation of Israel: Use of Israel's History in Matthew 1:1–4:11.* WUNT 2/57. Mohr Siebeck, 2008.
Kuhn, G. "Die Geschlechtsregister Jesu bei Lukas und Matthäus, nach ihrer Herkunft untersucht." *ZNW* 22.2 (1923): 206–28.
Kuhn, Karl A. "Beginning the Witness: The αὐτόπται καὶ ὑπηρέται of Luke's Infancy Narrative." *NTS* 49.2 (2003): 237–55.
Kurz, William S. "Luke 3:23–38 and Greco-Roman and Biblical Genealogies." In *Luke-Acts: New Perspectives from the Society of Biblical Literature Seminar.* Edited by Charles H. Talbert. Crossroad, 1984.
Kwon, Youngju. "Reimagining the Jesus Tradition: Orality, Memory, and Ancient Biography." PhD diss., Asbury Theological Seminary, 2018.
Lagrange, Marie-Joseph. *Évangile selon Saint Luc.* 3rd ed. Études bibliques. Victor Lecoffre, 1927.
Laurentin, René. *Structure et théologie de Luc I–II.* Gabalda, 1957.
Laurentin, René. *The Truth of Christmas Beyond the Myths: The Gospels of the Infancy of Christ.* Translated by Michael J. Wrenn and associates. Studies in Scripture. St. Bede's, 1986.
Licona, Michael R. "Historians and Miracle Claims." *JSHJ* 12 (2014): 106–29.
Licona, Michael R. *Why Are There Differences in the Gospels? What We Can Learn from Ancient Biography.* Oxford University Press, 2017.
Lincoln, Andrew T. *Born of a Virgin? Reconceiving Jesus in the Bible, Tradition, and Theology.* Eerdmans, 2013.
Lincoln, Andrew T. "Luke and Jesus' Conception: A Case of Double Paternity?" *JBL* 132.3 (2013): 639–58.

Lindsay, Hugh. Commentary to *Tiberius*, by Suetonius. Edited by Hugh Lindsay. Bristol Classical, 1995.

Lindsay, Hugh. Commentary and Introduction to *Caligula*, by Suetonius. Edited by Hugh Lindsay. Bristol Classical, 1993.

Litwa, M. David. *How the Gospels Became History: Jesus and Mediterranean Myths*. Yale University Press, 2019.

Lobur, John Alexander. *Cornelius Nepos: A Study in the Evidence and Influence*. University of Michigan Press, 2021.

Loisy, Alfred. *L'Évangile selon Luc*. Minerva, 1924.

Luz, Ulrich. *Matthew 1–7: A Commentary*. Rev. ed. Hermeneia. Fortress, 2007.

Machen, J. Gresham. *The Virgin Birth of Christ*. 2nd ed. Harper & Row, 1932.

Marshall, I. Howard. *The Gospel of Luke: A Commentary on the Greek Text*. NIGTC. Eerdmans, 1978.

Masson, Jacques. *Jesus, fils de David, dans les généalogies de saint Matthieu et de saint Luc*. Téqui, 1982.

McGing, Brian. "Philo's Adaptation of the Bible in His *Life of Moses*." In *The Limits of Ancient Biography*. Edited by Brian McGing and Judith Mossman. Classical Press of Wales, 2006.

McHugh, John. *The Mother of Jesus in the New Testament*. Doubleday, 1975.

Meier, John P. *A Marginal Jew: Rethinking the Historical Jesus*. 5 vols. ABRL. Doubleday, 1991–2016.

Metzger, Bruce M. *A Textual Commentary on the Greek New Testament*. 2nd ed. Deutsche Bibelgesellschaft, 1994.

Miller, Robert J. *Born Divine: The Births of Jesus and Other Sons of God*. Polebridge, 2003.

Moessner, David P. "The Appeal and Power of Poetics (Luke 1:1–4): Luke's Superior Credentials (παρηκολουθηκότι), Narrative Sequence (καθεξῆς), and Firmness of Understanding (ἡ ἀσφάλεια) for the Reader." In *Jesus and the Heritage of Israel: Luke's Narrative Claim upon Israel's Legacy*. Luke the Interpreter of Israel 1. Trinity Press International, 1999.

Moessner, David P. "'Eyewitnesses,' 'Informed Contemporaries,' and 'Unknowing Inquirers': Josephus' Criteria for Authentic Historiography and the Meaning of ΠΑΡΑΚΟΛΟΥΘΕΩ." *NovT* 38.2 (1996): 105–22.

Moessner, David P. *Luke the Historian of Israel's Legacy, Theologian of Israel's "Christ": A New Reading of the "Gospel Acts" of Luke*. BZNW 182. de Gruyter, 2016.

Moles, J. L. Commentary and Introduction to *The Life of Cicero*, by Plutarch. Edited and translated by J. L. Moles. Aris & Phillips, 1988.

Moles, J. L. "Luke's Preface: The Greek Decree, Classical Historiography and Christian Redefinitions." *NTS* 57 (2011): 461–82.

Murison, Charles L. Commentary to *Galba, Otho, Vitellius*, by Suetonius. Edited by Charles L. Murison. Bristol Classical, 1992.

Mussies, Gerard. "Parallels to Matthew's Version of the Pedigree of Jesus." *NovT* 28.1 (1986): 32–47.

Neirynck, Frans. "Maria bewaarde al de woorden in haar hart. Lk. 2, 19. 51 in hun context verklaard." *Collationes Brugenses et Gandavenses* 5 (1959): 433–66.

Nelson, W. David. *Mekhilta de-Rabbi Shimon Bar Yoḥai: Translated into English, with Critical Introduction and Annotation*. Jewish Publication Society, 2006.

Nepos, Cornelius. *On Great Generals. On Historians*. Translated by John C. Rolfe. LCL 467. Harvard University Press, 1929.

Nolland, John. *The Gospel of Matthew: A Commentary on the Greek Text*. NIGTC. Eerdmans, 2005.

Nolland, John. "Jechoniah and His Brothers (Matthew 1:11)." *BBR* 7 (1997): 169–78.

Nolland, John. *Luke 1–9:20*. WBC 35A. Word, 1989.

Oden, Thomas C., ed. *Incomplete Commentary on Matthew (Opus Imperfectum)*. Translated by James A. Kellerman. 2 vols. Ancient Christian Texts. IVP Academic, 2010.

Pao, David W., and Eckhard J. Schnabel. "Luke." In *Commentary on the New Testament Use of the Old Testament*. Edited by G. K. Beale and D. A. Carson. Baker Academic, 2007.

Pelling, Christopher. "Aspects of Plutarch's Characterization." In *Plutarch and History: Eighteen Studies*. Classical Press of Wales, 2002.

Pelling, Christopher. "Childhood and Personality in Greek Biography." In *Plutarch and History: Eighteen Studies*. Classical Press of Wales, 2002.

Pelling, Christopher. *Literary Texts and the Greek Historian*. Approaching the Ancient World. Routledge, 2000.

Pelling, Christopher. "'Making Myth Look Like History': Plutarch's *Theseus-Romulus*." In *Plutarch and History: Eighteen Studies*. Classical Press of Wales, 2002.

Pelling, Christopher. "Plutarch's Adaptation of His Source-Material." In *Plutarch and History: Eighteen Studies*. Classical Press of Wales, 2002.

Pelling, Christopher. "Plutarch's Method of Work in the Roman Lives." In *Plutarch and History: Eighteen Studies*. Classical Press of Wales, 2002.
Pelling, Christopher. "Truth and Fiction in Plutarch's Lives." In *Plutarch and History: Eighteen Studies*. Classical Press of Wales, 2002.
Penner, Todd C. *In Praise of Christian Origins: Stephen and the Hellenists in Lukan Apologetic Historiography*. Emory Studies in Early Christianity 10. T&T Clark, 2004.
Peters, John J. *Luke Among the Ancient Historians: Ancient Historiography and the Attempt to Remedy the Inadequate "Many."* Pickwick, 2022.
Peters, John J. "Luke's Source Claims in the Context of Ancient Historiography." *JSHJ* 18 (2020): 35–60.
Philo. *On Abraham. On Joseph. On Moses*. Translated by F. H. Colson. LCL 289. Harvard University Press, 1935.
Plummer, Alfred. *A Critical and Exegetical Commentary on the Gospel According to St. Luke*. 5th ed. ICC. T&T Clark, 1922.
Plutarch. *Lives*. Translated by Bernadotte Perrin. 11 vols. LCL. Harvard University Press, 1914–26.
Polybius. *The Histories*. Translated by Robin Waterfield. Oxford World's Classics. Oxford University Press, 2010.
Power, Tristan. "Poetry and Fiction in Suetonius' *Illustrious Men*." In *Writing Biography in Greece and Rome: Narrative Technique and Fictionalization*. Edited by Koen De Temmerman and Kristoffel Demoen. Cambridge University Press, 2016.
Quast, Udo, ed. *Ruth*. Vol. 4.3 of *Septuaginta: Vetus Testamentum Graecum*. Vandenhoeck & Ruprecht, 2006.
Quinn, Jerome D. "Is 'PAXAB in Mt 1:5 Rahab of Jericho?" *Bib* 63.2 (1981): 225–28.
Rahlfs, Alfred, and Robert Hanhart, eds. *Septuaginta: Editio altera*. Deutsche Bibelgesellschaft, 2006.
Räisänen, Heikki. *Die Mutter Jesu im Neuen Testament*. Annales Academiae Scientiarum Fennicae 2/158. Suomalainen Tiedeakatemia, 1969.
Rajak, Tessa. "Philon (4), 'Philo.'" *OCD*, 1134.
Ramsay, W. M. *Was Christ Born at Bethlehem? A Study on the Credibility of St. Luke*. 3rd ed. Hodder & Stoughton, 1905.
Reece, Steve. *The Formal Education of the Author of Luke-Acts*. LNTS 669. T&T Clark, 2022.
Rhodea, Greg. "Did Matthew Conceive a Virgin? Isaiah 7:14 and the Birth of Jesus." *JETS* 56.1 (2013): 63–77.

Rieske, Susan M. *"This Generation" and the Elect in the Book of Matthew: A Tale of Two Families*. LNTS 677. T&T Clark, 2026.
Riesner, Rainer. *Jesus als Lehrer: Eine Untersuchung zum Ursprung der Evangelien-Überlieferung*. WUNT 2/7. Mohr, 1981.
Rolfe, John C. Introduction to *On Great Generals. On Historians*, by Cornelius Nepos. LCL 467. Harvard University Press, 1929.
Rolfe, John C., and G. P. Goold. Prefatory note to Suetonius, *Lives of the Caesars, Volume II: Claudius. Nero. Galba. Otho. Vitellius. Vespasian. Titus. Domitian. Lives of Illustrious Men: Grammarians and Rhetoricians. Poets (Terence. Virgil. Horace. Tibullus. Persius. Lucan). Lives of Pliny the Elder and Passienus Crispus*. Rev. ed. LCL 38. Harvard University Press, 1997.
Rolfe, John C., Gavin B. Townend, and Antony Spawforth. "Cornelius Nepos." *OCD*, 380.
Rothschild, Clare K. *Luke-Acts and the Rhetoric of History*. WUNT 2/175. Mohr Siebeck, 2004.
Rowe, C. Kavin. *World Upside Down: Reading Acts in the Graeco-Roman Age*. Oxford University Press, 2009.
Russell, D. A. "Plutarch." *OCD*, 1165–66.
Saffrey, Henri D. "Plutarchus." *BNP* 11:410–27.
Sanders, E. P. *The Historical Figure of Jesus*. Penguin, 1993.
Schaberg, Jane. *The Illegitimacy of Jesus: A Feminist Theological Interpretation of the Infancy Narratives*. Harper & Row, 1987.
Schmidt, Daryl D. "Rhetorical Influences and Genre: Luke's Preface and the Rhetoric of Hellenistic Historiography." In *Jesus and the Heritage of Israel: Luke's Narrative Claim upon Israel's Legacy*. Edited by David P. Moessner. Luke the Interpreter of Israel 1. Trinity Press International, 1999.
Schneider, Gerhard. *Das Evangelium nach Lukas Kapitel 1–10*. 3rd ed. Ökumenischer Taschenbuch-Kommentar 3/1. Mohn, 1992.
Schniewind, Julius. *Das Evangelium nach Matthäus*. 11th ed. NTD 2. Vandenhoeck & Ruprecht, 1964.
Schreiner, Patrick. *Matthew, Disciple and Scribe: The First Gospel and Its Portrait of Jesus*. Baker Academic, 2019.
Schürer, Emil. *The History of the Jewish People in the Age of Jesus Christ (175 B.C.–A.D. 135)*. Edited by Géza Vermes and Fergus Millar. 3 vols. T&T Clark, 1973–87.
Schürmann, Heinz. *Das Lukasevangelium, erster Teil: Kommentar zu Kap. 1, 1–9, 50*. HThKNT 3. Herder, 1969.

Shuler, Philip L. "Philo's Moses and Matthew's Jesus: A Comparative Study in Ancient Literature." *Studia Philonica Annual* 2 (1990): 86–103.

Siffer-Wiederhold, Nathalie. "Le projet littéraire de Luc d'après le prologue de l'évangile (Lc 1,1–4)." *RevScRel* 79.1 (2005): 39–54.

Smith, Christopher, and Anton Powell, eds. *The Lost Memoirs of Augustus and the Development of Roman Autobiography*. Classical Press of Wales, 2009.

Smith, Henry B., Jr., and Kris J. Udd. "On the Authenticity of Kainan, Son of Arpachshad." *Detroit Baptist Seminary Journal* 24 (2019): 119–54.

Soares Prabhu, George M. *The Formula Quotations in the Infancy Narrative of Matthew: An Enquiry into the Tradition History of Mt 1–2*. Pontifical Biblical Institute, 1976.

Sparks, James T. *The Chronicler's Genealogies: Towards an Understanding of 1 Chronicles 1–9*. Academia Biblica. SBL, 2008.

Spong, John S. *Born of a Woman: A Bishop Rethinks the Birth of Jesus*. HarperSanFrancisco, 1992.

Steidle, Wolf. *Sueton und die antike Biographie*. Zetemata 1. Beck, 1951.

Steinmann, Andrew E. "Challenging the Authenticity of Cainan, Son of Arpachshad." *JETS* 60.4 (2017): 697–711.

Stendahl, Krister. "Matthew." *Peake's Commentary on the Bible*. Edited by Matthew Black. Thomas Nelson, 1962.

Stendahl, Krister. *The School of St. Matthew and Its Use of the Old Testament*. 2nd ed. Fortress, 1968.

Sterling, Gregory E. "Philo of Alexandria." In *The Eerdmans Dictionary of Early Judaism*. Eerdmans, 2010.

Steyn, Gert J. "The Occurrence of 'Kainam' in Luke's Genealogy: Evidence of Septuagint Influence?" *ETL* 65.4 (1989): 409–11.

Strack, Herman L., and Paul Billerbeck. *A Commentary on the New Testament from the Talmud and Midrash*. Edited by Jacob N. Cerone. Translated by Andrew Bowden and Joseph Longarino. 4 vols. Lexham, 2022.

Strauss, David Friedrich. *The Life of Jesus Critically Examined*. Translated by George Eliot. 4th ed. Sonnenschein, 1902.

Strauss, Mark L. *The Davidic Messiah in Luke-Acts: The Promise and Its Fulfillment in Lukan Christology*. JSNTSup 110. Sheffield Academic, 1995.

Suetonius. *Lives of the Caesars*. Volume 1, *Julius. Augustus. Tiberius. Gaius Caligula*. Translated by J. C. Rolfe. Rev. ed. LCL 31. Harvard University Press, 1998.

Suetonius. *Lives of the Caesars*. Volume 2, *Claudius. Nero. Galba. Otho. Vitellius. Vespasian. Titus. Domitian. Lives of Illustrious Men: Grammarians and Rhetoricians. Poets (Terence. Virgil. Horace. Tibullus. Persius. Lucan). Lives of Pliny the Elder and Passienus Crispus*. Translated by John C. Rolfe. Rev. ed. LCL 38. Harvard University Press, 1997.

Talbert, Charles H. "Miraculous Conceptions and Births in Mediterranean Antiquity." In *The Historical Jesus in Context*. Edited by Amy-Jill Levine, Dale C. Allison Jr., and John Dominic Crossan. Princeton Readings in Religions. Princeton University Press, 2006.

Talbert, Charles H. *What Is a Gospel? The Genre of the Canonical Gospels*. Fortress, 1977.

Theissen, Gerd, and Annette Merz. *The Historical Jesus: A Comprehensive Guide*. Translated by John S. Bowden. SCM, 1998.

Titchener, Francis. "Cornelius Nepos and the Biographical Tradition." Greece & Rome 50.1 (2003): 85–99.

van Unnik, Willem C. "Die rechte Bedeutung des Wortes treffen: Lukas 2,19." In *Verbum: Essays on Some Aspects of the Religious Function of Words. Dedicated to Dr. H. W. Obbink, Professor in the History of Religions and Egyptology, University of Utrecht, on November 14th, 1964*. Edited by Theodorus Petrus van Baaren. Studia theologica Rheno-Traiectina 6. Kemink, 1964.

Vermes, Géza. *Jesus the Jew: A Historian's Reading of the Gospels*. Fortress, 1981.

Waaler, Erik. *The Use of the Old Testament in Matthew 1–4*. WUNT 2/595. Mohr Siebeck, 2023.

Waetjen, Herman C. "The Genealogy as the Key to the Gospel According to Matthew." JBL 95.2 (1976): 205–30.

Wallace-Hadrill, Andrew. *Suetonius: The Scholar and His Caesars*. Duckworth, 1983.

Walton, John H. "Exodus, Date of." *Dictionary of the Old Testament: Pentateuch*. Edited by T. Desmond Alexander and David W. Baker. IVP, 2003.

Wardle, D. Commentary to *Life of Augustus*, by Suetonius. Edited and translated by D. Wardle. Clarendon Ancient History Series. Oxford University Press, 2014.

Wardle, D. *Suetonius' Life of Caligula: A Commentary*. Collection Latomus 225. Latomus, 1994.

Warmington, B. H. Commentary to *Nero*, by Suetonius. Edited by B. H. Warmington. 2nd ed. Bristol Classical, 1999.

Watson, Francis. *Gospel Writing: A Canonical Perspective*. Eerdmans, 2013.

Westlake, H. D. "ΛΕΓΕΤΑΙ in Thucydides." *Mnemosyne* 30 (1977): 345–62.

Wilson, Robert R. *Genealogy and History in the Biblical World*. Yale University Press, 1977.

Woldemariam, Fasil. "A Targeted Comparison of Plutarch's, Xenophon's, and Nepos's Biographies of Agesilaus, with Implications for the Historical Reliability of the Synoptics." In Keener and Wright, *Biographies and Jesus*.

Wolter, Michael. *The Gospel According to Luke*. Translated by Wayne Coppins and Christoph Heilig. 2 vols. Baylor-Mohr Siebeck Studies in Early Christianity. Baylor University Press, 2016–17.

Wong, Chan-Kok. "Philo's Use of *Chaldaioi*." *Studia Philonica Annual* 4 (1992): 1–14.

Wright, N. T. *Jesus and the Victory of God*. Vol. 2 of Christian Origins and the Question of God. Fortress, 1996.

Wright, N. T. *The New Testament and the People of God*. Vol. 1 of Christian Origins and the Question of God. Fortress, 1992.

Xenophon. *Scripta Minora*. Translated by E. C. Marchant and G. W. Bowersock. LCL 183. Harvard UP, 1925.

Ziegler, Joseph, ed. *Ieremias, Baruch, Threni, Epistula Ieremiae*. 3rd ed. Vol. 15 of *Septuaginta: Vetus Testamentum Graecum*. Vandenhoeck & Ruprecht, 2006.

INDEX OF MODERN AUTHORS

Adams, Sean A., 16, 171
Albrecht, Michael von, 27–28, 93
Alexander, Loveday, 171–73
Alfred, Chris, 42, 211, 223, 228
Allison, Dale C., Jr., 9, 136–38, 142–43, 147, 150–51, 155–56, 158–59, 161
Aune, David E., 48, 169–70
Aus, Roger David, 48

Baldwin, Barry, 110
Bauckham, Richard, 138, 144, 146–48, 171–73, 182–83, 186–90, 193
Baum, Armin D., 171
Berger, Klaus, 48
Bernier, Jonathan, 165, 195
Billerbeck, Paul, 138, 148, 151, 156
Blomberg, Craig L., 137
Bock, Darrell L., 172–74, 182–83, 193
Bond, Helen K., 15

Borg, Marcus J., 11–12
Bovon, François, 183
Bradley, James R., 35
Bradley, Keith R., 93–94, 111, 122, 211
Braithwaite, A. W., 106
Braun, Roddy, 150, 188
Brown, Raymond E., 2, 7, 137–38, 142–43, 147, 150–51, 153–56, 158–59, 175, 177, 183, 190
Bryan, Steven M., 139, 142, 146, 149, 151–52
Buckler, John, 223
Burridge, Richard A., 15, 48, 169
Byrskog, Samuel, 70, 177, 205

Carson, D. A., 137, 142, 157
Carter, John M., 97
Casey, P. M., 180
Cohen, Jonathan, 52–53, 61
Collins, John J., 180
Colson, F. H., 58–60

Cook, Brad L., 21, 223
Crossan, John Dominic, 9–11

Damon, Cynthia, 58
Davies, W. D., 9, 136–38, 142–43, 147, 150–51, 155–56, 158–59, 161
Dawes, Gregory W., 2
Dawson, Nancy S., 187, 189
De Temmerman, Koen, 18
Down, M. J., 154–55
Du Plessis, I. I., 173–74
Dunn, James D. G., 11

Edwards, James R., 172–73
Ehrman, Bart D., 156
Eidinow, Esther, 44
Elliott, J. K., 156
Erdmann, Gottfried, 178

Farrer, A. M., 176
Feldman, Louis H., 51–53, 55–58, 61
Feuillet, André, 177
Fitzmyer, Joseph A., 172, 178, 183, 190
France, R. T., 142, 145, 154–57, 164, 177
Freed, Edwin D., 10
Friedeman, Caleb T., 157, 176, 178–82, 187
Friedlander, Gerald, 54

Gascou, Jacques, 109–10, 228
Geldenhuys, Norval, 177
Ginzberg, Louis, 58, 61
Godet, F., 177
Goldwurm, Hersh, 151
Goodacre, Mark S., 157, 176
Goold, G. P., 94, 116, 122
Gossage, A. J., 223
Goulder, M. D., 176
Green, Joel B., 193

Gundry, Robert H., 137, 142, 149, 156, 159

Hadas, Moses, 58
Hägg, Tomas, 88
Hagner, Donald A., 137–38, 143, 158, 160
Hamilton, J. R., 67
Harnack, Adolf, 177
Hays, Richard B., 137, 183
Heater, Homer, Jr., 191–92
Henderson, John Jordan, 54
Hendrickx, Herman, 9
Hervey, Arthur, 187
Hidalgo, Esteban, 48, 51, 54, 60, 214
Hood, Jason B., 147
Hornblower, Simon, 44
Horsfall, Nicholas, 28, 40
Hubbard, Robert L., Jr., 150
Hurley, Donna W., 108

Jackson, John L., 30–31
Jeremias, Joachim, 138, 150, 186–87, 190
Johnson, Marshall D., 138, 189–90
Jones, C. P., 68

Kagan, Donald, 8
Keener, Craig S., 12–13, 15–19, 21, 42–43, 47–48, 54, 58, 87, 123, 132, 142, 147, 154, 171, 173, 202, 211, 214, 228–29, 231
Kennedy, Joel, 149
Köstenberger, Andreas J., 187, 189
Kuhn, G., 151
Kuhn, Karl A., 174
Kurz, William S., 185
Kwon, Youngju, 54

Lagrange, Marie-Joseph, 177
Laurentin, René, 137, 151, 156, 174, 177
Licona, Michael R., 15–17, 54, 68, 161, 202
Lincoln, Andrew T., 8–10, 13, 16, 18, 29, 48, 68, 72, 74, 88, 94, 98–100, 103–4, 107, 229, 231
Lindsay, Hugh, 102, 105, 110, 122
Litwa, M. David, 14–15, 19, 59, 78
Lobur, John Alexander, 28, 211
Loisy, Alfred, 178
Luz, Ulrich, 135, 137–38, 143, 160

Machen, J. Gresham, 156, 177, 193
Malinowitz, Chaim, 151
Marshall, I. Howard, 185, 190, 193
Masson, Jacques, 151
McGing, Brian, 48, 54, 60
McHugh, John, 156, 177
Meier, John P., 3–6, 9–10, 13, 16, 18, 29, 48, 68, 94, 98–99, 164
Merrill, Eugene H., 187, 189
Merz, Annette, 11
Metzger, Bruce M., 142, 145, 191
Miller, Robert J., 5–10, 13, 16, 18, 29, 48, 68, 88, 94, 98–99, 149, 229, 231
Moessner, David P., 170, 173
Moles, J. L., 17, 21, 85, 171, 202
Murison, Charles L., 116
Mussies, Gerard, 138, 169, 189

Neirynck, Frans, 178
Nelson, W. David, 53

Nolland, John, 142, 147, 151, 177, 183

Oden, Thomas C., 151
Otten, Jeremy D., 178

Pao, David W., 183
Pelling, Christopher, 16–18, 54, 58, 70, 76, 87–88, 132, 202, 223
Penner, Todd C., 170, 172
Peters, John J., 171–72
Plummer, Alfred, 187
Powell, Anton, 96
Power, Tristan, 118

Quast, Udo, 143, 146
Quinn, Jerome D., 146

Räisänen, Heikki, 177
Rajak, Tessa, 47
Ramsay, W. M., 177
Reece, Steve, 172
Rhodea, Greg, 156
Rieske, Susan M., 151–52
Riesner, Rainer, 177
Rolfe, John C., 27–28, 31–32, 40, 94, 116, 122
Rothschild, Clare K., 170–71
Rowe, C. Kavin, 172
Russell, D. A., 67

Saffrey, Henri D., 67–68
Sanders, E. P., 11, 165
Schaberg, Jane, 147
Schmidt, Daryl D., 170
Schnabel, Eckhard J., 183
Schneider, Gerhard, 183
Schniewind, Julius, 142
Schorr, Yisroel Simcha, 151
Schreiner, Patrick, 137
Schürer, Emil, 150
Schürmann, Heinz, 178

Shuler, Philip L., 60
Siffer-Wiederhold, Nathalie, 170
Smith, Christopher, 96
Smith, Henry B., Jr., 186
Smith, Morton, 58
Soares Prabhu, George M., 9, 137, 153–54, 166
Sparks, James T., 149
Spawforth, Antony, 27–28, 44
Spong, John S., 9
Steidle, Wolf, 109
Steinmann, Andrew E., 186
Stendahl, Krister, 137, 152
Sterling, Gregory E., 47, 58
Steyn, Gert J., 185
Strack, Herman L., 138, 148, 151, 156
Strauss, David Friedrich, 9
Strauss, Mark L., 193

Talbert, Charles H., 9, 48
Theissen, Gerd, 11
Titchener, Francis, 211

Townend, Gavin B., 27–28

Udd, Kris J., 186

van Unnik, Willem C., 177
Vermes, Géza, 10, 156

Waaler, Erik, 147
Waetjen, Herman C., 152
Wallace-Hadrill, Andrew, 109
Walton, John H., 65
Wardle, D., 95–101, 108, 110
Warmington, B. H., 112
Watson, Francis, 172, 176
Westlake, H. D., 20, 205, 208
Wilson, Robert R., 149–50
Wolter, Michael, 171, 173, 193
Wong, Chan-Kok, 52
Wright, Edward T., 15, 202
Wright, N. T., 11, 13, 164

Ziegler, Joseph, 146

INDEX OF ANCIENT SOURCES

This index does not include references from the appendixes.

OLD TESTAMENT

Genesis

2:7	185
4–5	183
4:25–26	185
4:26	185
5:6	185
5:9	185
5:12	185
5:15	185
5:18	185
5:21	185
5:25	185
5:28–29	185
5:32	185
10–11	183
10:22	185
10:24	185
11:10	185
11:10–26	150
11:12	185
11:12–18	150
11:13	185
11:14	185
11:16	185
11:18	184
11:20	184
11:22	184
11:24	184
11:26–27	184
15:7	52
38:8–9	156
46	188
46:21	188

Exodus

1:22	158
2:1	52
2:2	50, 54, 61
2:3–10	55
2:5	62
2:7–9	50
2:10	55
2:11–12	56
2:15	158
2:23	158
4:19	157–58

4:19–20	158	**1 Samuel**	
6:16–20	52, 150	22:5	190
6:23	147		
7:7	65	**2 Samuel**	
7:12	64	5:14	184
20:5	151	24:11–14	190

Numbers		**1 Kings**	
1:7	147	21:21–24	151
2:3	147	21:29	151
7:12–17	147		
10:14	147	**2 Kings**	
22–24	159	15:1	142
23:7	159	15:13	142
24:7	159	15:30	142
26	188	15:34	142
26:38	188	21:1–18	190
		21:18–19	145
Deuteronomy		21:23–25	145
25:5–6	156	24:7	149

Joshua		**1 Chronicles**	
7:1	150	1–3	139, 146, 183
7:24	150	1–9	138
		1:1	185
Judges		1:2	185
5:14	151	1:3	185
		1:4	185
Ruth		1:17	185
4	139, 146, 183	1:18	185
4:11	147	1:24	185
4:12	139–40, 143, 184	1:24–3:19	143
4:12–22	143	1:25	184–85
4:13	140, 143, 184	1:26	184
4:17	140, 143, 184	1:27	140, 184
4:18	140, 184	1:28	140, 184
4:18–19	143, 183	1:34	140, 184
4:18–22	150	2:1–2	140, 143, 184
4:19	140, 143, 184–85, 191	2:1–17	150
4:20	140, 184	2:4	139–40, 184
4:20–21	147	2:5	140, 143, 183–84
4:21	140, 143, 184	2:9	140, 143, 183
4:22	140, 184	2:10	140, 184–85, 191

2:11	140, 143, 147–48, 184	**Psalms**	
		60:7	151
2:11–12	146	72:10–11	159
2:12	140, 143, 184	78:2	142
2:15	140, 184		
2:21	151	**Isaiah**	
2:54–55	148	7:14	156
3:5	139, 141, 143, 146, 184	60:6	159
3:10	141, 143, 145–46		
3:11	141	**Jeremiah**	
3:12	141–43, 146	1:2	146
3:13	141	25:3	146
3:14	141–43, 145–46	37:1	149
3:16	141, 149		
3:17	139, 141, 184, 189	**Daniel**	
3:19	141, 184, 187	4:28	179
3:19–24	149, 186	7	179–80
3:21	187	7:1	179–80
6:7–9	150	7:2–27	179
6:33–43	150	7:28	178–81
7:6	188	8:16	178
7:10	190	9–10	178
7:22–27	150	9:21	178
8:1–2	188		
8:1–5	188	**Micah**	
14:4	184	5:2	154–55
15:5–10	149		
25:2	190	**Haggai**	
26:5	190	1:1	139
2 Chronicles		**Zechariah**	
33:20–25	145	1:1	150
36:10	141, 149	12:12	188

NEW TESTAMENT

Ezra		**Matthew**	
2:59–63	138	1	136
3:2	138	1–2	1, 4–5, 8, 10, 12–13, 135–36, 162–64
5:1	150		
7:3	150	1:1	144
8:18–19	149	1:2–3	143
Nehemiah		1:2–16	140–41, 143
7:61–65	138	1:2–17	1

1:2–2:23	1	2:16	5, 158, 160
1:3	139, 143	2:16–17	158
1:4	143, 147	2:16–18	153
1:5	143, 146, 148	2:17–18	154
1:6	139, 144	2:19	158
1:6–7	143, 146	2:19–21	158
1:7–8	146	2:20	157
1:8	143	2:23	154, 175
1:8–9	143	3–4	164
1:9	143, 146	3:16–17	164
1:10	143	4:1–11	164
1:10–11	143	4:12–16	155–56
1:11	149	4:14–16	154
1:12	139, 185	4:23–24	164
1:16	175	4:24	164
1:17	144, 151, 191	8–9	164
1:18	175	8:5–13	164
1:18–21	158	8:14–17	164
1:18–2:23	13	8:16	164
1:20	144, 175	8:16–17	155
1:20–23	175	8:17	154
1:21	158, 175	8:23–27	164
1:22–23	154, 156	8:28–34	164
1:23	175	9:27	144
1:24–25	175	12:17–21	154
1:25	175	12:23	144
2	136	13:34–35	155
2:1	5, 159, 175	13:35	142, 154
2:1–2	159	14–15	164
2:1–6	160	14:13–21	164
2:1–12	136	14:22–33	164
2:1–13a	147	15:32–39	164
2:2–12	158	15:22	144
2:4–6	158	17:1–8	164
2:5–6	5, 154	20:30–31	144
2:5a	155	21:1–6	155
2:5b–6	155	21:4–5	154
2:8	5	21:9	144
2:11	159	21:15	144
2:13–14	158	22:42–46	144
2:13–23	155, 160	27:9–10	154, 156
2:15	154	28:1–10	164

28:11–13	162
28:15	162
28:16–20	164

Mark
1:14	155
1:32–34	155
4:33–34	155
11:1–4	155

Luke
1–2	1, 4–5, 8, 10, 12–13, 176, 181, 194
1:1	172, 176
1:1–4	169–70, 192, 195–96
1:2	172, 203
1:5	175
1:5–25	180
1:5–2:52	1, 169, 174
1:19	179
1:26	179
1:26–38	180
1:27	175
1:30–35	175
1:31	175
1:32	175
1:34	175
1:34–35	193
1:35	175
1:39–56	180
1:57–80	180
2:1–21	180
2:4	5, 175
2:4–6	175
2:5–6	175
2:11	175
2:15	5, 180
2:17	180
2:19	176–82, 192–93, 196, 203
2:22–40	180
2:39	175
2:41–52	1, 174, 180
2:44	193
2:50	180
2:51	176–82, 192–93, 196, 203
3:21–22	194
3:23	182–83, 193, 196
3:23–37	186
3:23–38	169, 182, 184
3:27	187, 189
3:27–31	188
3:29–30	189–90
3:33	183, 186, 190
3:36	185
3:38	183
4–5	194
4:1–13	194
4:33–36	194
4:38–39	194
4:40	194
4:41	194
5:12–13	194
5:17–26	194
6:18	194
6:18–19	194
7–8	194
8:22–25	194
9:10–17	194
9:28–36	194
24:1–49	194
24:50–53	194

Acts
1–3	194
1:14	166, 174
1:18–19	156
1:21–22	174
7:22	56
7:25	193
8:20	193
14:19	193
16:13	193

16:27	193	3.12	179
17:29	193		
21:29	193	**Testament of Abraham B**	
		3.4	179

Hebrews

11:23	54

Testament of Reuben

1.4	179

OLD TESTAMENT PSEUDEPIGRAPHA

Testament of Simeon

2.1	179

Apocalypse of Abraham

title	150

Testament of Zebulun

3.4	156

Apocalypse of Moses

3.2–3	179

DEAD SEA SCROLLS

Aramaic Levi

7	179

1QapGen (Genesis Apocryphon)

VI, 12	179

2 Baruch

50.1	179

4Q174

1 II, 1–5	180

Ezekiel the Tragedian

37	56

11Q13

II, 18	180

4 Ezra

14.7–9	179

JOSEPHUS AND PHILO

Jubilees

8.1–5	185
41.4–5	156
47.4	62
47.9	56

Josephus

Against Apion

1.28–36	138
1.286	56

Jewish Antiquities

2.205	158
2.205–206	61
2.205–209	158
2.210	52
2.212–216	61, 158
2.221	55
2.228	56
2.229	52
2.230	62
2.230–237	57

Liber antiquitatum biblicarum

9.10	61, 158
9.12	55
9.13	61
9.14	55

Testament of Abraham A

3.4	179

2.231–232	54	1.33	53
2.232	51, 55	1.40	53
2.233–237	62	1.44	53
2.234	158	1.65–84	63
8.286	145	1.91–95	64
8.287	145	1.93	64
8.290	145	1.94	64
8.292	145	1.96	64
8.294	145	1.96–145	64
8.295	145	1.130	64
8.298	145	1.165–166	64
8.303	145	1.176–179	64
8.304	145	1.184–186	64
8.306	145	1.198–209	64
8.307	145	1.210–211	64
8.312	145	1.212	64
8.314	145	1.276	159
10.267–80	180	*On the Migration of*	
11.337	180	*Abraham*	
The Life		142	61
1–6	138	*On the Posterity of Cain*	
3–5	150	180	156
		That God Is Unchangeable	
Philo		16	156

On the Life of Joseph
1	47

On the Life of Moses
1.4	49, 51, 59, 63, 65
1.5	51
1.5.23	51
1.7	52
1.9	50, 54
1.10	55
1.10–11	55
1.12	63
1.13	50, 55
1.17	56, 63
1.18–24	56
1.19	63
1.21	57
1.23	57–58

RABBINIC LITERATURE

Mishnah
Qiddushin
4.4–5	138

Yevamot
4.13	138

Tosefta
Yevamot
8.4	151

Jerusalem Talmud
Ta'anit
4.2	138

Babylonian Talmud

Bava Batra
120a	61

Berakhot
31a	180

Ketubbot
62b	138

Megillah
14a	61, 158
14b–15a	148

Pesahim
4a	138

Qiddushin
4a	151
76b	138

Sotah
12a	55, 61
12b	61–62
12b–13a	61, 158

Yevamot
62b	151
70a	151

Minor Tractates of the Talmud

Avot of Rabbi Nathan A
2.4	61

Mekhilta of Rabbi Ishmael

Shirata
10.58–61	61, 158

Mekhilta of Rabbi Simeon

1.1	53
36.3	61

Sifre Numbers

78	148

Midrash Rabbah

Genesis Rabbah
19.7	52
98.8	138

Exodus Rabbah
1.18	61
1.19	61
1.20	55, 61
1.23	62
1.24	62
1.26	54, 57, 62

Leviticus Rabbah
1.3	61
20.1	61

Numbers Rabbah
8.9	148

Deuteronomy Rabbah
11.10	57, 61

Ecclesiastes Rabbah
4:9–12 §1	61
8:10 §1	148
9:2 §1	61

Song of Songs Rabbah
5.1	52

Pesiqta of Rav Kahana

23.10	52

Midrash Tanhuma Buber

Deut. 2.1	61

Midrash Tanhuma Printed Version

Gen. 2.5	61
Exod. 1.7	54, 62

Midrash Psalms

9.7	61

Pirqe Rabbi Eliezer

48	53–54, 57, 61–62

Targums

Targum Pseudo-Jonathan
Gen 37:11	179

Exod 1:15	158	57.18.2	102
Targum of the Writings		58.22.1	116
Ruth 4:20	148	58, frag. 1	105
		61.2.1	112
		61.2.3	112
		61.2.4	113

PATRISTIC AND OTHER EARLY CHRISTIAN SOURCES

Cicero
Epistulae ad familiares
4.4.4	85

Epistulae ad Quintum fratrem
1.1.21	96
1.2.7	96

Clement of Alexandria
Stromateis
1.23	58

Eusebius
Historia ecclesiastica
1.7.13–14	138
2.18.1–9	47
3.12	138
3.19–20	138
3.32.3–4	138

Praeparatio evangelica
9.27	58
9.27.3	51, 55
9.29.2	52

Cornelius Nepos
Agesilaus
1.1	34–35
1.2	34, 41

Alcibiades
1.1–2	30–32, 41
1.2–4	30
2.1	30–31
2.2	31
11.1–2	31

Justin Martyr
Dialogue with Trypho
108	163

Atticus
1–18	40
1.1–3	39
2–4	39
13.7	40
16.3	40
17.1	40
18.1–6	40
19–20	40
19.1	28, 40

Origen
Scholia in Matthaeum
1.5	146

Cato
1.1	38
2.4	38
3.1	38
3.5	38

GRECO-ROMAN SOURCES

Aristotle
frag. 556	71

De viris illustribus
pref. 1.1	27–28, 40

Cassius Dio
Roman History
45.1.2–3	101
45.1.3–5	101

Alcibiades
| 30 | |

Epaminondas
- 1.1 — 33
- 1.1–4 — 33
- 2.1–2 — 33
- 2.2 — 33
- 4.6 — 42

Hannibal
- 1.1 — 35–36, 41
- 2.3–6 — 36, 41
- 3.1 — 36
- 13.1–3 — 37–38

Miltiades
- 1.2–3 — 43

Pausanias
- 5.5 — 43

Themistocles
- 2.6–7 — 43

Thrasybulus
- 1.1 — 41–42

Diodorus Siculus
Library of History
- 4.8 — 35
- 4.8–39 — 35
- 12.84.1 — 32
- 13.37.2 — 32

Dionysius of Halicarnassus
Antiquitates romanae
- 6.3 — 111

Euripides
Hippolytus
- 11 — 71

Herodotus
Histories
- 1.7 — 35
- 2.44 — 35
- 2.146 — 35
- 4.195 — 20
- 7.204 — 35
- 8.131 — 35

Horace
Epistles
- 1.20.20 — 118

Satires
- 1.6.6 — 118
- 1.6.45–46 — 118

Livy
History of Rome
- pref. 6–7 — 76
- 2.19–20 — 111
- 2.42.5 — 111

Lucian
How to Write History
- 60 — 22

Pausanias
Description of Greece
- 6.11.2–9 — 6

Plato
Greater Alcibiades
- 103A — 32

Republic
- 521C–531C — 57

Plutarch
Aemilius Paulus
- 25.1–2 — 110

Agesilaus
- 3.5 — 35

Alcibiades
- 1.1 — 32
- 1.2 — 32

Alexander
- 1–2 — 5
- 1.1 — 77
- 1.1–3 — 16
- 2.1 — 35, 77
- 2.2 — 77
- 2.2–3 — 77
- 2.3 — 77, 90

2.4	77	*Lycurgus*	
2.6	77	1.1	81
3	88	1.1–3	81
3.1–2	78	1.3	81
3.3	78	1.3–4	35
3.4	79	1.4	81
3.5	79	2.3–3.1	81
4.1–4	79	5	68
4.4–5	79	*Marcellus*	
4.4–8.4	79, 86	1.1	86
5.1–2	79	*Pelopidas*	
6–7	5	16.5	35
8.2	80	*Romulus*	
9.1	79	1.1–2.1	72
14.5	90	2.1	73
21.4–23.6	79	2.2–4.3	73
25.1	90	2.3	73
25.3–4	90	2.5	88
50.2–3	90	2.6	73
52.1	90	3.1	74–75
Cicero		3.1–8.6	76, 131
1.1	84	3.2	74
1.2–4	84	3.3	74
1.3–4	86, 130	3.4	74
2	88	4.2	74, 88
2.1	84	4.3	74
2.2	85, 89	6.1	75
2.3	85	6.1–2	75
14.4	85	6.2	75
20.1–2	85	8.6	75
32.4	85	8.7	75, 89
45.1	85	*Solon*	
Coriolanus		1.1–2	19
37.3	89	*Themistocles*	
38.1	89	1.1	82
38.2	89	1.2	82
38.3–4	89	1.3	83
Lucullus		2.1	83
2.3	90	2.2	83
12.1–2	90	2.3	83
23.3–4	90	2.4	83
24.6–7	90	2.6	83

Index of Ancient Sources

Theseus
1.1	73
1.1–2	69
1.1–3	20
1.2	72
1.3	69, 73, 76
2	88
2.1	70
3.2	71
4.1	72
6	88
6.1	72
36	88

Polybius
Histories
2.1	37
3.11	37, 41

Suetonius
Augustus
1	95
1.1–8.1	98–99, 102
2	98
2.1–2	95
2.3	19, 95
3	98
3–4	96
3.1	96
3.2	96
4	98
4.1	97, 105
4.2	96–97
5	97
6	97, 121
7	98
7.1	98
8.1	98
16.2	98
69.2–70.1	98
79.2	100
94	5, 98–99, 102
94.1–9	99, 169
94.1–11	99
94.1–97.3	99, 103
94.3	99
94.4	100
94.5	101
94.6	101
94.7	101
94.8	102
94.10–96.2	99
97.1–3	99

Gaius Caligula
1–7	108
1.2	108
2	108
3.1	108
4	108
5	108
8.1–2	108
8.1–5	119
8.2	109
8.3	109
8.5	109
60	121

Horace
1.1–5	118

Julius
32	121
56.7	169

Nero
1.1	110
1.2	111
2.2	111
6.1	111
6.1–2	121
6.2	112
6.4	113
7.1	113
8	112
19.1	121

20–24	114	5.6	107
20.1	113–14	5.7	107
22.1	113	*Virgil*	
36.1	121	1	116
40.1–3	121	3–4	117
41.2	121	5	117
46	121	6	117
52	169	17	117
57.1	112	17–18	117
Otho		*Vitellius*	
10.1	93	1.1	115
Tiberius		1.2	115
1–4	102	2.1	115
2.1	102	2.2	115
2.3	102	3.2	115–16, 121, 131
3.2	102	9	121
4.2–3	103	14.5	121
5	102, 108	18	121
6.1	103		
6.3	103	**Tacitus**	
6.4	103	*Annals*	
7	103	4.34.5	98
14	103–4	6.1	116
14.1	103	11.11.5	113
14.2	104, 169	11.11.6	113
14.4	104	12.8.3	113
43–44	116	13.3.5	114
52	113	13.31.1	108
57.1	104, 169	16.22.3	108
57.2	105		
Vespasian		**Thucydides**	
1.1	105	*Peloponnesian War*	
1.1–2.1	107	5.43	32, 41
1.2	106		
1.3	106	**Xenophon**	
1.4	106	*Agesilaus*	
2.1	107	1.2	35, 41
5	107	8.7	35
5.2	107–8	*Hellenica*	
5.3–7	107	3.3.3	35
5.4	107	6.3.6	35

www.ingramcontent.com/pod-product-compliance
Lightning Source LLC
Chambersburg PA
CBHW021352271225
37262CB00002B/3